Computing with Parallel Architectures: T.Node

EURO

C O U R S E S

A series devoted to the publication of courses and educational seminars organized by the Joint Research Centre Ispra, as part of its education and training program.
Published for the Commission of the European Communities, Directorate-General Telecommunications, Information Industries and Innovation, Scientific and Technical Communications Service.

The EUROCOURSES consist of the following subseries:

- Advanced Scientific Techniques
- Chemical and Environmental Science
- Energy Systems and Technology
- Environmental Impact Assessment
- Health Physics and Radiation Protection
- Computer and Information Science
- Mechanical and Materials Science
- Nuclear Science and Technology
- Reliability and Risk Analysis
- Remote Sensing
- Technological Innovation

COMPUTER AND INFORMATION SCIENCE

Volume 2

Computing with Parallel Architectures: T.Node

Edited by

D. Gassilloud

and

J. C. Grossetie

Commission of the European Communities,
Joint Research Centre,
Institute for Systems Engineering and Informatics,
Ispra, Italy

W K A P   —   A R C H I E F

07923-1225-2

KLUWER ACADEMIC PUBLISHERS
DORDRECHT / BOSTON / LONDON

Based on the lectures given during the Eurocourse on
'Computing with Parallel Architectures'
held at the Joint Research Centre Ispra, Italy, September 10–14, 1990

ISBN 0-7923-1225-2

Publication arrangements by
Commission of the European Communities
Directorate-General Telecommunications, Information Industries and Innovation,
Scientific and Technical Communications Service, Luxembourg

EUR 13439
© 1991 ECSC, EEC, EAEC, Brussels and Luxembourg

Published by Kluwer Academic Publishers,
P.O. Box 17, 3300 AA Dordrecht, The Netherlands.

Kluwer Academic Publishers incorporates the publishing programmes of
D. Reidel, Martinus Nijhoff, Dr W. Junk and MTP Press.

Sold and distributed in the U.S.A. and Canada
by Kluwer Academic Publishers,
101 Philip Drive, Norwell, MA 02061, U.S.A.

In all other countries, sold and distributed
by Kluwer Academic Publishers Group,
P.O. Box 322, 3300 AH Dordrecht, The Netherlands.

Printed on acid-free paper

Printed in the Netherlands

CONTENTS

PREFACE

One of today challenges in computer science is parallelism. Sequential processors are reaching their physical limits and definitive advantages can be brougth defining parallel computation models and designing parallel computers. The CEC funded the Esprit project Supernode to develop a low cost, high performance, multiprocessor machine. The result of this project is a modular reconfigurable architecture based on transputers: T.Node.

T.Node can be considered a european success, and CEC has decided to continue to encourage the transputer community, manufacturers as well as researchers and end users. In this context, the book gives a flavour of the state of the art in T.Node programming.

First, we present the architecture, the system software and the programming environment of T.Node. In a second part we have conferences showing various trends to design system software for multiprocessor machines. Third, some real case applications on T.Node are presented in the field of image processing, image synthesis, particle physics simulation. Neural computing is not a new topic but efficient implementations are. We show in a last section how neural nets can be simulated and put at work on a transputer machine.

Eurocourses are held at the Ispra Joint Research Center on parallel computation under the sponsorship of the Institute for Systems Engineering and Informatics (ISEI). It is hoped that in this context the Institute and particularly the 3D imaging group can play a stimulating role in sponsoring and promoting the diffusion of knowledge in novel areas of computer and information sciences.

D. GASSILLOUD   J.C.GROSSETIE

T.NODE: PAST, PRESENT AND FUTURE.

G. DUDKIEWICZ, S. FLIELLER
Telmat Informatique, ZI Rue de l'Industrie,
68360 Soultz
France

ABSTRACT. Telmat Informatique is an active partner since 5 years in the European research on the parallel architectures. The Supernode architecture is one result of this research: this architecture is now diffused at 60 exemplars. This papers presents the history of the research on the parallelism at TELMAT, its results and the new project which are developed today.

Introduction

The new high performance processors and the computers with parallel architectures let us foresee important modifications in the well defined structure of the Information Processing Systems industry.

Europe has a very important technical card to play in this game: transputers and a variety of parallel systems using this processor to provide high performance computers.

Parallel processing is the centre of the research in Europe in the field of Information Processing Systems. Like all technological borders, this one is turbulent and sometimes deceitful.

Many creative and talented researchers propose constantly new architectures. Only a few of them are prototyped and a small part are used as support of experimentations.

The market of parallel computers is very recent. You can find a variety of technical ingenuities, the possibilities of these architectures seem to be without limits: the youth explains the diversity of the architectures, but experience tell us that only a few of them will survive.

We enter today in a critical phase. The next two or three years will decide which of these architectures can arrive to maturity. We hope that the way gone over today by the Supernode will enable us to demonstrate that it deserves a leading position in this market.

TELMAT History

The history of TELMAT is linked with the developments done in the french researches

1

D. Gassilloud and J. C. Grossetie (eds.), Computing with Parallel Architectures: T.Node, 1–10.
© 1991 ECSC, EEC, EAEC, Brussels and Luxembourg. Printed in the Netherlands.

centres, at the beginning, and also in other european countries today. In its research of innovations, TELMAT has assumed several technological transfers with success.

In fact, at its creation in 1981, the exchanges with the research centres has been very frequent. Early in 1983, the first realisation of TELMAT in Information Processing Systems has been the SM90, revolutionary computer at its time, which proposed a multi-processor architecture under Unix. This architecture is always alive today with some technological adaptations: the STE30, graphical workstation, and the Txxx systems.

This processus of industrialisation of architectures outcoming from the research is continued in 1984 with a 3D synthesis computer, CUBI, which also includes transputers to provide a high computing power.

In 1985, the exchanges with the world of the research takes an european dimension with the first participation of TELMAT in an Esprit project which will be discussed more in details in this paper.

In the idea of keeping companies with human size and in order to facilitate the constitution of responsible and competent teams, a holding has been created in 1986. The structure of the holding is today in Figure 1.

A short description of the expertises of each company gives an overview of the diversity of the activities in the TELMAT Holding. This diversity, among others, warranties the perenity of the holding:

- *TELMAT INFORMATIQUE* industrialise Information Processing Systems. The company develops, realises and manufactures its products. TELMAT INFORMATIQUE develops two lines of products: the Unix systems and the parallel computers based on transputers.
- *TELMAT COMMUNICATIONS* delivers the telecommunications world with measurements and networks supervision systems.
- *CAPTION* is concentrated on the graphics with products in image processing and image synthesis. Another part of this team is largely involved in several Esprit projects.

Today the TELMAT holding has a staff of more then 200 people (Figure 2).

On 30 people involved in the parallel task force, 1/3 are hardware conceptors and 2/3 are software developers.

The Esprit Supernode I Project

The transputer has become a very popular european micro-processor and is now used for the design of supercomputers in many projects in the UK, in Germany and in France, es

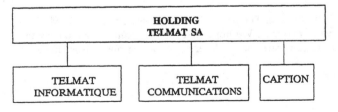

Figure 1. Structure of the TELMAT holding.

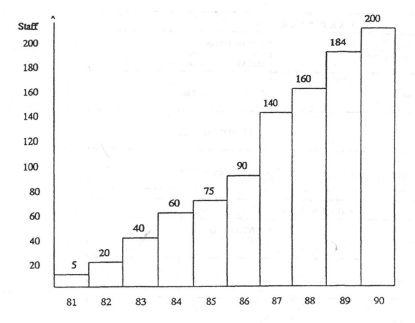

Figure 2. Evolution of the staff in the TELMAT HOLDING.

pecially. It is difficult to imagine such a development without the European Research program ESPRIT. Esprit has proposed the environment and the resources to facilitate the convergence of today separated interests in different countries in the EEC.

The objective of the Esprit P1085 "Supernode" project was to develop a multi-processor, high performance, low cost supercomputer. In this french and British project were involved the Royal Signals and Radar Establishment (RSRE), Inmos, Thorn-Emi, the University of Southampton, Apsis, the University of Grenoble (Imag) and TELMAT Informatique.

The high quality of the project in terms of collaboration can be analysed from several point of view, in particular the technical success which has permitted to bring a performant industrial product to the market before the end of the project. It is also interesting to study the raisons of this universally recognized success.

The first raison can be seen in the maturity of the technology which has been used: the T414 transputer was available on the market at the beginning of the project and Inmos knew what they were looking for with the next generation of processors, the T800 transputers. Added to the fact that the work achieved in the application field had clearly illustrated where this processor can be used in the areas of supercomputing, it is obvious that the hardware technology was well-known: that has facilitated the technical specifications in the initial phase of the project.

The second raison of this success can be seen in the technical complementary of the different partners in the project, this is represented on Figure 3 which gives the role of each partner in the Supernode I project.

HARDWARE	
1. Architecture of Supernode	SOUTHAMPTON RSRE : switch TELMAT : disk server
2. Transputer with FPU	INMOS : T800
3. Fast I/O	THORN EMI and RSRE
4. Industrialisation	THORN EMI and TELMAT

SOFTWARE	
5. Low level	SOUTHAMPTON RSRE IMAG
6. Operating System	IMAG
7. High Level Langage	IMAG

APPLICATIONS	
8. Signal Processing	RSRE
9. Image Processing	RSRE and THORN EMI
10. Engineering	SOUTHAMPTON
11. CAD-CAM	APSIS
12. Graphics	TELMAT

Figure 3. Work of each partner in Supernode I project.

The third raison appears in the convergence of interests between the several partners. Each one gave its technological expertise towards a common goal, the EEC funding

has catalysed this convergence of interests. All partners had the will to access to a technical result, only possible through such a collaboration. Figure 4 of next page gives an indication of the contributions and the benefits of each partners in the project, illustrating this convergence of interests.

A big part of this success is due to the quality of the management which has leaded the emergence of ideas towards this common goal and has managed the conflicts which are unavoidable in a three-years project: "You've got conflict whenever you put two people together", says Gordon HARP, who took on the task of managing the project.

ENTITY	BRINGS	GETS
INMOS	- Expertise in VLSI - Transputer - Occam	- Development of T800 - Occam Debugger - Feeback for the next generation of processors - Applications - Marketfor the T800

RSRE	- Management
	- Experience in
	    Parallel Programming
	- Design on VLSI
	- Algorithms of
	    Signal processing
		- Parallel computer
		    and software
		- Expertise in high level
		    langages
		- Early informations on T800

THORN-EMI	- Experience on Hard and Soft for Image Processing - Development of fast I/O - Applications in I.P. - Debbugers for Soft and hard	- Experience on transputer - Industrial product - Ethernet Soft

APSIS	- Experience in CAD-CAM
	- Ethernet Soft
	- Applications in CAD-CAM
		- Experience on transputer
		- Products in CAD-CAM
		- Experience in connection
		    of Transputers to local
		    networks

SOUTHAMPTON	- Experience with
	    Parallel Architectures
	- Design of Supernode
	- Scientif applications
	    in Physics
		- Testing of Ideas
		- Parallel Computer for
		    applications

IMAG	- Experience in high-level
	    Langages
	- Experience in Parallel
	    Programming
		- Parallel Computers
		- Machine parallèle
		- Licence on a software
		    product

TELMAT	- Industrialisation and
	Manufacturing of machines
	- Graphics
	- Dévelopment of Software
	    Environment
	- Application in Image
	    Synthesis
		- Experience with transputer
		- Commercial product

Figure 4. Give-and-take of each partner in the Esprit Supernode P1085 project.

6

Supernode has been the first european collaboration which result was an industrial product commercialised, demonstrating the possibilities of Europe in this domain. This project has enabled the realisation of a massively parallel architecture based on the transputer technology, including low-level system software and applications. Started in December 1985, this project has permitted TELMAT to created a new line of products, the T.Node.

THE T.NODE

The modular approach of the T.Node enable to propose a large variety of products in terms of performance on several segments of the Information Processing Systems market. This is illustrated by Figure 5 where the T.Node is present on all the domains of performance: from micros-computers to the Cray supercomputers. This figure shows also the interesting price/performance of the T.Node.

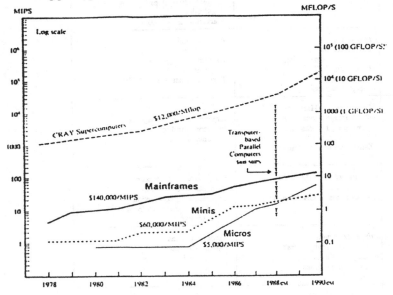

Note:
The figure is not intended to give an exact comparison of performance between different categories of computers. Rather, its purpose is to illustrate the fact that transputer-based machines can offer a wide range of performance at low cost. There is no single scale of conversion of Mflop/s (million of floating point operations per second) to MIPS (million of instructions per second) which is valid for all computers, given that the instruction sets of different makes of machines vary considerably in complexity and performance realised by each instruction. For the transputer-based machines, the scale is roughly 1 Mflop/s = 1f MIPS. Here we use this equivalence to draw the transputer-based machines against micros, minis and mainframes whose performance is given in MIPS (left-hand axis) and against Cray Supercomputers whose performance is given in Mflop/s (right-hand axis).

Sources: Financial Times, *30 December 1987;* Electronics, *18 February 1988; Johnson and Durham, 1986;*

Figure 5. Modularity and Price-performance of transputer-based Computers.

The second major characteristic of the T.Node consists in the **reconfigurability**: the user can determine the number of transputers and the connexions between processors adapted to the problem. This point is very important: it is well-known that there is not a single topology for an optimal solution for all types of problems. This possibility offered by the Supernode architecture is in particular very useful in the development phase of software, because it enables to set immediately new configurations.

Commercial Phase

The Supernode project, ended in December 1988, was promised to be followed by a commercial phase as successful as the technical work. After the industrialisation phase of the system, the Supernode has been launched on the market by TELMAT under the name T.Node.

The first configurations has been delivered by TELMAT to the partners of the Supernode project: RSRE, Southampton, Liverpool, Apsis and Imag.

The two first Mega.Node has been manufactured for Southampton (128 transputers) and RSRE (256 transputers) at the beginning of 1989.

The research teams have found with the T.Node a support for their experimentation at low cost compared with parallel computers available on the market. The following list of customers is not exhaustive, but gives an overview of the major french laboratories working with T.Nodes:
- IMAG with the laboratories TIM3, LGI and LIP;
- CRIN in Nancy;
- LRI in Orsay;
- LAAS in Toulouse;
- LITP in Paris;
- IRISA in Rennes;
- LABRI in Bordeaux;
- LIB in Besancon;
- INT in Evry.

Most part of these laboratories are involved in the "Greco C3" (Cooperation - Concurrence - Communication) with which TELMAT has started this year a common work on the use of the T.Node system. The first phase of that collaboration consists in the evaluation of the T.Node and its Operating System Helios, in order to define in which field these research teams can contribute to enhance the use of the T.Node.

In the same time, research teams in a more application oriented field have been equipped with T.Node systems:
- ULP in Strasbourg;
- LGME in Strasbourg;
- ENSPS in Strasbourg;
- LPC of Collège de France in Paris;
- OSC in the Faculté des Sciences in Dijon;
- LMS in Orsay.

The interest of the T.Node system for these laboratories consists in the use of a local computing power available in their offices to solve problems of which nature allows the use of parallel systems like the T.Node with performances comparables, or better, than vectorial supercomputers very expensive.

In 1989, the EEC has launched the PCA (Parallel Computing Action) in order to promote these technologies through Europe. This action has permitted TELMAT to deliver T.Node systems in several european research laboratories in Greece, in Denmark, in Spain and in Germany.

This year, the main objective is to bring the industry to the use of T.Node systems. Some systems have been installed:
- Thomson DTC (Genevilliers);
- Syseca Temps Rèel (Saint-Cloud);
- Syseca Logiciels (Louveciennes);
- Philips (Limeil-Brevannes);
- Caption (Rennes);
- Ibsi Electronique (Paris).

Some T.Node systems have also found users in various fields like the medical domain (CHS Rouffach) or the military domain (CPM, CERT/ONERA).

This list must be completed by the Joint Research Centre in Ispra, research centre of the EEC with which TELMAT has signed a collaboration contract for the development of applications and also for the creation of an european expertise centre on the use of this type of computers in order to promote these technologies by organising training courses and work-shops.

Development of Applications

One of the main field of interest for transputers is the field of graphical applications where the computing power of the T.Node enables to solve problems of a high degree of complexity. The T.Node and its software environments have guaranteed with success the realisation of applications in various fields; these successes of parallel processing reenforce our conviction: transputers will rapidly become a majeure competitor in the development of many industrial applications.

Image Processing. Image processing is a large set of various techniques and applications; in some cases the Input and Output are images (the Output being a modification of the Input), in some other, recognition for example, the Input is an image but the Output a description of the Input.

The major application fields of image processing have been tested: *Data Processing* in recognition of printed or manuscripts character: the T.Node is used as a general purpose computer to test algorithms developed by other industrial partners for automatic selection of postal mailing in a research centre of the french post in order to achieve this job automatically. More than 50 transputers are used to read the post code; 140 are necessary to read the complete address.

Biology: software for the classification of images from electronic microscopes enables to process the dates in a few minutes instead of several days: the T.Node allows in this case to process a higher number of samples, enhancing the classification of the images.

Industrial Automatization for automatic inspection and assembling of components: and Esprit project of vision machine and on-line inspection is now preparing a system able to detect the defective parts in the manufacturing of parts using the T.Node. The manual techniques of inspection are very slow and can, at the moment only check some samples. This system will allow to compare a video image from a camera on the production line to a reference stored in data base via an synthesis image.

Medical: the cerebral cartography needs very high computing power because it uses 32 EEG signals which are registered simultaneously and processed in real time by a FFT (Fast Fourier Transform). These signals are visualised on a 3D scalp in image synthesis. Due to the computing power of the T.Node system, the doctors can visualise in real time the evolution of the activity by representing each level of electrical activity by a colour. The 3D representation allows an easier interpretation of the signals.

Military applications in cartography and survey of the battle field have been assembled to propose a complete system of radar signals processing in order to visualise in real time the image seen by a radar including the parts which are not detected. This system enables the processing in real time of radar signals to been exploited in embedded systems.

Another field which has seen many industrial applications been developed is the *simulation*. For instance, Petri networks are used to design an application on a network of transputers: the product resulting from this study will allow simulation and validation of distributed systems on the T.Node. The porting of software simulating experiences in High Energy Physics have also been undertaken. Another significative example is a simulator of VLSI completely written in Ocean.

Classification software of various records can be processed in a few minutes instead of several days: the T.Node enables a large number of samples to be processed reducing the time of computation.

Developments of *neural networks* have largely been tested with transputers: various researches are now undertaken in this field with some nice success: automatic sleep analysis, for instance, or some very interesting results in recognition of fuzzy shapes.

Image synthesis is really adapted to parallel processing. The parallelism is inherent to this type of algorithms: in the case of the ray-tracing there is a product available (T.Light). The T.Node allows the processing of very complex images in a few seconds.

The New Projects

The developments today at TELMAT on the hardware are oriented towards four directions. The results, in term of products, will be available in the last trimester of this year.

The *neural module* associates transputers to specific neuro-mimetics chip to realise the resolution and the learning with automates on-chip.

The graphic card with a resolution 1280 x 1024 x 8 bits will be available with an X.Window interface and a graphic library.

A direct extension to the VME bus will enable the opening of the T.Node towards the VME world and the direct Ethernet or FDDI connection, or video acquisition.

TELMAT participates also to the *Supernode II Project* to develop software for the T.Node.

The *release 2.0 of Helios* will be available end of 1990, including some new features for the connections to networks: Ethernet and TCP-IP; and a set of new servers with the possibility to integrate minis-servers to enhance performance et introduce new Unix fonctionnalities.

The release 3.0 of *T.Node Tools* will also be available at the end of this year. This release will be compatible with the version 2.2. It will propose the multiplexing of the links toward the controller of the T.Node, the possibility to execute simultaneously several environments on the T.Node, the dynamic resource sharing and software tools to propose pseudo-dynamic switching. Dynamic switching is studied to be integrated in the release 3.1 of the T.Node Tools.

CONCLUSIONS

In perspective, the future of the T.Node is really promising looking to the interest around the transputer, the technical evolutions and the growing market towards industry. But Europe, which has here a chance to become a leader in the field of Information Processing Systems, must put together is forces: at the level of research, but also on an industrial view to propose industrial standards which will permit to ensure the homogeneity of the products of the several manufacturers proposing today their transputer products to the market.

BIBLIOGRAPHY

Molina (1989), The Transputer Constituency, PICT, Edinburgh University.
MD Prospective (1989), Parallel and Multiprocessing Status 88, Meylan.
Flieller, T.Node Industrial version of Supernode (North Holland, Amsterdam, 1989) Computer Physics Communications 57(1989) 492-494.
Harp, J.G. et al., Phase 1 of the development and application of a low cost, high performance multiprocessor machine, ESPRIT 86: Results and Achievements (North-Holland, Amsterdam, 1987) pp. 551-562.

PROGRAMMING T.NODE

Denis GASSILLOUD
Joint Research Center
ISEI TP 361
21020 ISPRA (Varese) ITALY

Abstract

The Esprit P1085 Supernode project has developed a modular reconfigurable architecture based on transputers. This highly parallel machine is now manufactured and distributed by TELMAT Informatique under the trade name T.Node. This paper presents the architecture and gives an introduction on the programming environments available for T.Node.

1 INTRODUCTION

Since more than six years the INMOS transputer family of components associated with the OCCAM programming language has brougth a new dimension to parallel programming.

The purpose of the Esprit P1085 project, partially funded by CEC, was to develop (and create applications for) a low cost, high performance multiprocessor machine. The project involved RSRE, Inmos, Thorn-EMI, University of Southampton, University of Liverpool, APTOR, University of Grenoble and Telmat Informatique. The objective was to develop a highly parallel architecture based on transputers, and associated system software and applications. To achieve this, Inmos developed the T800 transputer, based on the T414, and the whole consortium defined the machine architecture. Started in Decembed 1985, this 3 year long project produced a significant industrial product: **T.Node** (1)(7).In a first section we detail the hardware.

Software packages have been developed to take advantage of the architecture by making effective use of the T.Node original hardware features. These low level softwares are called T.Node Tools (TNT) and are presented in a second section.

Three directions for system software are supported. T.Node Tools are designed to be used in all three environments. Each of these directions corresponds to a peculiar use of T.Node.

The Transputer Development System (TDS), an INMOS product including the OCCAM compiler, is associated with T.Node Tools to provide a complete OCCAM

11

D. Gassilloud and J. C. Grossetie (eds.), Computing with Parallel Architectures: T.Node, 11–27.
© 1991 *ECSC, EEC, EAEC, Brussels and Luxembourg. Printed in the Netherlands.*

development tool for T.Node. OCCAM and TDS are presented in the second section with the T.Node Tools.

Other languages are provided with parallel C, Fortran and Pascal from 3L. There is a complete set of tool for these languages, including compiler, linker, libraries and runtime support. Now we provide also a stand-alone toolset product from INMOS. These toolset are used either to design embedded application or to re-use dusty decks.

Last, HELIOS from Perihelion Software is implemented on T.Node to offer a complete homogeneous system. This operating system gives a reliable basis to develop program for T.Node and provides the user with some standards adapted to parallelism. Helios is detailled in section three.

2 T.NODE ARCHITECTURE

T.Node is a non shared memory, MIMD, highly parallel machine based on transputers. One of its most important characteristics is its ability to reconfigure network topology, using an electronic switch. This architecture offers a range of 16 to 1024 processors, delivering from 24 to 1500 Mflops peak performance. To achieve these performances, a hierarchical structure has been adopted.

2.1 TRANSPUTER

The T800 transputer is a 32-bit microprocessor, with on-chip memory and FPU (IEEE 754 standard), delivering 10 Mips and 1.5 Mflops peak performance. It has been designed in order to provide concurrency. It has an integrated microcoded scheduler which shares processor time among concurrent processes. It is used as a building block in multiprocessor systems. Communication between transputers is supported by 4 bidirectionnal, serial, asynchronous, point to point connection links. With such a component it becomes easy to design a parallel system. On largest arrays, however, message routing communication introduces important overheads. The alternative solution is circuit switching, which has been adopted.

2.2 SWITCHING DEVICE

All transputer links are connected to a specific device called an electronic switch. This switch consists of a pair of 72x72 asynchronous switches, each implemented by 2 components. Each component is functionnaly equivalent to a 72x36 crossbar. The electronic switch is controlled by a dedicated transputer: the controller. (This is why, in T.Node, there are two types of transputers: control transputers, referred to here as controllers, and non-specific worker transputers, called workers.) The switch can structure any network topology among transputers in a rearrangeable, non blocking way. It can work in 3 modes: static, pseudo-dynamic and dynamic. In static mode, the network topology is fixed before run time, with no modifications during program execution. In pseudo-dynamic mode, the overall network topology may be modified during run-time, requiring the links to be quiescent. In dynamic switching, ad hoc connection is established in a part of the network, without alteration of the remaining communications. Such an asynchronous device needs system communication in order to synchronize the transputers to be connected. Such system communication could be multiplexed with user communication on links, but this introduces overheads. To avoid multiplexing, T.Node has implemented a specific feature: the control bus system.

2.3 CONTROL BUS SYSTEM

All transputers are connected to this bus, via a specific component, a memory-mapped gate array, releasing links from system messages. This bus has a master/slave protocol, where the master is the control transputer, and allows fast synchronization among transputers. Additional features like selective reset, and message broadcast are also supported by the control bus. Futhermore, this bus allows the entire network to be brought to a rapid halt, and debugging information to be extracted, without disturbing transputer link states. This possibility is used to provide a debugger with breakpoints.

2.4 BASIC MODULE: A NODE

The basic module is a reconfiguring network of 36 transputers, one of wich is the control transputer. This module has a control structure and communication facilities with the outside world. This type of machine is called a node. (fig. 1)

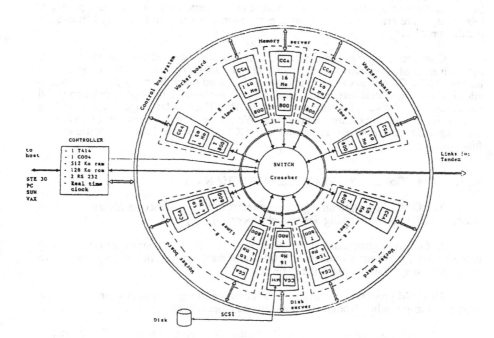

Figure 1: A Node

14

To create larger machines based on this node structure, the position held by each worker can be replaced by an entire basic module. This is the principle of the hierachical architecture used to produced multi-node machines.

2.5 MULTI-NODE

In a multi-node machine, an external level of switches implements a 3-stage Clos Network. This external level expands the network to 1024 transputers, while maintaining the network's dynamic reconfiguration feature. An external level control bus system, now controlled by an external level controller, connects all node controllers, while observing the master/slave protocol. In consequence, each node controller is master of its local control bus and slave of the overall control bus. The physical implementation of this outer level control bus sytem is realized using the same memory-mapped gate array as in single nodes.

3 OCCAM: FROM CSP TO SILICON

In a sequential machine, a program is compiled in a sequence of instructions to be executed step by step on a processor. To adequately model the concurrency of the real world, it would be preferable that a processor simulate a lot of concurrent processes and better, to have many processors all working at the same time on the same program. Obviously there are also huge potential performance benefits to be derived from such parallel processing.

Conventional programming langages are not well equiped to construct programs for such multiple processors as their very design assumes the sequential execution of instructions. OCCAM is the first language to be based upon the concept of parallel, in addition to sequential execution, and to provide automatic communication and synchronisation between concurrent processes. The OCCAM language is also a suitable method for designing concurrent programs. We present here the concepts of OCCAM, the programing environment associated with OCCAM and the T.Node specific system functions.

3.1 OCCAM CONCEPTS: PROCESSES AND CHANNELS

The OCCAM programming language arises from the concepts founded by Tony Hoare in CSP (Communicating Sequential Processes) (2).

In OCCAM programming we refer to the parts of a program as processes. A process starts, performs a number of actions and then finishes. In OCCAM more than one process may be executing at the same time.

OCCAM processes use channels for communicating values. A channel is a one-way, point-to-point link from one process to one other process.

Channels are patient and polite. If an input process finds that no value is ready it will wait until one is supplied, without any explicit instruction from the programmer. Equally an output will not send until the receiver is ready. This introduces the time factor into programming. A channel can pass values either between two processes running on the same processor, or between two processes running on different processors. In the first case the channel would in fact be just a location in memory, rather like a variable. In the second case the channel could represent a real hardware link, such as a transputer link or other serial communication line. Both cases are represented identically in an OCCAM program. For more about OCCAM please refer to (3)(4).

3.2 OCCAM & THE HARD REALITY

INMOS development of the transputer has been closely related to OCCAM, its design and implementation. The transputer reflects the OCCAM architectural model, and may be considered an OCCAM machine. OCCAM is the language of the transputer and as such, when used to program a single transputer or a network of transputers, provides the equivalent efficiency to programming a conventional computer at assembler level.

CSP considers a parallel program to be equivalent to a number of ordinary sequential programs running concurrently while exchanging messages over synchronous message channels. The trouble is, current transputer hardware and software only partially embody the CSP model. A program running on a single transputer, faking parallelism by time slicing, can contain as many processes and message channels as memory permits, which for most practical purposes is unlimited.

When it comes to distribute the processes onto different transputers for real parallelism, though, we find we are limited because the chip has only four communications links. This hard constraint severely cramps the way we can write programs and results in the loss of some of the advantages on the CSP model. To reduce the number of channels used, we might have to rewrite our single-processor program and/or force the processes to share the physical links by multiplexing many messages onto the same channel. This is a limitation of the transputer architecture that will surely disappear in the next generation of processors.

An OCCAM channel describes communication in the abstract, and does not depend upon its physical implementation. We can thus write and test a program using channels without having to worry about exactly where the different processes will be executed. The program can be developed on a single processor. When it is finished and proved you may decide to distribute various processes in the program onto different processors,and do so by making a few simple declarations at the beginning of the program.

3.3 TDS

TDS is the INMOS Transputer development system (5). TDS runs in two parts, a server provides access to the resources of a host workstation, a core TDS runs on a transputer board attached two the host. This board is linked to T.Node (figure 2).

The basic TDS interface between user and machine is an OCCAM oriented editor. This editor can be considered as a structured coding help. A utilities set is emulated by templates from the editor. Several utilies sets are available. One of these set includes an OCCAM compiler. It also makes it possible to configure and execute a program on a transputer network.

OCCAM extensions have been made in TDS. Among other things, program configuration primitives are available. It is therefore possible to assign a process to a physical processor by invoking the PLACED PAR primitive. It is also possible to place a logical communication channel between processes on a physical link connecting two transputers. For instance:

PLACED PAR

    PROCESSOR 0
      PLACE canal.to.host AT link1.out:

      PLACE canal AT link0.in:
      P0(canal)

    PROCESSOR 1
      PLACE canal AT link0.out:
      P1(canal)

This explicitly says that the P0 process will be executed on processor 0 and the P1 process on processor 1. canal represents the channel between the process P0 and P1. The PLACE instruction is used to assign the channel to a processor link. The processes P0 and P1 can therefore communicate through link 0 of processor 0 and 1. The TDS configurer is a system tool used to build the program binary code corresponding to such a description. In this program binary code, link0 and link1 are translated to addresses.

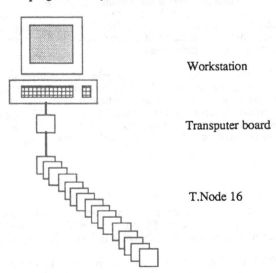

Workstation

Transputer board

T.Node 16

Figure 2: TDS network

The TDS environment supplies a system tool used to load a configured program made of several PLACED processes onto a transputer network. Using that tool implies that all necessary connection between the network different transputers have been set up.

This is the point where T.Node becomes interesting. Instead hand wiring transputers (as it is still sometimes done on some transputers boards), instead making static connections once at boot time (as it is usually done nowadays), T.Node hardware configuration can be tunned for each application.

3.4 TNT

T.Node Tools is a toolset developed to make the best use of T.Node features. It was previously made under TDS but it was rewritten for integration in Helios. We present in this section the main functions of TNT under TDS, first the T.Node logical and physical configuration, and second the T.Node debugger

To program T.Node there is two configuration phases. The first phase is handled by the T.Configurer. In TNT, T.Configurer is a compilation phase. The TDS configurer has been deeply modified in order to produce T.Configurer. T.Configurer inputs are, however, the same. The programmer distributes the program on a processor set by using the TDS configuration language. To do so he PLACEs the processes onto the processors and the communication channels between processes on the communication links between processors. T.Configurer takes as input the configuration program and all the already compiled processes. T.Configurer does not modify the process placement, but it rearranges the channel placements so that the configuration suits the T.Node. It generates configuration information. Taking the same example as above, the configuration program will be:

```
#USE SNconfig

PLACED PAR

    VAL processor IS 0:
    ... define south.out and west.in for processor
    PROCESSOR processor
        PLACE canal.to.host AT south.out:
        PLACE canal AT west.in:
        P0(canal)

    VAL processor IS 1:
    ... define north.out for processor
    PROCESSOR processor
        PLACE canal AT south.out:
        P1(canal)
```

SNconfig is a library used to define the T.Node hardware, south.out, west.in are constants extracted from this library. The user does not worry about what they actually are.

T.Configurer outputs have the same form as TDS configurer outputs. In content, they differ perceptibly. The link placement has been rearranged in order to adapt the connection orders to T.Node architecture. The program code is configured consequently (ready for loading).

Once a program has been configured, T.Node is not yet ready for execution. It is sufficient to program the switch before loading the user program onto the network. It is also necessary to establish the connections between the T.Node network and the outside world. An intermediate step is therefore introduced between the configuration and program loading. The tool responsible for this task is called T.Switcher. Before loading, used transputers must be reset. This task is also done by T.Switcher, using the control bus and associated software.

The T.Debugger is used to debug OCCAM programs on *live* transputer networks, as opposed to the debugger supplied with the TDS which has post mortem facilities only. Network debugging makes full use of the T.Node control bus which allows communication between the controller and individual worker transputers without using transputer links. As well as providing a communication path, this bus also has control facilities such as the means to reset or analyse individual processors. The control bus was designed very much with break and continue debugging in mind. Such debugging is not really possible on networks of transputers without additional hardware support.

The T.Debugger has a source browsing and monitor page features that users of the TDS post mortem debugger will immediately be familiar with. It also has an additional line driven mode. As far as the user is concerned, the main additional feature is the break and continue debugging. Internally, the main difference between the two debuggers is the way in which they access the network. The post mortem debugger uses an analyse worm through transputer links, whereas the break and continue debugger uses the T.Node control bus hardware.

The most important facilities offered are: break and continue debugging of a live transuputer network; compile time break point and debug messages; the whole network may be halted on command from the keyboard, or when a processor reaches a breakpoint; when the network is halted, processes, variables, memory, and registers may be examined and altered; this can be performed either symbolically at the OCCAM source code level, or at a machine intruction/register level; a source browsing and monitor panel user interface based on that of the TDS post mortem debuggger; suppport of a user EXE running in parallel with the debugger on the host computer, sharing the keyboard and screen ressources; an additional command line driven user interface; use of the special facilities provided by the T.Node control bus hardware.

4 HELIOS ON T.NODE

Helios is the first operating system specifically designed for the transputer to become widely available. It is a fully distributed, multi-tasking system that supports multiple processors and multiple users. It provides an excellent programming environment to T.Node applications. We present here the main functions of Helios (reprinted from Perihelion (6)).

Helios incorporates several key computer industry standars: the Helios interface is an implementation of the proposed POSIX standard for UNIX; the Helios compilers (FORTRAN, C Pascal, Modula-2) all meet existing or proposed ANSI and ISO standards; and the Helios graphics interface is the X Window System. Together, these ensure that Helios is straightforward to learn and use, and that software can be readily ported to and from Helios.

Although appearing similar to UNIX at the user level the underlying implementation is entirely different in order to handel multiple processors. T.Node Tools as they are described above have been integrated in the implementation of Helios on T.Node. This chapter highligths how this implementation takes advantage of T.Node particularities. The enhanced facilities of the networking system include: the boot of an unlimited number of processors, the distribution of task forces accross unlimited number of processors, the support for selective reset/analyse and the support for multiple users of the T.Node network.

4.1 UNDERLYING PRIMITIVES

Helios is based on the client-server model for operating systems. Inter-process communication is handled by message passing, although this underlying mechanism is effectively hidden by the layers of system software above it. A client process wishing to access a system resource, such as opening a file, sends a mesage to a server process requesting this action be performed on its behalf. The server replies with another message to indicate success or failure. Subsequently the client can read or write this file by sending further messages to the server.

This mechanism is convenient for a number of reasons. This server is responsible for handling the resource, for example keeping locks on files. This is easy to arrange when the server runs as a distinct process within the machine. The client may either behave in a simple fashion and send message and then wait for the reply; alternatively the client may engage in asynchronous I/O and perform some other action while waiting for a reply message to arrive from a server. The interface for servers is consistent, thus making it simple for extra servers to be added into the system to handle any added hardware.

The underlying Helios design uses this client-server model, but with the additional feature that the processes which act as clients and servers may reside in different processors. The client always makes the same call to send a message to a server, but the actual delivery mechanism may either pass the message to a process in the same transputer or transmit it through any number of other transputers before reaching the final destination. The actual location of the destination process is unknown to the sender, as is the route by which it is sent.

Other servers run on one or more or several processing nodes within the network. Some servers must run on nodes with particular hardware attached; for examples the file system needs the disc device connected while a window manager must run in a processor with video memory attached. Other servers with no particular hardware requirement may be distributed to share the load equitably.

It is also possible to have processing nodes which do not run Helios all the time.

One or more processors may be reset and loaded with a program written in a language such as OCCAM. Links connected to these nodes are specified as "dumb" links and a program is written which runs under Helios and supports a private protocol down the dumb links. This provides the connection between the program runnning on naked hardware and Helios. It is especially usefull where specific hardware configurations must be used at certain times, but not at others. It is also useful when interconnecting processors which have too few memory to run the Helios kernel.

T.Nodes are normally connected to other computer systems which act as hosts. Helios treats these host systems just like a transputer processing node, and achieve this by running a program called the I/O Server within the host system. This program, written in C, causes the host processor to appear to the rest of the network just like another node running Helios. Messages sent to the link adapter connected to the host are replied in the same way as messages sent to real transputer nodes.

The I/O Server provides support for Helios servers runing on the host. As far as the rest of Helios network is concerned, the host processor is a normal Helios node running servers. These are usually servers for consoles, file systems, serial ports and so on. They are implemented by the I/O Server communicating with the host operating system. In particular, the file server is implemented by mapping Helios requests onto the existing file system. This has the advantage of using the host filing system disc format, and also allowing to any remote filing system supported over other networks such as Ethernet. Helios File server is also implemented on T.Node disc server, using a UNIX file system format.

Any Helios network may contain any number of T.Node workers and host nodes. The transputer links may be regarded as a local area network connecting different hosts. On T.Node Helios network processors may be configured in any topology and may be subdivided into any number of subnetworks. Separate subnetworks can be combined into a single connected network. A simple example is described in figure 3, where there are one T.Node with 16 Helios nodes, two naked nodes, and two host systems. One Helios node is runnning nothing except the base system, while other servers are distributed around the network.

4.2 USER INTERFACE

There are two main user interfaces within Helios. The first is the shell, which provides a command line interface at which commands and parameters may be typed. The other interface is the graphical interface provided by X Window System, although the shell runs within an X Window window in this case as well.

The shell is intended to be as similar as possible to the Unix *csh*. It provides pipes as a way of communicating between programs, and redirection of standard input, output and error streams. Jobs may be run in the background and shell scripts executed.

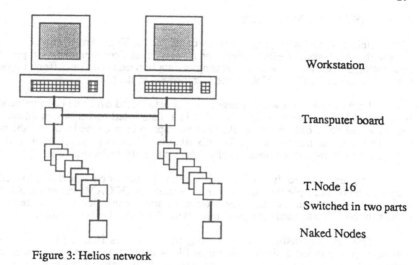

Workstation

Transputer board

T.Node 16
Switched in two parts

Naked Nodes

Figure 3: Helios network

4.3 PARALLEL PROGRAMMING

Helios was designed from the outset to support multiple processors and it provides built-in mechanisms for handling the resource of multiple processors. One of the design aims for Helios was ability to run the same binary code on different transputer installations, independent of the topology or the number of processors.

4.3.1 NETWORK SERVER

Each computer running Helios runs a network manager: the Network Server responsible for the physical configuration of Helios networks, and the distribution of system images. It consists of distributed components each of which controls a small section of a network. Particular responsabilities include the initial booting of Helios networks and subsequent re-booting of faulty nodes, the control of the Reset/Analyse signals within Helios networks, the control of configuration and reconfiguration of Helios networks. The specific work done to control the T.Node takes part of the Network Server actions.

The Network Server is handed a blueprint file which describes the resources within the network: the resource map. This includes the number of processors and how they are connected, but also other information about each processing node such as the type of processor, amount of external memory, existence of video memory and so on.

4.3.2 TASK FORCE MANAGER

Helios works with program units called tasks. Tasks are compiled and linked separately. All tasks are either clients or servers. Tasks communicate via pipes using conventional reads and writes. The passing of data between tasks on different processors is handled automatically by Helios, and is transprent to the user.

A set of tasks, known as a task force, is distributed over one or more processors by the Task Force Manager or TFM. This is a distributed server which automatically maps the task force onto the network. TFM attemps to balance the load over the network so as to minimize multi-tasking. The distribution of tasks is transparent to the user, though the user may, if required, specify where particular tasks should run.

Any task is fixed during its lifetime to the processor on which it is loaded. tasks may consist of multiple threads, which are similar to OCCAM processes. All threads within a task must run on the same processor, and communicate via shared memory synchronised using semaphores. New threads can be created automatically.

TFM is responsible for managing the resources indicated by the network manager. It is handed a similar blueprint file whenever a job is to be executed, and attempts to match the resources required with those available. For example, a job may require three processors connected so that the central one has video memory. The TFM decides on a suitable mapping from the requested network to that available in the current system. The decision on the way in which the mapping is done depends on the current load in the system as well as the physical resources available.

The normal interface to Helios is via the shell described earlier. When requested to do so, the shell will execute commands by passing them to the TFM rather than simply spawning a child process in the same processor. In this way a simple shell command of the form: *ls* / *more* will result in the *ls* command running in one processor, the original shell in another and the *more* command in yet another, assuming sufficient processors are available. Output from *ls* is sent to *more* via a pipe between the two processors. Pipes are implemented as direct message passing between the two processors, with efficiency enhanced by removal of redundant copying.

4.3.3 COMPONENT DESCRIPTION LANGUAGE

More complicated examples are possible though the use of a special language called the Component Distribution Language or CDL. This is a simple high level language with a syntax based on the UNIX Cshell, which allows any task force to be described in a language and hardware independant way. The language independance means that task forces can include tasks written in more tha one language. The hardware independance means task forces may be run on a single processor, as easily as on a multi-processor network, without any change to the CDL description. But the description can also include any special resources needed by each component.

The CDL provides a powerful and versatile methos for creating parallel programs. It includes contructs to automatically create pipelines ans farms, and can be used to program networks of any topology and complexity. Simple task networks can be described at the command line level since the Helios shell supports a subset of CDL commands.

An example of the use of CDL can be shown using the standard technique of dividing up a program into a master task which distributes work, and a number of slaves which handle work in parallel. Two programs, master and slave, are separately compiled. The CDL system is the used to specify the parallelims. The CDL compiler would be given an input line such as *master [5] | | | slave*
which will cause Helios to load a copy of the master, the load balancer and five copies of the slave into suitable spare processors. Pipes are provided to link the master to the load balancer, and the balancer to each of the slaves.

A command given in CDL is in general more complicated than this simple example, because of the way in wich attributes can be specified for each of the different parallel parts, but this simple case shows how it allows tasks to be distributed among processors. Note that the use of the CDL and pipes is independent of the language used; indeed master and slave could be written in different languages.

4.4 SPECIALS FOR T.NODE

This section describes the details of the T.Node support software. A Network is composed of several transputer boards connected to a T.Node machine. The software provides Reset/Analyse and link configuration for one or mutliple users. The software may be extended at some future stage to support the other features of the T.Node control bus.

T.Control Server is a Helios server to control the T.Node hardware it works with a Reset/Analyse driver and a link configuration driver

T.Control Server runs on the root processor of the system subnet and can accepts control requets from other networks. It incorporates the T.Configurer and T.Switcher software modules from the T.Node Tools, which process the same network requests as under TDS. T.Control Server communicates directly with the T.Kernel software resident on the controller via a dumb system link. The standard server library support routines handle most T.Control Server operations. Reset/Analyse and link configuration drivers are clients of the T.Control Server.

The Reset/Analyse driver is loaded automatically by the Network Server when a user starts up. It is responsible for resetting and analysing individual transputers within that user's subnet. The Reset/Analyse driver has no direct access to the appropriate hardware, so it must perform all its work by sending messages to the T.Control Server. When the driver is loaded by the Network Server, it opens a stream (a way to access the server) for future communications according the user There are three orders sent to the T.Control Server: *reset-node'*, *analyse-node* and *reset-all*. The exchanges of messages are totally transparent for the user.

The link configuration driver is loaded also by the Network Server to perform network configuration. It is used for setting up the initial network configuration so that Helios can boot up the network. Setting up and clearing individual connections once Helios is up and running is supported in the second release.

During initialisation, the link configuration driver opens a stream to the T.Control server just like the Reset/Analyse driver. Then it scans the user resource map to determine the desired connections. The table of connections is sent to the T.Control Server which processes it via the T.Configurer. The T.Configurer running under Helios has the same functionnalities as under TDS inside the T.Node Tools. It processes the network connections to reorder them, being compatible with the T.Node machine specifications. As a result, actual connections can be different from those specified by the resource map. The link configuration driver has to modify the network map in memory, using the real connectivity rather than specified by the original resource map.

The link configuration driver needs three other routines: *Connect*, *Disconnect* and *Enquire*. All these routines involve sending messages to the T.Control Server. All the connect messages are ordering by the Network Server as it reads the resource map updated at initialisation time. The T.Control Server process these messages, calling the T.Switcher.

4.5 PRODUCTS

There is a steadily growing range of sotware products provided by third parties and supported by Helios:

Helios C

Helios C is the recommanded compiler for use with T.Node running Helios. It is a high specification C compiler which conforms to the proposed ANSI standard (X3J11). ANSI conformance brings important advantages such as function prototyping, as well as improves code portability. Helios C provides a powerful C development environment for the transputer, with excellent UNIX compatibility.

Helios Source Debugger

The Helios Source Debugger is a powerful source level symbolic debugger for Helios C compiler, which can debug distributed programs running silmutaneously on multiple processors.

Meiko FORTRAN

Meiko FORTRAN is a high specification FORTRAN compiler for use with T.Node running Helios. It provides a complete ANSI FORTRAN 77 implementation (ANSI X3.9-1978), including all the standard intrinsic functions and I/O operations. It also includes rhe many commonly used extensions to standard DORTRAN; as a result, most existing FORTRAN programs will readily recompile under Meiko FORTRAN.

Prospero PASCAL

Prospero PASCAL for Helios is an ISO standard Pascal compiler for use with T.Node running Helios. It conforms fully to the ISO 7185 standard, level 0. In addition, a comprehensive set of language extensions is supported, including dynamic string types, double-precision floating point, random access files, separate compilation, bit manipulation and parallel programming.

Rowley Modula 2 Compiler

Rowley Modula-2 is a high specification Modula-2 compiler for use with T.Node running Helios. It is a fast and compact two pass compiler that generates high quality code. Rowley Modula-2 conforms to Niklaus Wirth's Edition 3 of the language, whilst anticipating the pending BSI and ISO standard.

Helios TDS Server

The Helios TDS Server is a software utility that enables the standard INMOS TDS (version D700D) to be run from Helios. By using the multitasking facilities of Helios, users may run multiple TDS jobs concurrently.

Helios AMPP

Helios AMPP is an assembler macro pre-processor for use with Helios.

Topexpress VecLib

The performance of scientific and engineering application programs can be dramatically enhanced by using the Topexpress Vector Library. The Library which contains over 100 single precision, double precision and complex vector primitives, is written in optimised T800 assembler. VecLib routines are callable from all Helios languages and OCCAM. Included with the Library is an executive which maximises performance by dynamically loading library code into on-chip RAM.

Basic Language System

BLS is a powerful application development system for PC hosted T.Node. It is a user-friendly, interactive programming environment based on an advanced and extended implementation of the Basic language.

Helios PC Graphics Library

The Helios PC Graphics Library enables software running on T.Node under Helios to user standard PC graphic boards: CGA, EGA and VGA. Heliso programs call a special graphic library, which is compatible with the graphics library provided by Microsoft C on PCs. The program output is then displayed on the host PC graphic system.

X Window for Helios-PC

X Window for Helios PC bring all the power of the X Window graphics system to users of T.node from a PC host. This is a complete and efficient implementation of the X Window System V.11-R2.

5 CONCLUSION

A real effort has been made to provide users with consistent programming environments for T.Node. We have presented here two ways to program T.Node. The first one (OCCAM TDS and T.Node Tools) is low level but very efficient. The second one (Helios C) is of higher level and is still evoluting concerning process mapping strategy and automatic load balancing tunning. These two ways are not uncompatible because we can use TDS from Helios.

Now one question remains, which language under which system do I need? There are multiple criteria to make a choice, it is necessary for the user to think about some questions. Is the T.Node shared among several users? If yes, then Helios is obligatory. Is the execution time critical? If yes, OCCAM is obligatory. Is the T.Node used to design embedded program for a dedicated machine? Are there dusty deck programs to be ported? If yes, it is to bet that the parallelisation will not be of a fine grain, use Helios or 3L. What is the programming language to be used? What is the future of the developped program (port to other processors)? Must the application have true results ? If yes use OCCAM. Must the application be reliable? Are specific hardware (graphics, I/O, disks) to be integrated in your T.Node? If yes, think about the servers available and their associated programming language

"Cut it simple" as said Ockham, but Aristoteles: "World 's diversity is its real wealth".

6 REFERENCES

(1) HARP J.G. et al, Phase 1 of the Development and Application of a Low Cost, High Performance Multiprocessor Machine ESPRIT 86 Results and Achievements, Elsevier Science Publishers B.V.

(2) HOARE C.A.R., Communicating Sequential Processes, Comm ACM 21,8 (August 1978), 666-677.
See also Comm ACM 26,1 (January 1983), 100.

(3) INMOS OCCAM2 Reference Manual, Prenctice Hall, ISBN 0-13-629312-3.

(4) POUNTAIN D., MAY D., A Tutorial Introduction To OCCAM Programming, BSP/INMOS, ISBN 0-632-01847-X.

(5) INMOS, Transputer Development System, Prenctice Hall ISBN 0-13-928995-X.

(6) Perihelion Software Ltd., The Helios Operating System, Prenctice Hall ISBN 0-13-386004-3.

(7) TELMAT Informatique, T.Node User Manual, BP12 68360 SOULTZ FRANCE (+33 89 76 51 10).

THE DESIGN OF COMMUNICATING PROCESSES

Guy-René PERRIN
Laboratoire d'Informatique
Université de Franche-Comté
25030 Besançon cédex
France

This work is supported by the French CNRS Research Program C^3.

Abstract

These last few years have seen the development of many parallel architectures. Among them, processor arrays seem to be very promizing. The programmation of these machines requires to design processes to be mapped on the nodes, communicating by message passing along the links of the architecture. The aim of this presentation is to give a contribution for a rationalized design of such programs. Refinement techniques are proposed from problem abstract specifications to synchronous or asynchronous communicating processes.

Keywords

Communicating Processes, Specification, Refinement, Equations, Data Dependencies.

Introduction

These last few years have seen the development of many parallel architectures. Among them, processor arrays seem to be very promizing. These architectures are composed of processors locally and regularly connected, with distributed memory. The programmation of these machines requires to design processes to be mapped on the nodes, communicating by message passing along the links of the architecture.

Many programming languages and operating systems are studied for these multiprocessors. From a design methodology point of view, it is worth bearing in mind the distance which currently separates these tools from safe and high level *academic* tools.

29

D. Gassilloud and J. C. Grossetie (eds.), Computing with Parallel Architectures: T.Node, 29–49.
© 1991 ECSC, EEC, EAEC, Brussels and Luxembourg. Printed in the Netherlands.

The most advanced progresses are made in the *parallelization* domain. Sequential program transformations for vectorized machines, or systolic array synthesis methods are current examples of such results. On the other hand, works about parallel program design are at the beginning. The required effort will be less of deterrent if high level linguistic tools are provided, supported by methods implemented on software environments defined to *assist design* of programs.

The aim of this presentation is to give a contribution for a rationalized design of such programs. Going from a formal specification of some problem to an implementation of some solution, requires to take good care to introduce convenient formalisms and development techniques (see for example Chandy and Misra (4)). Looking at the target machines, either in terms of program transformations as automatic parallelizations in compilers, or in terms of parallel programmation, the common techniques are based on the expression of data dependencies. In the first case these dependencies are deduced from a semantical data flow analysis of a given program. In the second one they have to be deduced from the problem terms in the same time as the data themselves.

An intermediate abstract expression level to express data and dependencies may be used in terms of equations such as

$$x[k] = f(..., y[k'], ...)$$

which defines some occurrence k of a variable x depending on some occurrence k' of a variable y.

Prefiguring architecture evolutions, specially in parallel computing, the study of Karp, Miller and Winograd (12) on *Uniform Recurrence Equations*, defines a formal frame where the now classical notions of data dependency, potential parallelism and computation scheduling are introduced. This formalism is used in most works about transformation, implementation or synthesis of algorithms, specially for systolic, vectorized, or SIMD ones ((8), (14), (17), (6), (18), etc.). In these studies, statements define linear recurrence relations between some variable occurrences, running on integral convex domains :

$$x[k] = f(..., y[\rho(k)], ...)$$

From such data definitions, synthesis methods consist in defining a valid timing of the calculations in a synchronous parallelism model, with respect to the data dependencies they induce.

More generally, many problems are expressed as equation systems : vector or matrix computations in linear algebra, differential equations or boolean equations in automaton science. Computer scientists have discovered the power of such formalisms for data flow interpretations. See for example the language LUCID (2), or the synchronous programming languages, as LUSTRE (16), for reactive systems.

In the context of programming processor arrays, we are concerned with synchronous or asynchronous programs, in which data dependencies may be less constrained. Hence, they both depend on the problem terms and on the computation circumstances. But what we have to do for the design of communicating processes is to specify and construct the required data dependencies for the algorithm correctness, and possibly the algorithm efficiency. So equation systems as hereabove should not entirely define data and their dependencies, but only invariant properties to be satisfied :

$$\textit{definition :} \qquad x[k] = f(..., y[k'], ...)$$
$$\textit{invariant :} \qquad k \text{ and } k' \textit{ satisfy some property.}$$

In other words, a problem specification defines in a descriptive style (for example by using a first order predicates language) the property the result satisfies. Conversely, a program defines in a functional or imperative style (for example uniform recurrence equations) the way a computation leads to a correct result. In the design process, some intermediate statement may then be composed on one hand by some computation definitions, in terms of equations, and on the other hand by some properties to be satisfied by data dependencies for the effective implementation to be correct. This *stepwise refinement* process goes on until all needed *operational* aspects are defined, according to some effective architecture. These operational aspects can be either a recurrence equation system, totally defined, from which a timing function may be deduced, or a set of equations defining the node computations and a set of communication operations, depending of the target environment.

1. Programming with equations

1.1. OBJECTS AND FUNCTIONS

An *equation* defines a variable occurrence x from a function f on variable occurrences as u, by :

$$x = f(..., u, ...)$$

The semantics of a *variable* is a mapping which defines a possible infinite set of values, in a set specified by the variable type. Each element of this set, called a *variable occurrence*, can be selected by an index which runs over some domain $\mathbb{D}$ of $\mathbb{Z}^p$. The symbol "=" links two identical occurrences, which may be substituted one for the other. A function is a composition of operations, which are defined in its argument types.

Then we can define a *recurrence equation* as an equation in which the same variable name occurs each side of the symbol "=". We note :

$$x[k] = f(..., x[\rho(k)], ...)$$

such equations, where ρ is a function mapping over $\mathbb{Z}^p$. The "..." mark some other arguments (variables, constants or other occurrences of x).

A *program* is then expressed as a recurrence equation system, each of them being defined over a sub-domain of the indices set :

$$x_u[k] = f_u(..., x_v[\rho_{u,v}(k)], ...) \qquad [1]$$
$$u, v \in \mathcal{U}, \ k \in \mathbb{D}_u, \ \rho_{u,v} \in \mathbb{D}_u \to \mathbb{D}_v$$

32

Example - gcd (a₀..., aₙ)

$$x_p[0] = a_p$$

$$x_p[k] = \begin{cases} x_{p-1}[k-1] < x_p[k-1] & \rightarrow & x_p[k-1] \cdot x_{p-1}[k-1] \\ \\ x_{p-1}[k-1] \geq x_p[k-1] & \rightarrow & x_p[k-1] \end{cases} \quad k > 0$$

p : 0.. n, k-1 stands for k minus 1 modulo n+1.

◊

1.2. COMPUTING EQUATIONS

1.2.1. *Synchronous interpretations.*

Some synchronous interpretations can be defined for a few target architectures, as systolic arrays (13) or more general processor arrays. Such architectures are characterized by a regular structure, local connections and a global external clock.

Example - gcd (a₀..., aₙ)

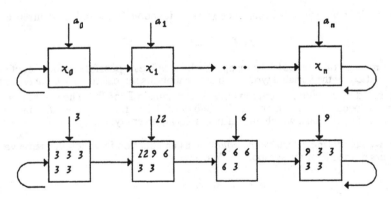

*A synchronous linear array for the gcd problem
and a few computation steps for (3, 12, 6, 9)*

◊

Exercise - A new definition of the gcd problem, where each variable definition involves two other variables.

$$x_p[0] = a_p$$

$$x_p[k] = \begin{cases} x_{p-1}[k-1] \leq x_{p+1}[k-1] < x_p[k-1] & \rightarrow & x_p[k-1] \cdot x_{p+1}[k-1] \\ x_{p+1}[k-1] < x_{p-1}[k-1] < x_p[k-1] & \rightarrow & x_p[k-1] \cdot x_{p-1}[k-1] \\ x_{p-1}[k-1] < x_p[k-1] & \rightarrow & x_p[k-1] \cdot x_{p-1}[k-1] \\ x_{p+1}[k-1] < x_p[k-1] & \rightarrow & x_p[k-1] \cdot x_{p+1}[k-1] \\ else & \rightarrow & x_p[k-1] \end{cases} \qquad k > 0$$

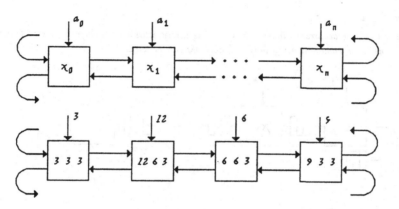

A synchronous processor array for the gcd problem

◇

In an abstract programming point of view we could say that synchronous processor arrays are infinitely fast machines, running deterministic calculations. Such interpretations consist in defining some injective mappings :

$$sem : \quad \biguplus_{u \in U} \mathbb{D}_u \rightarrow S * T$$

where S is the surface of the target array, and T some time domain (5).

Example - $gcd (a_0..., a_n)$

The injective mapping is the trivial one from $\quad \biguplus_{p \in 0..n} \mathbb{D}_p \quad to \quad 0..n * \mathbb{N}$

◇

In the particular domain of systolic arrays and efficient mappings, the literature is rich about architecture synthesis. The implementation of the calculations defined by recurrence

34

equations supposed to be linear ones, that is the array and the data stream definitions, consists in transforming the system to obtain uniform recurrence equations, in which the affine mapping is a translation. Classical synthesis techniques process in three steps : define a dependence graph, derive a convenient timing in $\mathcal{T}$, by defining a linear timing function, and then allocate computations to $\mathcal{S}$. This points are developped in the section 2.

1.2.2. *Asynchronous interpretations*.

Different sorts of asynchronous interpretations can be imagined, that consider non deterministic computations depending of their scheduling.

Example · gcd $(a_0,..., a_n)$

Assuming that the occurrence index k has no time interpretation, as in synchronous languages, a processor network communicating buffered messages can be used.

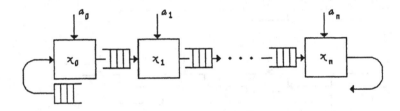

◇

This first example seems very close to the previous synchronous interpretation. In fact it defines a very different semantics. In a synchronous interpretation the semantics is an iterative program controlled by $\mathcal{T}$:

$$
\begin{aligned}
&\textit{for any } t \textit{ in } \mathcal{T} \textit{ loop} \\
&\qquad \textit{compute the set of } x_u[k] \\
&\qquad\quad \textit{such that } \textit{sem } <u,k> = <s,t> \\
&\textit{end loop;}
\end{aligned}
$$

In the asynchronous interpretation, the program is a function network (11) whose semantics is the histories of the buffered messages. More generally, asynchronous interpretations model non deterministic temporal behaviours of algorithms running on distributed architectures (MIMD machines). Such an interpretation may be presented as a straightforward generalization of the preceeding equation systems [1], such as :

$$
x_u[k] = f_u (..., x_v[k_{u,v}], ...)
$$
$$
u, v \in \mathcal{U}, \ k \in \mathbb{D}_u, \ k_{u,v} \in \mathbb{D}_v \qquad\qquad [2]
$$
$$
k \text{ and } k_{u,v} \text{ satisfy some relation } \mathcal{R}.
$$

Suppose you apply the substitution rule, you may rename arguments by introducing local variables, as following :

$$x_u[k] = f_u (..., y_{u,v}[k], ...)$$
$$y_{u,v}[k] = x_v[k_{u,v}]$$ [3]

$$u, v \in \mathcal{U}, \ k \in \mathbb{D}_u, \ k_{u,v} \in \mathbb{D}_v$$
k and $k_{u,v}$ satisfy some relation $\mathcal{R}.$

This last statement expresses communication specifications between processes. If the occurrence indices run over an inductive domain and the functions f_u and the relations $\mathcal{R}$ (in some sense) are monotonic, such fix-point equation system have a minimal solution which can then be computed by a recurrence path.

Such abstract parallel program specifications, in terms of processes and communications can be progressively derived from the problem terms. This point will be developped in the section 3.

2. Synchronous computations

Processor arrays composed of nodes locally and regularly connected are close to systolic arrays. So, problems expressed by recurrence equations can have nice solutions on these architectures. The techniques to design these synchronous programs come from systolic array synthesis results.

2.1. SYNTHESIS OF SYSTOLIC ARRAYS

The convex occurrence domain $\mathbb{D}$ associated with a system of linear recurrence equations is represented in the affine space $\mathbb{Z}^p$ (in practice p = 2 or 3). The points using the same occurrence as data for the associated calculations are joined by vectors called the *generating vectors*. These vectors define either a line or a plane. The set of points using some ocurrence are joined with the point associated with its calculation by a set of vectors called *inductive vectors*.

The inductive vectors joining a point with all the points which use the associated data define one or several *angular sectors*. Associated with the generating vectors, they define the *routing* of data in the array.

A *timing* is defined by a linear function of the occurrence indices. Any timing has to satisfy a few necessary conditions as : an occurrence can be used only after its calculation, data streams must flow in a regular way, etc.

These conditions are expressed more formally by solving a set of inequations, as :

for any inductive vector Ψ_x *associated with a variable* x: $\Psi_x \cdot \vec{\theta} > 0$

where $\vec{\theta}$ is a vector associated with the timing function. To validate these properties some transformations of the equation system, or of the domain definition, can be applied.

To obtain a systolic solution we may introduce other constraints for the architecture model. For example : no data broadcast, to define pure systolic arrays, neither control stream nor programmable cells :

- the first condition is expressed by a property of the generating vectors : $\vec{\Phi}_x \cdot \vec{\theta} \neq 0$,
- the second one may be satisfied by choosing a suitable *allocation direction*.

The systolic arrays are then obtained by *projection* of the domain relatively to the choosen allocation direction $\vec{\xi}$.

Example - The Gaussian elimination algorithm.

The problem is to solve the linear system $Ax = b$ where A is a $n \times n$ matrix and b a n vector. In order to solve it, the Gaussian elimination algorithm first transforms A into an equivalent triangulate matrix and then solves the triangular system. We are only concerned here by the triangularization of A. Since the transformation affects vector b, we consider that A is a $n \times n+1$ matrix whose last column is b. The elements of the resulting triangular matrix $A=(a_{ij})$ are defined as the final recurrence step $a(i,j,n-1)$ of the following system of recurrence equations :

$$a(i,j,0) = \begin{cases} a_{ij} & \text{if } j < n+1 \\ \\ b_i & \text{if } j = n+1 \end{cases} \qquad 1 \leq i \leq n, \quad 1 \leq j \leq n \qquad [0]$$

$$a(i,j,k) = a(i,j,k-1) \cdot a(i,k,k-1) / a(k,k,k-1) \times a(k,j,k-1) \qquad [1]$$
$$1 \leq k \leq n, \quad k+1 \leq i \leq n, \quad k+1 \leq j \leq n+1$$

When analysing equation [1], we observe that for any given i_0 and k_0 the point $a(i_0, j, k_0)$ uses the same values $a(i_0, k_0, k_0-1)$ and $a(k_0, k_0, k_0-1)$. To improve the efficiency of the solutions we transform these equations in such a way that each value $a(i_0, k_0, k_0-1) / a(k_0, k_0, k_0-1)$ is calculated only once. We substitute the sytem [1'-2] for the equation [1].

$$a(i,j,k) = a(i,j,k-1) \cdot c(i,k,k) \times a(k,j,k-1) \qquad [1']$$
$$1 \leq k \leq n, \quad k+1 \leq i \leq n, \quad k+1 \leq j \leq n+1$$

$$c(i,k,k) = a(i,k,k-1) / a(k,k,k-1) \qquad 1 \leq k \leq n-1, \quad k+1 \leq i \leq n \qquad [2]$$

An optimal pure systolic timing is defined by the linear function $t(i,j,k) = i+j+k-3$. By projecting points relatively to the direction $\vec{\xi} = (1,1,1)$ we obtain the following systolic array :

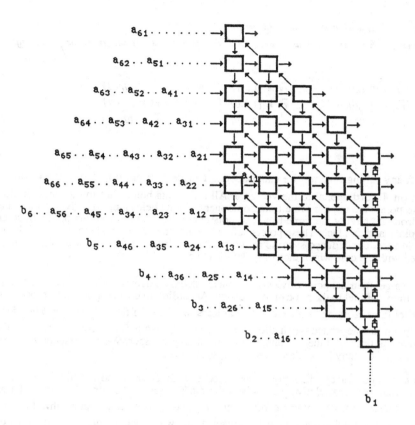

◇

2.2. SYNCHRONOUS SOLUTIONS

The *potential parallelism* of an algorithm is the maximal number of simultaneous calculations allowed by a given scheduling. The mapping of algorithms on processor arrays has then to take into account this potential parallelism relatively to the target architecture. The following study presents some results about space-optimal mappings. It is based on a geometrical model of computations.

2.2.1. *Geometrical tools.*

The convex domain $\mathbb{D}$ is supposed to be a polyhedron bounded by linear inequalities. The associated equations define its faces. From these equations we can determine its *ray vectors* which generate its edges. In the following, we consider convex polyhedra defined from these ray vectors $\vec{r}_q$

38

Example - The Gaussian elimination algorithm.
The convex polyhedron of $\mathbb{Z}^3$ associated with this problem is defined from the following ray vectors:

$$\vec{r1} = (0,1,0) \qquad \vec{r4} = (1,0,1) \qquad \vec{r7} = (0,0,1)$$
$$\vec{r2} = (1,0,0) \qquad \vec{r5} = (1,0,0) \qquad \vec{r8} = (0,1,1)$$
$$\vec{r3} = (1,1,1) \qquad \vec{r6} = (0,1,0) \qquad \vec{r9} = (0,1,0)$$

◇

With any timing function we can associate τ successive cutting planes of the convex polyhedron $\mathbb{D}$, orthogonal to the vector $\vec{\theta}$. All the points belonging to the same cutting plane are points having the same time component. Points belonging to a given face of the polyhedron and having the same time component are then the intersection points of some cutting plane and this face. These points define either a line or the whole face. If they define the whole face, the deduced systolic array is space-optimal. In the following we are only interested with the case where they only define a line.

From a geometrical point of view, any linear allocation decomposes the domain $\mathbb{D}$ into a set of lines parallel to the allocation direction. According to convex polyhedra properties, the parallel lines crossing $\mathbb{D}$ intersect with at least two faces of the polyhedron. Therefore, for any given line generated by an allocation direction $\vec{\xi}$, two points define respectively the first activation time, and the last one, of the allocated processor. We call respectively *first face,* and *last face,* any hyperplane containing such points.

These geometrical considerations about allocation direction are now used to determine a space-optimal mapping relatively to a given timing. The results hereunder are given for an allocation direction $\vec{\xi}$ whose time component is equal to 1. They can be generalized for any vector $\vec{\xi}$ (7). To simplify the rest of the presentation, we only consider the case in which there is only one first and one last face. We note $\vec{\mathcal{F}}$ and $\vec{\mathcal{L}}$ the orthogonal vectors of these two faces. We note $\vec{\mathcal{F}}_s$ and $\vec{\mathcal{L}}_s$ the vectors that generate the simultaneously active points in these faces.

For any timing function t and for any time $t0$ we define the number of simultaneous calculations $p(t0)$. The potential parallelism p is then defined by :

$$p = max_{1 \le t0 \le \tau} p(t0)$$

Property - For any time $t0$, the number of calculations occurring at $t0$ is equal to :

$$p(t0) = \sum_{h=1}^{t0} nf(h) - \sum_{h=1}^{t0-1} nl(h)$$

where for any h in $1..\tau$, $nf(h)$ and $nl(h)$ are defined as following :

$$nf(h) = Card\ \{k \in \mathbb{D}\ /\ t(k) = h\ and\ \vec{\mathcal{F}}.k + f = 0\}$$
$$nl(h) = Card\ \{k \in \mathbb{D}\ /\ t(k) = h\ and\ \vec{\mathcal{L}}.k + l = 0\}$$

where $\vec{\mathcal{F}}.k + f = 0$ (respectively $\vec{\mathcal{L}}.k + l = 0$) is the equation of the plane generated by the ray vectors of the first (respectively last) face.

These values $nf(h)$ and $nl(h)$ are defined at intervals $\mathcal{D}_{ij} \subset [1..\tau]$ where $\mathcal{D}_{ij}$ is the time interval whose extremities are the intersection of a line generated by $\vec{\mathcal{F}}_s$ (respectively $\vec{\mathcal{L}}_s$) and the edges e_i and e_j of $\mathbb{D}$:

$$nf(h) = \sum_{q=0}^{\left\lfloor \frac{\delta_{ij0}}{\vec{r}_i . \vec{\theta}} \right\rfloor} \left\lfloor \frac{\vec{r}_j . \vec{\theta} - (\delta_{ij0} - q\, \vec{r}_i . \vec{\theta})\, mod\ \vec{r}_j . \vec{\theta}}{\vec{r}_j . \vec{\theta}} \right\rfloor \qquad h \in \mathcal{D}_{ij}$$

where, if v_{ij} is the vertex intersection of the edges e_i and e_j we note $\delta_{ij0} = |h - t(v_{ij})|$; r_i and r_j are the ray vectors associated with e_i and e_j.

Note that in this value, i and j may be exchanged. Note also that the value $nl(h)$ is characterized in the same way. The demonstration of this property is given in (7).

2.2.2. Space-optimal mappings.

For any allocation direction $\vec{\xi}$ whose time component is 1, by applying the allocation function on both vectors $\vec{\mathcal{F}}_s$ and $\vec{\mathcal{L}}_s$, we can represent them at the level of the systolic architecture associated with $\vec{\xi}$. For any time h we call $\mathcal{L}_h$ the line generated by $\vec{\mathcal{L}}_s$ at h, and $\mathcal{F}_{h+1}$ the line generated by $\vec{\mathcal{F}}_s$ at $h+1$. These lines characterize a cone containing the active calculations at h, and whose top is a virtual calculation.

A mapping allocates the calculations of $\mathcal{L}_h$ and the calculations of $\mathcal{F}_{h+1}$ to the same processor of the array. We note np the number of processors needed for this mapping. This value np is determined by considering $nf(h)$ and $nl(h-1)$ for all values of $h \in [1..\tau]$, as expressed in the following algorithm :

$np := 0;$
$for\ h := 2\ to\ \tau\ do$
$\quad if\ nl(h\text{-}1) > nf(h)\ then\ np := np + nl(h\text{-}1)\text{ - }nf(h);$

We deduce from this algorithm that :

$$np = \frac{1}{2} \left[nf(1) + \sum_{h=2}^{\tau} |\ nf(h) \text{ - } nl(h\text{-}1)\ | + nl(\tau) \right]$$

Theorem -

$np = p$, then for any allocation direction $\vec{\xi}$ whose time component is 1, this mapping is space-optimal.

In the general case where the time component of $\vec{\xi}$ is > 1, this mapping is completed with a grouping of non simultaneous calculations on the same processor. This technique is defined in (15). Such allocation is determined by defining a set of allocation direction sequences of the form $\{\vec{\xi}_1, \vec{\xi}_2, ..., \vec{\xi}_p\}$ such that :

$- p = \vec{\xi}.\vec{\theta}$

$- |\vec{\xi}_m.\vec{\theta}| = 1 \quad \forall\ m \in 1..p$

$- \sum_{m=1}^{p} \vec{\xi}_m = \vec{\xi}$

Example - The Gaussian elimination algorithm.
For the allocation direction $\vec{\xi} = (1,1,1)$ *the first and last faces are represented hereunder :*

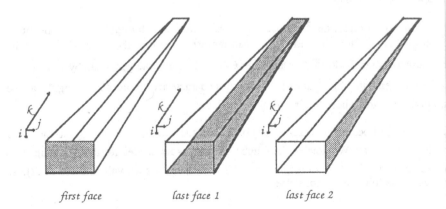

first face   last face 1   last face 2

The orthogonal vector of the first face is $\vec{F} = (0,0,1)$ and the orthogonal vectors of the last faces are $\vec{L}_1 = (1,0,0)$ and $\vec{L}_2 = (0,1,0)$. We calculate the unimodular vectors $\vec{F}_s$, $\vec{L}_{1s}$ and $\vec{L}_{2s}$:

$$\vec{F}_s = (f1,f2,f3) \qquad \text{with} \qquad f3 = 0$$
$$f1 + f2 + f3 = 0 \quad \Rightarrow \quad \vec{F}_s = (1,-1,0)$$

$$\vec{L}_{1s} = (l1,l2,l3) \qquad \text{with} \qquad l1 = 0$$
$$l1 + l2 + l3 = 0 \quad \Rightarrow \quad \vec{L}_{1s} = (0,-1,1)$$

$$\vec{L}_{2s} = (l1,l2,l3) \qquad \text{with} \qquad l2 = 0$$
$$l1 + l2 + l3 = 0 \quad \Rightarrow \quad \vec{L}_{2s} = (-1,0,1)$$

The potential parallelism is defined from these expressions of $nf(h)$ and $nl(h)$:

$$\forall \; h \in [1..n-1] \qquad nf(h) = h$$
$$\forall \; h \in [n..n+1] \qquad nf(h) = n - 1$$
$$\forall \; h \in [n+2..2n-1] \qquad nf(h) = 2n - h$$
$$\forall \; h \in [1..n-2] \qquad nl(h) = 0$$
$$\forall \; h \in [n-1..n] \qquad nl(h) = \left\lfloor \frac{h-n+1}{2} \right\rfloor + 1$$
$$\forall \; h \in [n+1..2n-1] \qquad nl(h) = \left\lfloor \frac{h-n+1}{2} \right\rfloor + h - n$$
$$\forall \; h \in [2n..3n-5] \qquad nl(h) = \left\lfloor \frac{3n-1-h}{2} \right\rfloor + \left\lfloor \frac{3n-3-h}{2} \right\rfloor + 1$$
$$\forall \; h \in [3n-4..3n-3] \qquad nl(h) = \left\lfloor \frac{3n-3-h}{2} \right\rfloor + 3n - 2 - h$$

For example, this potential parallelism is equal to $p = 10$, for $n = 6$. The time component of the systolic allocation direction is $\vec{\xi} . \vec{\theta} = 3$. Therefore, in order to respect the calculation scheduling, we consider the two cones $[L_{1h}, F_{h+3}]$ and $[L_{2h}, F_{h+3}]$ for any $h \in [1..3n-3]$. Mappings can be deduced from these cones. To complete the mapping we apply the grouping technique according to these decompositions of the vector $\vec{\xi}$,

$$\vec{\xi}_1 = (0,1,0), \quad \vec{\xi}_2 = (0,1,0), \quad \vec{\xi}_3 = (1,-1,1)$$
$$\vec{\xi}_1 = (0,0,1), \quad \vec{\xi}_2 = (0,0,1), \quad \vec{\xi}_3 = (1,1,-1)$$

which determines a space-optimal array (composed of 10 processors for $n = 6$):

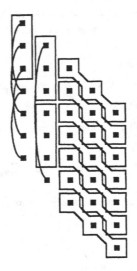

◇

3. A stepwise refinement technique to design asynchronous computations

We consider the specification of a problem as a first order predicate $\mathcal{P}$:

$$x \text{ such that } \mathcal{P}(x).$$

The transition from such a specification to a solution involves the definition of variables whose some occurrence value satisfies $\mathcal{P}$. We express this property as the conjonction of a termination property and a partial correctness one. Let us introduce some definitions and notations for the solution expressions.

3.1. SOLUTION SPECIFICATIONS

In the following $X = \{x_u, u \in \mathcal{U}\}$ denotes a finite set of typed variables, and $occX$ the set of the occurrences of X. Any element of $occX$ is a finite set as $\tilde{X}_{ku, u \in \mathcal{U}} = \{x_u[ku], u \in \mathcal{U}\}$. We note $\tilde{x}_k$ such an occurrence, and $\tilde{x}_{ku}$ to stipulate an occurrence whose index in x_u is ku. The indices ku of a variable x_u are supposed to belong to a countable and totally ordered domain $\mathbb{D}_u$, with a least element noted 0. We note $ku+1$ the successor of ku in this order. We note $\tilde{X}_0 = \{x_u[0], u \in \mathcal{U}\}$.

A *solution specification* is expressed as following :

$$(SAFE) \quad \forall \; k = \{ ku, \; u \in U \} \; \bullet \; Q(\tilde{x}_k)$$

$$(LIVE) \quad \exists \; k = \{ ku, \; u \in U \} \; \bullet \; term(\tilde{x}k)$$

The partial correctness property *(SAFE)* is expressed by a predicate Q characterizing the value of each occurrence of the variables x_u, and in particular the result one. This property is an invariant. It allows to precise how we determine an occurrence value from another one. The property *(LIVE)* is expressed by a predicate *term* on the variable occurrences. This predicate characterizes a state called *final state* in (4).

The design of a such a specification involves first the definition of the set of variables (the processes of the future program) and then the choice of both predicates Q and *term*. These properties must verify :

$$\forall \; k \; \bullet \; (Q(\tilde{x}_k) \wedge \; term(\tilde{x}_k)) \; \Rightarrow \; P(\tilde{x}_k)$$

Example - gcd $(a_0 ..., a_n)$
For this problem specification : $\quad x$ *such that* $x = gcd(a_0, ..., a_n)$
we define the following solution specification :

$$X = \{ x_0 ..., x_n \}$$

$$(SAFE) \quad \forall \; k_0 ..., k_n \; \bullet \; gcd(x_0[k_0], ..., x_n[k_n]) = gcd(a_0 ..., a_n)$$

$$(LIVE) \quad \exists \; k_0 ..., k_n \; \bullet \; x_0[k_0] = ... = x_n[k_n]$$

◇

3.2. STRATEGIES

We characterize now *strategies* (4), that are specifications from which we can build a program. We precise then the property *(LIVE)* by characterizing convenient occurrence sequences, for which the predicate *term* is eventually true for some occurrence $\tilde{x}_k$

For that we use the induction on well-founded sets. A *well-founded set* is a set F with an order relation $\leq$ such that any decreasing sequence is stationary. Intuitively, for the property *term* to be eventually true, it is sufficient to define an ordered set *occX* of variable occurrences. Hence we associate some element in a well-founded set with each variable occurrence and we show that the defined sequence decreases.

A strategy has the following general form :

$$(SAFE) \quad C_u(\tilde{X}_{k_u}) \rightarrow \quad x_u[k_u+1] = f_u(\tilde{X}_{k_u}) \quad u \in U$$

$$(LIVE) \quad \forall k \cdot ((\forall k' \cdot k \leqslant k' \Rightarrow \alpha(\tilde{X}_{k'}) \leq \alpha(\tilde{X}_k))$$
$$\wedge \ (term(\tilde{X}_k) \vee (\exists k' \cdot k < k' \wedge \alpha(\tilde{X}_{k'}) < \alpha(\tilde{X}_k))$$
$$)$$

with $\alpha : occX \rightarrow \mathcal{F} = \prod_{u \in U} \mathcal{F}_u$ where the $\mathcal{F}_u$ are well-founded sets.

Example - gcd $(a_0, ..., a_n)$

$$x_p[0] = a_p$$

$$x_p[k_p] = \begin{cases} x_q[k_q] < x_p[k_p-1] \ \rightarrow \ x_p[k_p-1] \cdot x_q[k_q] \\ \\ x_q[k_q] \geq x_p[k_p-1] \ \rightarrow \ x_p[k_p-1] \end{cases} \qquad k_p > 0$$

$p, q : 0.. n$ *such that :*
if some occurence k_r *of a variable* x_r *(r in 0.. n) is such that* $x_r[k_r] < x_p[k_p]$, *there exists an occurrence* $k'_p > k_p$ *satisfying* $x_p[k'_p] \leq x_p[k_p]$.

◇

At this point, a stepwise refinement technique (3) can be used by weakening the invariant property Q. Such a refinement using some predicate Q', assuming $Q' \Rightarrow Q$ is correct if and only if :

$$\forall k \cdot (Q'(\tilde{X}_k) \wedge \ term(\tilde{X}_k)) \Rightarrow \mathcal{P}(\tilde{X}_k)$$

This refinement is suitable if a strategy can be deduced from it.

Example - finding the root of a real function f by a partitionning method of an interval $]a, b[$.

$X = \{x_0, ..., x_n\}$ *defines the partition of the current interval.*

$\alpha : occ[a, b) \rightarrow \mathbb{R} :$ *defines the length of the current interval.*

$Q \equiv \forall k \in \mathbb{N} \cdot (\forall p \in 0..n \cdot (x_p[k] \in]a[k], b[k][\wedge \ f(a[k]) * f(b[k]) \leq 0))$
defines a decreasing sequence of intervals and leads to a synchronous iterative algorithm.
$Q' \equiv \forall k \in \mathbb{N} \cdot (\exists p \in 0..n \cdot (x_p[k] \in]a[k], b[k][\wedge \ f(a[k]) * f(b[k]) \leq 0))$
defines a refinement which leads to an asynchronous algorithm.

◇

3.3. DISTRIBUTING PROGRAMS

In order to design abstract parallel solutions, in terms of communicating processes satisfying such a strategy, we introduce local variables and communication specifications, which have to be a correct refinement of the strategy. This step leads to statements whose safety part has the following form :

$$C_u(\tilde{y}_{u,k_u}) \rightarrow x_u[k_u+1] = f_u(\tilde{y}_{u,k_u}) \quad u \in \mathcal{U}$$
$$P_{u,v}(y_{u,v}, x_v)$$

where $\tilde{y}_{u,k_u}$ is an occurrence of the variable set $\{y_{u,v}, u \in \mathcal{U}\}$.

Example - *gcd* $(a_0, ..., a_n)$

In the gcd previous statement we can substitute y_p *variables for the* x_p *ones. The conditions are then* $y_p[k_p] < x_p[k_p-1]$ *and the predicates* $P_{p,q} \equiv TRUE$.

Note that these two conditions can be substituted one for the other. We obtain then :

$$x_p[0] = a_p$$
$$x_p[k_p] = x_p[k_p-1] - y_p[k_p] \qquad k_p > 0$$
$$y_p[k_p] = x_q[k_q] \qquad q \in 0..n \ such \ that \ x_q[k_q] < x_p[k_p-1]$$

◇

The next refinement step consists in defining an abstract *array topology*, and possibly reinforcing the *(LIVE)* property. Such a reinforcement restrains the possible target solutions by defining :

$$y_{u,v}[k_u] = x_v[k_{u,v}] \quad with \ k_{u,v} = \tau (k_u)$$

The definition of τ requires some expression about the computation circumstances. This asynchronous parallelism modeling can be easily expressed by associating some *time stamp* with any variable occurrence. A time stamp may be considered as a value in an infinite, ordered discrete set as $\mathbb{N}$ to handle time. For any variable x and any occurrence k, we note $t(x[k])$ its time stamp. Examples of very used functions to reinforce a communication specification may be :

$$-\tau (k_u) = least \ \{ \ k' \ / \ t(x_v[pre_{u,k}] < t(x_v[k']) \le t(y_u[k_u]) \}$$

where $pre_{u,k}$ is the last occurrence of x_v used to define some previous occurrence of y_u. This function defines a very common asynchronous *fifo* communication.

$$-\tau (k_u) = greatest \ \{ \ k' \ / \ t(x_v[pre_{u,k}] < t(x_v[k']) \le t(y_u[k_u]) \}$$

This function defines an other communication primitive where messages can be lost.

46

Example · gcd (a₀..., aₙ)

Any connex graph for the abstract array is convenient for the previous strategy. Then, for any p in 0.. n, if we define the used variable set as {p-1, p+1} we determine parallel solutions to be mapped on a bidirectionnal ring of nodes.

Because of the decreasing condition expressed in the definition, the second function τ can be proposed to reinforce the parallel expression of the gcd problem.

◇

From such functions which implement communication specifications, we can easily deduce an *operational expression* of convenient communication primitives. For the last example, we give the pre-post definition of a communication operation, from an abstract data set X, representing the values possibly used :

$$\{pre :: \quad not \; empty? \; (X)\}$$
$$value :: \quad last \; (X)$$
$$\{post :: \quad []\}$$

Last transformations consist in expressing *processes* in a CSP style (10).

Example · gcd (a₀..., aₙ)

From syntactical transformations the solution leads to the following program CSP, which is proposed in (1) :

$GCD :: [P(i: 0.. n)]$
where each process is defined as :

$P_i ::$ 　$[\; x := a_i \; ;$

　　　　$rsl := true; \; rsr := true;$

　　　　$*[\; rsl \; ; \; P_{i-1} \, ! \, x \; \rightarrow \; rsl := false$

　　　　$[] \; rsr \; ; \; P_{i+1} \, ! \, x \; \rightarrow \; rsr := false$

　　　　$[] \; P_{i-1} \, ? \, y \rightarrow [\; y \geq x \; \rightarrow \; skip$

　　　　　　　　$[] \; y < x \; \rightarrow \; x := x \cdot y; \; rsr := true; \; rsl := true$
　　　　　　　　$]$

　　　　$[] \; P_{i+1} \, ? \, y \rightarrow [\; y \geq x \; \rightarrow \; skip$

　　　　　　　　$[] \; y < x \; \rightarrow \; x := x \cdot y; \; rsr := true; \; rsl := true$
　　　　　　　　$]$

　　　　$]$
　　$]$

◇

Exercise - *From the famous paper of Dijkstra :* '*Finding the correctness proof of a concurrent program*' *(9).*

y denotes a vector of $n+1$ components y_i for i in $0..n$. With the identifier $\mathcal{F}$ we denote a vector-valued function of a vector-valued argument. The algorithm solves the equation $y = \mathcal{F}(y)$, or, introducing the components $\mathcal{F}_i$ of $\mathcal{F}$:

$$y_i = \mathcal{F}_i(y) \qquad i \text{ in } 0..n$$

It is assumed that the initial value of y and the function $\mathcal{F}$ are such that the repeated assignements $y_i := \mathcal{F}_i(y)$ lead in a finite number of sets to a vector solution y.

From this statement, we propose the followwing solution specification :

$$\mathcal{Y} = \{y_0, ..., y_n\}$$

(SAFE)   TRUE

(LIVE) $\exists k \cdot (\forall i \in 0..n \cdot y_i[k] = \mathcal{F}_i (y_0[k], ..., y_n[k]))$

The hypothesis suggests the following strategy :

(SAFE) $y_i[k+1] = \mathcal{F}_i (y_0[k], ..., y_n[k])$

(LIVE)   hypothesis

By distributing the variables the following statement leads to the classical synchronous Jacobi iteration :

(SAFE) $y_i[k+1] = \mathcal{F}_i (x_0[k], ..., x_n[k])$
          $x_i[k] = y_i[k]$

(LIVE)   hypothesis

The derivation of a correct asynchronous solution can be obtained from a new specification expression, which is a refinement of the first one, by reinforcing the (SAFE) and (LIVE) properties to introduce a vector h that defines the termination conditions.

$$\mathcal{Y} = \{y_0, ..., y_n\}$$
$$\mathcal{H} = \{h_0, ..., h_n\}$$

(SAFE) $\forall k_0, ..., k_n \cdot (\forall i \in 0..n \cdot (h_i[k_i] \lor y_i[k_i] = \mathcal{F}_i (\tilde{\mathcal{Y}}_{k_i}))$

(LIVE) $\exists k_0, ..., k_n \cdot (\forall i \in 0..n \cdot \neg h_i[k_i])$

The proof of correctness of the following strategy can be referred to the proof by Dijkstra :

48

$$(SAFE) \quad y_i[k_i] = \mathcal{F}_i(\tilde{\mathcal{Y}}_{k_i}) \;\rightarrow\; y_i[k_i+1] = y_i[k_i]$$
$$h_i[k_i] = false$$

$$y_i[k_i] \neq \mathcal{F}_i(\tilde{\mathcal{Y}}_{k_i}) \;\rightarrow\; y_i[k_i+1] = \mathcal{F}_i(\tilde{\mathcal{Y}}_{k_i})$$
$$\mathcal{H}[k_i+1] = (true, true, ..., true)$$

$(LIVE)$ hypothesis

Last, by distributing the variables, the following abstract program is correct, assuming the used occurrence indices k'_i are growing :

$$(SAFE) \quad y_i[k_i] = \mathcal{F}_i(\tilde{X}_{k_i}) \;\rightarrow\; y_i[k_i+1] = y_i[k_i]$$
$$h_i[k_i] = false$$

$$y_i[k_i] \neq \mathcal{F}_i(\tilde{X}_{k_i}) \;\rightarrow\; y_i[k_i+1] = \mathcal{F}_i(\tilde{X}_{k_i})$$
$$\mathcal{H}[k_i+1] = (true, true, ..., true)$$

$$x_i[k_i] = y_i[k'_i]$$

$(LIVE)$ hypothesis

◇

Conclusion

This presentation is an attempt to progress in the general problem of designing communicating processes to be mapped on regular distributed architectures. While some particular target solutions receive good answers, specially in synchronous computations, for other ones related with asynchronous computations the studies are just at the beginning.

The main points we have put foreward in this presentation concern some technical steps to go from a given problem abstract specification, in terms of a system of recurrence equations, to some operational concrete parallel solutions.

Our current work in this domain aims to define a software environment to assist design of parallel programs. At the specification level we are defining a functional language to express equations and variable domains. A denotational semantics is defined in terms of time stamped variables. Formal transformations are defined to transform the equation systems until concrete parallel solutions in different contexts : systolic and synchronous processor arrays, by geometrical considerations, or asynchronous computations expressed as OCCAM processes. These transformations have to be expressed and applied through a metalanguage whose objects are statements and architecture constraints.

This work is developed in the PERCEVAL project by Ph. Clauss, S. Damy, M.C. Eglin, S. Grisouard, J. Julliand, C. Mongenet and E. Violard.

References

(1) Apt, K.R., Francez, N., and Roever, W.P. de, (1980), A proof system for communicating sequential processes, ACM Toplas, 2, 3, 359-385.

(2) Aschcroft, E.A. and Wadge, W.N., (1976), Lucid : a formal system for writing and proving programs, SIAM Journal on Computing.

(3) Back, R.J.R. and Sere, K., (1989), Stepwise refinement of action systems, in Mathematics of program construction, LNCS 375.

(4) Chandy, K.M. and Misra, J., (1988), Parallel Program Design, Prentice Hall Ed.

(5) Choo, Y. and Chen, M.C., (1988), A theory of program optimization, TR-608, Univ. of Yale.

(6) Clauss, Ph. and Perrin, G.R., (1988), Synthesis of process arrays, in CONPAR'88, Manchester.

(7) Clauss, Ph., (1990), Synthèse d'algorithmes systoliques et implantation optimale en place sur réseaux de processeurs synchrones, Thesis, Univ. of Franche-Comté.

(8) Delosme, J.M. and Ipsen, I.C.F., (1985), An illustration of a methodology for the construction of efficient systolic architectures in VLSI, Sd Inter. Symposium on VLSI technology systems and applications.

(9) Dijkstra, E.D.W., (1979), Finding the correctness proof of a concurrent program, in LNCS 69.

(10) Hoare, C.A.R., (1978), Communicating Sequential Processes, Com. ACM, 21, 8.

(11) Kahn, G., (1974), The semantics of a simple language for parallel programming, in IFIP Information Processing.

(12) Karp, R.M., Miller, R.E. and Winograd, S., (1967), The organization of computations for uniform recurrence equations, J. of ACM, 14, 3.

(13) Kung, H.T., (1979), The structure of parallel algorithms, Advances in Comp., 15, 1.

(14) Mongenet, C. and Perrin, G.R., (1987), Synthesis of systolic arrays for inductive problems, in Conf. PARLE, Eindhoven, LNCS 259.

(15) Perrin, G.R., Clauss, Ph. and Damy, S., (1989), Mapping programs on regular Distibuted Architectures, in Hypercube and Distributed Computers, Elsevier Sc. Pub.

(16) Plaice, J.A., (1988), Sémantique et compilation de Lustre : un langage déclaratif synchrone, Thesis INP Grenoble.

(17 Quinton, P., (1988), Mapping recurrences on parallel architectures, in Third Inter. Conf. on Supercomputing, Boston.

(18) Thalhofer, K., (1989), RGL : A Specification Language Based on Recurrence Equations, Research report, Univ. of Erlangen-Nürmberg.

DOMAIN DECOMPOSITION ON TRANSPUTER ARRAYS AND EMERGING ARCHITECTURES

J.S. REEVE
Dept. of Electronics and Computer Science
University of Southampton
Southampton, U.K.

ABSTRACT. Most problems in CFD fit neatly onto transputer arrays as the computational domain can readily be sub-divided and the data set distributed evenly over a number of processors. Results using three different algorithms (vortex shedding, finite volume and spectral elements) are presented. The commonality of the parallelised methods is discussed, and tools under development that exploit the common structure are described.

1. MIMD Architectures and Their Uses

The formal model Communicating Parallel Processes (CSP) (Hoare (1985)) developed at Oxford University provides a neat and consistent model of parallel programming. Each of the parallel processes in the model can only access its own memory, thereby removing any contention at a stroke. If one process want to read or write another processes data it can only do so by mutual agreement. This means that if process A wants to know the value of variable b in process B's data space then by prearrangement B must send A a message telling it the value. The native language of the transputer, Occam, was developed to implement a restricted subset of CSP. On the lowest level each parallel process is a sequentially executed program that can interact with other processes by communication only over one way channels. Once a process has elected to send (or receive) data on a channel, then it is committed to it until the process attached to the other end of the channel is ready to receive (or send) the data. At this point the two processes are synchronised and the data exchange takes place, after which each process continues.

MIMD (multiple instruction multiple data) architectures are amenable to three broad classes of program design. Either code is distributed, or data is distributed or the program is replicated. Of course programs are often hybrids containing phases of each design type. Code distribution views the program as a flow of data through code modules that "add value". This is usually referred to as algorithmic design paradigm. Domain decomposition or geometric parallelism is a design paradigm for data distribution algorithms, where each transputer has the same code but works on a different subset of the data. Program replication or farming is where the same program needs to be run several times with different initial conditions. Programs that seem likely candidates for farming are not always able to be implemented, because of memory restriction, however farming

51

D. Gassilloud and J. C. Grossetie (eds.), Computing with Parallel Architectures: T.Node, 51–63.

52

is one way of guaranteeing very efficient use of the processors.

The ratio communication-time to work-time always dominates efficiency formulae of parallel algorithms, so it is easy to increase processor efficiency by swamping it with work, and not so easy to increase overall speed-up which requires that more processors do less work each. For an introduction to practical occam programming and the efficiency of algorithms see (Kerridge (1987), Hey (1989), Pritchard (1987), Pritchard (1988)).

2. Geometric Parallelism

Geometric designs are almost always used for physical simulations, where there is a one map between the physical space and the transputer array. Two dimensional problems are the more naturally suited to transputer because of the restriction to four links per transputer. For higher dimensional problems there is a large communications overhead, because of the restricted connectivity. Very often too, a problem that seems ideally suited to a pure geometric solution is marred by one or two bits of information being by all parts of the grid. Additionally each transputer involved in the simulation needs to be logically connected to the host and/or graphics display monitor.

The efficiency of geometric solutions is roughly proportional to the ratio of information inside each segment to the amount on the edges, i.e. a perimeter to area effect, or a surface to volume effect in three dimensions.

Lets say for instance, that the problem is a grid of $N \times N$ data points and these are distributed on an array of $L \times L$ transputers. Define T_{calc} as the time to update one data point and T_{comm} as the time to transmit one data point then, the time to update the data on the whole array is:

$$T_{update} = (N \times N) \, T_{calc}/(L \times L)$$

and the communication time needed is:

$$T_{talk} = (N/L + 1) \, T_{comm}$$

provided that each data point needs only neighbouring points and that communication in each direction overlaps. The total time for the calculation, assuming no overlap between communication and calculation is:

$$T_{total} = T_{update} + T_{talk}$$

The ideal total time:

$$T_{ideal} = (L \times L) \, T_{calc}$$

The efficiency E is then the ratio of T_{ideal} to T_{total}, that is:

$$E = 1/(1 + g \, (1 + g) \, t)$$

where:

$$g = L/N$$

is the geometric factor, and:

$$t = T_{comm}/T_{calc} \cdot$$

For values of gt << 1 the efficiency can be written as:

$$E = 1 - W_{egdes}/W_{inner}$$

where:

$$W_{edges} = LT_{comm}$$

measures the work on the edges and:

$$W_{inner} = NT_{calc}$$

measures the internal work. Clearly speed-up is not nearly as easily gained as scaleup, where a larger problem can be done in the same time on more processors.

3. The Travelling Salesman

Not all geometric algorithms involve a direct mapping of the simulation space onto the distributed data set. One interesting counter example is the Travelling Salesman problem as tackled by Allwright and Carpenter.

Given a set of towns and a road network between them, what is the shortest path that a travelling salesman must take in order to return home having visited each town only once. This travelling salesman problem is NP-complete. That is there is almost certainly no algorithm that solves the problem in a time that is polynomial in the number of cities. A more modest aim is to solve the problem approximately using the simulated annealing technique. In this approach variations about an arbitrary initial path are considered. The variations are path reversals on a short segment that are effected by pair exchanges. Exchanges that reduce the path length are kept, but exchanges that increase the path length are only accepted with a probability:

$$p(L,T) = \exp(- L/T)$$

where L is the change in path length L, and T is a parameter usually referred to as the temperature because of its role in the Metropolis algorithm from which it is derived. The system starts off at a high temperature and the algorithm proceeds selecting random exchanges until equilibrium is reached. That is until there is little or no progress in reducing L. The temperature is then lowered and the process repeated. When the temperature reaches zero the local minimum reached is usually within around five percent of the exact answer.

The apparent global nature of the cost function make this an unusual problem to try and distribute, but if the inter-town exchanges are paired so that the path doesn't break up into a series of closed loops, then the cost function can be evaluated locally. The path is a one dimensional structure that is distributed on a ring of processors. The town is sequentially labelled around the path then the trial exchanges:

$$(2,3) \text{ with } (n,n - 1) \text{ and } (3,4) \text{ with } (n - 1, n - 2)$$

and so on until:

$$((n - 3)/2, (n - 1)/2)$$

is exchanged with:

$$((n + 3)/2, (n + 1)/2)$$

See Figure 1 for a schematic view of the procedure. We have assumed an odd number of towns without loss of generality.

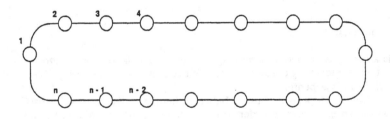

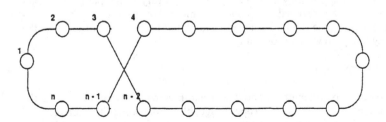

Figure 1. A ring of towns before and after an exchange.

4. The CFD Problems

The flow problems considered are for viscous incompressible flows, using both vortex shedding and spectral element techniques, and inviscid compressible flows using the finite volume technique.

Computationally, the simplest method is vortex shedding (Chorin (1978)) off a two dimensional object. The Navier-Stokes equations are written in the form:

$$\partial \omega / \partial t + (\vec{u} \cdot \nabla)\omega = R^{-1}\nabla^2 \omega$$

where:

$$\omega = \nabla \times \vec{u}$$

and

$$\nabla^2 \psi = -\omega$$

This enables the vortex potential function to be expressed as a sum of vorticities of the form:

$$\psi = \sum_{j=1}^{N} \psi_j$$

The method works by splitting off the viscous and convective parts.

$$D\omega / Dt = 0$$

and

$$\partial \omega / \partial t = R^{-1}\nabla^2 \omega$$

The algorithm consists of tracking vortices shed by the object as they move in the potential flow, with added diffusion induced by the viscous term which is modelled by Gaussian noise. Normally this algorithm has time complexity $O(N^2)$, but by zone refinement the complexity is reduced to $O(N \ln N)$, so the ideal complexity on P processors is $O(N \ln N / P)$, which is very nearly achieved. In this problem, each processor needs information from every other processor, but by organising a ring around all the processors all processors can share data in P time steps. The results from this simulation are quite promising and quantities like drag and lift are confirmed by experiment.

The second problem we consider here is inviscid compressible flow, of the type that might be encountered off the surface of an aerofoil. The system is described by the Euler equations:

$$\frac{\partial \vec{U}}{\partial t} + \frac{\partial \vec{F}}{\partial x} + \frac{\partial \vec{G}}{\partial y} = 0$$

$$U = \begin{pmatrix} \rho \\ \rho\,u \\ \rho\,v \\ \rho\,E \end{pmatrix} ; F = \begin{pmatrix} \rho\,u \\ \rho\,u^2 + p \\ \rho\,uv \\ \rho\,uE + pu \end{pmatrix} ; G = \begin{pmatrix} \rho\,v \\ \rho\,uv \\ \rho\,v^2 + p \\ \rho\,vE + pv \end{pmatrix}$$

and the energy:

$$E = \frac{p}{(\gamma - 1)\rho} + \frac{u^2 + v^2}{2}$$

assuming an ideal gas. Where in the above   is the fluid density and u and v are the x and y components of the velocity and p is the pressure. Using the finite volume method (Peyret and Taylor (1986)) the physical space is broken up into regions, and the fluxes through each is conserved. The computational space is broken up into larger regions to be handled by each processor. The algorithm requires that data is exchanged between edges of the processor regions. The last method we consider is the spectral element method (Patera (1984)) applied to incompressible, viscous flows. The Navier-Stokes equation is solved by using a Lagrange interpolation formula for the velocity, the coefficients of which are determined by a variational principle. So we write for the velocity field:

$$\vec{v}(x,y) = \sum_{j=0}^{N} \sum_{i=0}^{N} \vec{v}_{ij} h_i(x) h_j(y)$$

and determine the v_{ij} by variation. This leads to a complicated set of equations that are solved at each time step by the conjugate gradient method. To parallelise the algorithm, the simulation domain is broken down into regions managed by each transputer. The efficiency of the algorithm is dominated by the "surface to volume" ratio of work communicated between regions to work done within a region. This method requires edge and corner swapping, as well as distribution of the convergence estimate by each processor.

5. The Program Structure

As first reported (Reeve (1989)), all the above problems have the common program structure outlined below. Each does not all use all of the facilities but a subset of them.

In pseudo code then, on each processor, the main code looks like:

```
SEQ
    get_initial_conditions(from_host_processor)
    FOR time = 0 FOR period
        SEQ
            work_out_display
            put_display(to_graphics_processor)
            PRI PAR
                swap_edge_&_corner_information(with_neighbours)
```

```
            work_out_inner_segment
            work_out_edge_segments
            circulate_convergence_data(on_data_ring)
```

Notice that the algorithm works in lock step and deadlock is readily avoided. The communications steps fall into one of three classes.

The first is on spanning trees from host to workers for initial data and the reverse for sending data back to the disc, and a separate tree from workers to the graphics system. Templates for communication on a tree are, for a spanning out tree:

```
    SEQ
        input_from_parent ? message
        SEQ i = 0 FOR no_of_daughters
            output_to_daughter[i] ! message
```

and for a spanning in tree:

```
    SEQ i = 0 FOR no_of_daughters
        SEQ
            input_from_daughter[i] ? message
            output_to_parent ! message
```

The second communications class is the edge and corner swapping between touching segments. This is simply:

```
    SEQ
        PAR i = 0 FOR no_of_edges
            PAR
                input[i] ? his_edge
                output[i] ! my_edge
        ... glean_corner_information
        PAR i = 0 FOR no_of_corners
            PAR
                input[i] ? his_corner
                output[i] ! through_corner
```

The third communications class is the data share ring, which needs a buffer on each site if cyclic deadlock is to be avoided, while ensuring maximal throughput.

```
    PAR
        SEQ
            internal_2 ! my_data
            SEQ i = 0 FOR NoOfWorkers
                SEQ
                    internal_1 ? ring_data
                    internal_2 ? (ring_data < > my_data)
```

```
SEQ i = 0 FOR NoOfWorkers
    SEQ
        internal_2 ? ring_data
        out ! ring_data
SEQ i = 0 FOR NoOfWorkers
    SEQ
        in ? ring_data
        internal_1 ! rind_data
```

For the spectral element method in particular, provision must be made for local grid refinement. It is possible to locally refine the grid (Maday et al. (1988)) and introduce a mismatch between sub-domains, as in Figure 2 for instance. The introduction of a mortar function on these non-conforming edges (or planes) preserves the accuracy of the numerical method, but degerates the communications to computation time ratio of the whole simulation, since each edge swap now consists of a number of swaps on sub edges. The depth of the nonconformity determines the number of extra time steps involved in each edge swap.

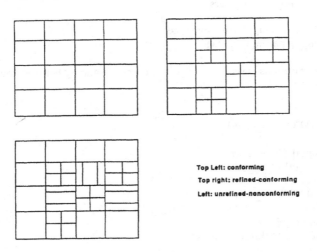

Top Left: conforming
Top right: refined-conforming
Left: unrefined-nonconforming

Figure 2: Conforming and Non-conforming Domain Decompositions

6. A CASE Toolset for CFD

One problem with massive parallelism is that the processes must be distributed among processors, and if that involves a shape or data space that is not a simple rectangle, then there has to be user support for processor placement. The CASE tool described in this section is based on the spectral element technique described in Section 3, as it is a superset of the others (if the common data ring is added), and the method of partitioning doesn't degrade the accuracy of the solution, even if a non conforming grid is specified. For methods requiring

them, conforming grids can, of course, be constructed. The CFD CASE toolset currenuy under development consists of
    a. a CAD system for carving up the dataset.
    b. a Preprocessor to extract communication paths.
    c a System Builder and Loader.
    d. Graphics Display Support.

The CAD works by allowing the user to specify boundary walls, and inflow and outflow segments. The enclosed region can then be sectioned off into gross regions, and these in turn can be bifurcated repeatedly until the total number of processors is reached, as shown in figure 3. A system configuration file is used to specify the availability of graphics and disc (host) processors. These are attached to the worker array previously specified by the user, by attaching the links equidistantly around the perimeter of the flow space. The CAD is only available on SUN systems. PC users have to type in a configuration file but this situation will change when the CAD is converted to Xwindows.

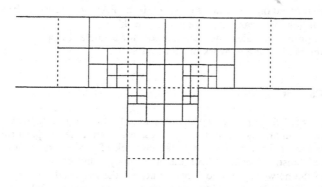

Figure 3: Bifurcation of a Channel Join (artries in 2-d)

The preprocessor takes the distribution of transputers as specified by the CAD and works out the communications trees for use by the communications library. The output of the preprocessor is a number of files that the user incorporates into the program.

The Builder and Loader pick up the files specified by the user on the CAD. These files are the program names of the worker and host programs as well as the names of boundary and inflow and outflow processes. The Loader then places the appropriate programs on each transputer and puts in all the local channels. FORTRAN, C and OCCAM are currently supported.

The Graphics Library simply contains routines that dump data into video ram and flip screens on each iteration. The users must convert the data for display on each worker, so that all work involved in the program is distributed.

In short provided the problem is a subset of the common structure outlined in the previous section, the it can probably use the tools as provided.

7 The Configuration Problem

The transputer implementation of the OCCAM model as described above suffers from the resctricted number of link per processor. It is the programmers responsibility to ensure that all the logical process to process connections required are made. If the communications scheme is simple and works in lock step, as for instance with the geometric paradigm on a two dimensional grid, then there may be little problem. However even for a conceptually simple master plus slaves design, the user is obliged to construct a communications harness to make all the logical connections of the master to each slave.

One other important restriction on transputer occam is the lack of global synchronization. On one processor it makes sense to write:

```
SEQ
    PAR
        ... process one
        ... process two
    ... process three
```

so that process three will only proceed when processes two and three are complete. As it is currently implemented on transputers however, if the PAR were a PLACED PAR then there is no way of "joining" again after the parallel "fork".

These two problems makes the occam model for a single transputer fundamentally different from the model for a network of transputers.

8. The Valiant Concept

(Valiant (1989, 1988, 1989)) has shown that provided that there is sufficient redundancy of parallel processes in an algorithm, then it is possible to emulate the performance of an ideal parallel processor, i.e. a totally connected network of processors, on a realistic machine. A suitable realistic machine is an n dimensional hypercube with $p = 2^n$ processors. The diameter of the network is n and it turns out that the required excess parallelism in n. This excess parallelism is required to ensure that each processor is fully occupied while messages related to the other processes on the same processor are being routed. As all the processors are now guaranteed to be busy all the time, it follows that this realistic machine is working with optimal efficiency, so the algorithm executes in a time proportional to the ideal time, where the constant of proportionality incorporates the ratio of the number of processors in the ideal machine to the number of processors in the realistic machine.

One key ingredient to the validity of the above argument is the assumption that messages can be delivered in time proportional to n. In general, algorithms will not have nicely balanced communications characteristics and hot spots will develop, reducing the effective maximum bandwidth of the network that is available when all links are busy. These communications bottlenecks can be eliminated in a network that uses two phase random routing. In the first phase messages are passed from the source to a random interim destination, and then in the second phase they go from the interim node to the final destination. The net effect is to use sufficient of the available bandwidth in the network to guarantee delivery in the required time.

Having a virtual shared memory system of transputers is another desirable property. This would require distributing the data over the memory space of the entire machine using a suitable hashing function to minimise the distribution of accesses among the memory banks. Even with randomised memory locations, the worst case number of clashes increases with machine size, so the additional feature of bulk synchronization has been proposed. This restricts the number of read or writes to n per time interval and the number of clashes becomes manageable. The work of Valiant and others has shown the possibility of building a general purpose MIMD machine that implements the XPRAM model of complexity theory. An XPRAM machine is a bit too complex for implementation yet however, and a necessary interim step is the construction of a general purpose MIMD machine with strictly local memory.

9. Emerging Technology

The next generation of transputers will be designed with Valiants theory in mind. The new processor, the H1 will support virtual links so that processes on one transputer can have logical channel connections to processes on other transputers, without the programmer having to provide through routing support. Other features of the H1 include many to one channels for resource sharing such as writing to disc or screen. There will no longer be a need to place channels and occam for a distributed network of transputers will begin to look like occam for a single transputer. Dynamica process creation will also be possible, that is the number of replications of a PAR statement need not be a compile time constant.

The through routing logic will be in hardware on another component, the C104, shown schematically in Figure 4, currently under development. Two fairly recent concepts, worm-hole routing and interval labelling enables fast compact implementation in silicon. Worm-hole routing is when messages are passed on through a node without being stored, so as soon as the header is read the message is shuffled through the node, so no buffering is necessary. Interval labelling (see Figure 5), in which a simple comparison is all that is required to go from source to destination, provided that the network can accommodate a suitable labelling scheme. The main networks for this type of approach are trees, n-cubes and 2-d arrays. Of course spanning trees can be defined for any network, but the number of links used in the routing scheme is less than the maximum. A machine of H1s attached to a C104 provides users with any desired logical network of the same number of processors. It will also be possible to connect C104s together to make a machine of any size.

The change in architecture to a more benign machine will allow many of the standard algorithms to be simplified and extended, and any through routing software to be thrown out. It will be interesting to see just how the new and old machines compare and whether or not two phase random routing degrades the performance of algorithms that have only local communications.

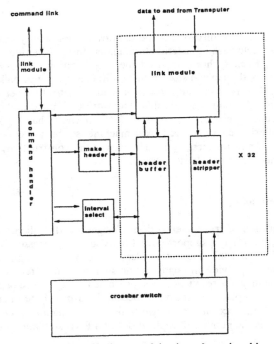

Figure 4. Schematic block diagram of the through routing chip.

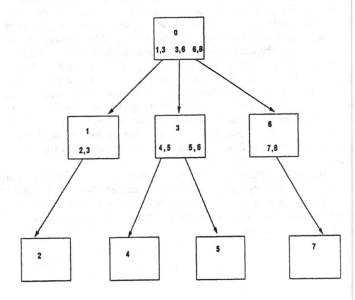

Figure 5. An example of interval labelling on a tree.

10. References

Hoare, C.A.R. (1985), Communicating Sequential Processes, Englewood Cliffs NJ., Prentice Hall.

Kerridge, J. (1987), Occam 2: A Practical Approach, Blackwell Scientific Publications, Oxford.

Hey, Anthony G.J. (1989), The Role of MIMD Arrays of Transputers in Computational Physics, Computer Physics Communications Vol. 56, 1-24.

Pritchard, D.J. (1987), Practical Parallism Using Transputer Arrays, Proceedings PARLE Conf. Eindhoven, Lecture Notes in Computer Science, Vol. 258, G. Goos and J. Hartmanis, Eds. (Springer, Berlin).

Valiant, L.G. (1989), Bulk Synchronous Parallel Computers, Parallel Processing and Artificial Intelligence. M. Reeve and S.E. Zenith, Eds. Wiley, Chichester.

Valiant, L.G. (1988), Optimally Universal Parallel Computers, Phil. Trans. Roy. Soc. A326 373.

Valiant, L.G. (1989), General Purpose Parallel Architectures, Handbook of Theoretical Computer Science. J. Van Leuwen Eds., North Holland, Amsterdam.

Pritchard, D.J. (1987), Mathematical Models of Distributed Computation, Proceedings 7th Occam User Group, Grenoble.

Chorin, A.J. (1978), Random Vortices and Random Vortex Sheets, SIAM-AMS proceedings, Vol. 11, p. 19.

Peyret, R. and Taylor, T.D. (1986), Computational Methods for Fluid Flows, Springer-Verlag, New York.

Patera, A.T. (1984), A Spectral Element Method for Fluid Dynamics ..., J. Comp. Phys., Vol. 54, p. 468.

Reeve, J.S. (1989), Some Parallel Communications Schemes, Proceedings 2nd Australian Occam User Group, Melbourne.

Maday, Y., Marriplis, C. and Patera, A. (1988), Nonconforming Spectral Element Methods ..., ICASE Report No. 88-59.

PROGRAMMING DISTRIBUTED COMPUTERS
A SINGLE PROGRAM APPROACH(*)

C. JARD
IRISA/CNRS
Campus de Beaulieu
35042 Rennes Cedex - France

1. Introduction

Distributed-memory parallel computers (DMPCs for short) receive presently much attention since they can provide computing power in a more cost-effective than traditional supercomputers designs and have the potential to still improve their performances. So, parallel computing on DM-PCs is becoming more and more important. In Europe, a lot of such multi-computers are now installed, and a peculiar effort is brought to the development of the Transputer technology.

However, recent advances in architectures have not been met with corresponding (and necessary) advances in software techniques. The main problem in multiprocessing is not only to build a computer, but also how to use it. Furthermore, we are not only interested in offering distributed services (as in distributed systems over computer networks), but in developing parallel algorithms and programs that can be executed efficiently. To build good languages and compilers for programming DMPCs is a real challenge. Very little industrial compilers are near to their end. We expect that research laboratories and universities will strongly contribute to that domain.

We report our experience in developing a compiler and a distributed run-time kernel for distributed computers, called Echidna is a software package available for more than one year, which aims at supporting DMPC programmers. It is basically oriented towards the prototyping of distributed software on real parallel machines. Applications are described using an ISO formal description technique called Estelle. We begin to present and justify the concept of experimentation of distributed algorithms for which our Estelle compiler has been designed. Then we discuss how the Estelle constructs are mapped onto C structures and how they are interpreted by a distributed runtime kernel. We conclude presenting typical uses of Echidna.

2. Languages for DMPCs

Programming languages are implemented on machines through runtime kernels. Those

---

(*) This work contributed to the French Research program C^3 on Parallelism and Distributed Computing.

D. Gassilloud and J. C. Grossetie (eds.), Computing with Parallel Architectures: T.Node, 65–78.

provide basic services which are invoked during execution and define some kind of operating system.

The question of the exact desired level of the system interface if of great interest for DMPCs, and is mainly related to architectural aspects.

There are at least three different approaches to languages for distributed computers:

- One may consider that completely new concepts and languages must be designed. This is particularly emphasized when considering massively parallel machines (we guess that the existing distributed computers prefigure multi-computers of hundred thousands asynchronous processors). "Geometrical programming" is the most popular expression to refer this kind of prospects.
- An other way of thinking is to hide the parallelism to the programmers. Programming in parallel is too difficult and dangerous when using DMPCs. We prefer to use traditional sequential languages or, better, languages with implicit parallelism (data flow languages, rule based formalisms, ...). The main work is charged to the compiler. A great effort is brought to build such parallelism/compilers, but obtaining efficient MIMD codes is a workhorse which uses a lot of optimisation techniques.
- The actual method of programming in the use of parallel languages. One has to describe explicitly distribution and communication. Programming correct software using this way is often a challenge: it is however in general the only service provided by the existing programming environments for DMPCs. Nevertheless, we think that the situation could be improved in the next years when real distributed implementations of parallel languages will be available. We detail this point in the following.

When distributed systems first appeared, they were programmed in traditional languages, usually with the addition of a few library procedures for sending and receiving messages. As distributed applications became more commonplace and more sophisticated, this ad hoc approach became less satisfactory. Researchers all over the world began designing new programming languages specifically for implementing distributed applications. Unfortunately, very little of these parallel languages have been ported on DMPCs: one of the main reasons is probably the difficulty of designing efficient distributed implementations.

In the present situation, the control and data are explicitly (by hand) distributed over the processors and memories. It is often a low level distribution and highly machine dependant. Parallel programming is reduced to a sequential programming with the use of a specific kernel. The program behaviours are then defined by the combination of the semantics of the application level (the sequential processes) and the kernel level (which has no real formal semantics).

It is the case for the existing programming environments on the iPSC or Supernode machines: parallel-C, parallel-Fortran, parallel-Lisp and even parallel-Ada!

There are been therefore considerable work on the subject of parallel programming, allowing to describe the distributed application as a single program. The single program approach to programming multiple computers allows the advantages of language level software engineering developments to be fully realized across machine boundaries. Among the advantages, one may think about abstract data types, separate compilation, extensive compile-time error checking and even program verification.

We conclude that the lack of parallel constructs integrated to a programming lan-

guage, and its replacement by a system library is dangerous:
- The offered primitives are often low-level with respect to constructs available in the modern parallel languages.
- This induces programs which have no (a priori known) semantics.
- And then they cannot be integrated in a programming methodology (verification, simulation, debugging, ...).

In contrast, the use of parallel languages like Occam, Ada, Estelle, ... allows:
- Abstraction (machine independence).
- Formal analysis: the potential behaviours of the program are defined by the language semantics.
- Performance: code optimization could compete in the future with the human capabilities.

3. The Echidna Project: Tools for Experimentation

The Echidna project aims at providing tools to prototype distributed algorithms on parallel machines. It provides an Estelle compiler for various DMPCs (Jard and Jézéquel (1989)) and a set of software tools to observe the behaviours of the distributed algorithm under experimentation.

The formal description models the distributed system as a whole: we only consider closed systems. Since we are not interested in producing code for heterogeneous networks (as in (Vuong et al. (1988), Richard and Claes (1989)) for example), we can work on the full algorithm, where remote communication belongs to the formal model. This allows to produce executable parallel codes directly.

Having a rather good experience in studying Formal Description Techniques for protocols, we chose the Estelle language, now an ISO standard (ISO, (1986)), to describe our distributed algorithms. As communicating automata is the natural semantics of loosely coupled distributed systems, Estelle is particularly well suited for our purpose. On the other hand, Estelle is a superset of the ISO Pascal, with some ADA concepts (class-instance mechanism, kind of modularity, ...). This allows to write efficient compilers producing efficient codes.

Numerous works have been done around Estelle concerning automated verification, simulation or prototype implementation (see the survey (Bochmann (1987))).

Several Estelle tools have been developed in the U.S., Canada and Europe (Diaz et al. (1985)).

So, with the very same formal description, we will be able to verify, simulate, or even implement a distributed algorithm: we are ensured to work on the very same object.

Our contribution to that research area is to be able to translate automatically Estelle description into parallel executable codes for distributed systems in order to perform experimentation. In the framework of experimentation, the target parallel machine must be general purpose, powerful and with an easily customizable environment. Our machine model consists in a set of sites (processors or machines) only communicating by message passing through an end to end reliable communication network. There is no loss of messages. They are exchanged within a finite but unpredictable delay, and the communication channels are FIFO queues.

Different machines may implement this abstract experimentation station model. We have focussed our development on the Intel iPSC hypercube supercomputer since it has been available in our laboratory for three years. We have also developed systems for networks of SUN-workstations (above TCP/IP), PC's and the Transputer world through the FPS T-40 hypercube machine held in Grenoble, France and the T-node supercomputer.

For portability reasons, we decided to generate C code, all the considered machines having an efficient C compiler (which was not the case for Pascal). Mapping Pascal constructs of Estelle into C is a tedious task but this allows to generate a compact code which can be easily interfaced with other programs and libraries.

4. The Computation Model

4.1. OUR ESTELLE MODEL

We present here our considered Estelle subset. We assume that full Estelle is known to the readers (see (Courtiat et al. (1987)) and (Budkowski and Dembinski (1987)) for presentations).

A system is either a set of parallel sub-systems running asynchronously, either a set of tasks. Asynchronous parallelism is required between physical sites. It is Estelle programmer's responsibility to define mapping of processes on physical sites: if the first parameter of a module is an integer, it is interpreted as the node identifier where the process must be run, the actual placement being done during task creation (initialisation) - each node is supposed to own a unique identify (a positive integer), and one node owns the identity 0. A centralised machine is assumed to be node 0 of a one node network.

We do not consider the dynamic part of Estelle: the system architecture remains unchanged after initialisation. So there are two classes of modules: the structuring modules (refinements) which have no transition part and disappear after the configuration phase, and the real processes (leaves) which perform transitions but without dynamic statements like init, connect, detach, ... Several Estelle concepts may then be simplified: sharing variables between children of a module becomes impossible, and distinction between processes and activities is irrelevant.

Such a static subset has already been considered in Veda (Jard et al. (1988)) and Xesar (Richier et al. (1987)) tools and seems to suit well for the context of experimentation. It considerably simplifies our parallel implementation. Implementing full Estelle would be an interesting prospect if the success is confirmed.

The compiler translates the formal description into a set of data structures (expressed in the C programming language), which fully describe the specification constants, types, channel definitions, module specifications and their associated body definitions. Those data structures are then compiled by the local C compiler, and linked with the DRTK to be loaded and run on the target distributed system.

The DRTK allows the execution of an Estelle program on a distributed system (see Figure 1). It consists of three parts: the scheduler, the Estelle runtime and the system interface. We detail their features in the following sections.

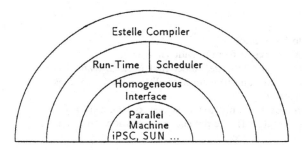

Figure 1. The Echidna compiler.

4.2. THE DISTRIBUTED DRIVER

The entry point of the executable code is on each node the main() function, whose text is:

```
main()
{
    int seed,duration;
    getOptions();
    init(seed);
    configuration();
    startScheduler(duration);
    terminate(0);
}
```

GetOptions() parses the command line to find options and parameters for the execution of the protocol, such as the duration of the execution, the seed for the random generator (in order to achieve reproducible experiments), or an alternate behaviour for the scheduler ...

Init() realizes the general initialisation of the experiment.

Configuration() is an external function, generated by the compiler. Upon invocation, it creates the root task of the Estelle specification and run its initialize part, which creates its child modules and recursively initialize them. When this resulting tree structure is achieved, only the leaf tasks that must be run on a node are actually set up in the active process list of this node to be scheduled by the local scheduler.

In the distributed execution of an Estelle specification, there are two levels of parallelism:

- Inter-nodes parallelism which is the real parallelism of the machine (the distributed driver runs in parallel on each site).
- intra-node parallelism or pseudo-parallelism: the parallelism simulated by a local scheduler.

StartScheduler() actually starts the task scheduling, according to the policy selected on the command line by the user, within deterministic or non-deterministic and synchronous or asynchronous. So the scheduler performs on each node the following simplified algorithm:

> Repeat Until EndofExperiment
> - Accept remote messages from outside (if some);
> - For each process of this node, select first fireable transition or choose at random one transition of all fireable transitions of maximal priority;
> - For each process (or only for a subset of them if asynchronously is simulated), fire the chosen transitions (if any);
> end repeat

4.3. THE ESTELLE RUNTIME

The aim of the Estelle Runtime is to build a virtual machine allowing the execution of an Estelle program, above the C runtime of the real machine. It provides the Estelle and Pascal primitive functions and objects that do not exist in the C programming language: set manipulation, error detection and recovery, good random generator (for non-deterministic), process manipulation ....

Furthermore, the runtime recognizes remote communications in order to route them through the network: when a message (interaction) is sent on an interaction point (ip), which is connected to an ip located on an other node, the message is routed by the underlying network (supposed to be FIFO without any loss nor alteration of messages) to the destination node. There, the function AcceptRemoteMessages() invocated at each iteration of the scheduler, will accept the message and queue it at the destination ip.

This runtime is made of 1000 lines of C, and is straight portable on every machine where a classical C compiler is available.

4.4. THE INTERFACE WITH THE SYSTEM

The aim of this module is to provide an implementation of the parallel machine model (as defined in Section 1.2.), building an homogeneous interface with the underlying distributed system, whichever it is. It deals with remote communications, local clock, I/O and node identifiers.

If the real distributed system is close enough to the model, this module can be quite short (100 lines of C for the iPSC/2). But if not so close, this interface will be more complex, as for example with a SUN network (TCP/IP above ethernet), where we had to develop a software package from the socket concept. For the T-node implementation, we had to build an asynchronous message passing system above the rendez-vous mechanism. This was performed as efficient as possible using Helios and 3LC.

Anyway only this part of the DRTK is to be adapted for each system, so the Echidna tool still remains easily portable.

When there is only one node, Echidna appears as an Estelle simulator which can be run on small computers (like PC).

5. The C Representation of Estelle Objects

The Estelle specification is a kind of black box without any external interaction.

If we look inside this black box during an execution, we can see some objects which interact each others:
- The tasks (or process), made of the association of a body to a module.
- The interactions points (ip), which are the interfaces between tasks and the outside world.
- The messages, or interactions, that tasks exchange on channels linking their ip's.
- The transitions, which are atomic guarded actions that can be performed by the tasks.

We will now describe in some details how those objects are represented with the C programming language.

A task is made of a specification (module) and a body. The module is created upon declaration within its nesting module (its father). When the father module initialize its children, it provides them a body (see below the Estelle instruction init).

At run time, a task is represented by a control block which stores:
- Some private data for the DRTK: process number, node identifier, activity state, transition descriptor list, ...
- The module ip's descriptors.
- The child module descriptors (pointers to control blocks).
- The local variables of the process, including the main state of the automation.
- The parameters transmitted at initialisation time.

The C representation of this control block is implemented by the following generic type:

```
typedef struct context {
    ker_workspace kw; /*private space for the DRTK (invisible)*/
    union for all modules type of {
        list of (ip *) lip;
        union for all the possible bodies of each module of {
            list of (struct context *) lt;
            list of (local variables) lv;
            list of (parameters) lpar;
        }
    }
} context;
```

The interaction points are the interfaces between tasks. They are used in a generic fashion and implemented as a DRTK private type. They are only known in the generated code as predefined descriptors.

An interaction point is made of:
- A unique ip identify over the whole system.
- The node identify where the ip is located.
- A pointer to its connected ip, if this ip is located on the same node.
- The unique identify of its corresponding ip.
- The node identify where the corresponding ip is located.
- A pointer to the task owner of the ip.
- An unbounded queue storing messages received at this ip.

The DRTK provides primitives to create ip's, to release them (when owner tasks are not initialised on this given node), to attach and connect them. The ip's which remain on a node after the configuration step are stored in a global list. Upon reception of an external message, this list will be search in order to find out the destination ip.

5.4. THE MESSAGES

Messages are the interactions exchanged between tasks through their ip's. A message is made of:
- A static block holding:
    . the total size of the message;
    . the destination ip identify;
    . the message type.
- A varying block, generated by the compiler to store the message parameters.

The DRTK provides primitives to manage messages: create, delete, copy, local or remote send, add to an ip queue, and accept remote messages.

5.5. THE TRANSITIONS

An Estelle transition is a < condition,action > pair. A condition is made of a (possibly empty) clause list, within when (message available on a ip), provided (Boolean condition on the first message on the queue or on any local variable of the task), from (condition on the main control state of the automaton), delay (specifying a time constraint for the firement of the transition) and priority (relative priority with respect to the other transitions of the same task).

An action is an optional change of the automaton main control state, followed by a compound Pascal statement, where specific Estelle instructions may take place (e.g. message sending ...).

The Estelle langage makes it possible to gather different transitions under the same text with any clause. The conditions and actions parts of such a transition group (that we call meta-transition) are the very same but for one or more index variables. So, a meta-transition is conceptually equivalent to a multidimensional array of transitions, and a simple transition (without the any clause) will be interpreted as a meta-transition with only one element.

Anyway, an Estelle transition will be referenced by the number of its meta-transition and a key identifying this transition within its meta-transition. This key looks like an access to a multidimensional array, and allows to set up the values for the indexes of the any clauses of the meta-transition.

We have chosen to generate only two C functions for each such meta-transition: evaluation and launch of the transition. Those functions take as parameters the task control block descriptor, and the transition identifying key. The code is hence the very same for all the transitions of a meta-transition.

Guard Evaluation. The guard evaluation function starts setting up some temporary variables corresponding to the any clauses indexes, according to the parameter key. Then, it uses the functions provided by the DRTK to test the specified clauses. If they are all verified, it returns the priority of the transition, else it returns the value -1.

If we have a spontaneous transition without priority clause, the guard evaluation function is simply a NOP function which returns the minimal priority.

The initialize part of a module is represented by such a spontaneous transition, fired only once during the initialisation step of the task.

Transition Firing. The action part is translated in a C function, which, as the guard evaluation function, starts setting up any clauses indexes. Then it performs the associated compound Pascal statement, including the optional control state change.

6. The Generated Code

6.1. NON-PASCAL INSTRUCTIONS TRANSLATION

6.1.1. *Within Guards. When.* This clause is found in guards to test if a given message is available on an ip, and to open visibility on its parameters. It is translated within a guard evaluation function to:

```
{
   msg*m;
   if(((m=get_msg(ipDescriptor))= =NIL)||
      (m    msg_kind!=WantedType))return(-1);
      TempVariable₁=m    FormalParameter₁;
            ...
      TempVariableₙ=m    FormalParameterₙ;
      /*tests on message parameters as specified*/
}
```

From, Provided. Those clauses allow to test the main control state of the automation and any other local variable of the task. They are directly translated to proper C tests.

Priority. As described above, the priority is computed and returned by the guard evaluation function.

Delay. This clause is not currently implemented.

Any. The unfactorisation of this kind of meta-transition is implemented as described in the previous paragraph.

6.1.2. *Within Actions.* Following instructions can only be found in the action parts of transitions.

Init. This module initialisation instruction associates a body to the considered module instance. Here is its syntax:

init < ModuleInstance > with < body > (parameters)

It is translated to the following C block:

```
if(mk_proc(&context,Site,ContextSize,TransitionList,
    SubModuleNumber,ipNumber) = = OnThisNode) {
context    FormalParameter₁ = ActualParameter₁;
                ...
context    FormalParameterₙ = ActualParameterₙ;
init_proc(context);/*fire the task initialisation transition*/
}
```

Connect and Attach. Connect allows a module to realise the connection between its sub-modules ip's, and Attach to link up a sub-module ip with a nesting module ip. Those instruction are implemented with direct invocations of corresponding DRTK primitives.

Output. This instruction allows a task to send a message on one of its ip. Here is its syntax:

Output < ipName > . < InteractionName > (MessageParameters)

It is translated to a C block which creates a message with the right tas selector, then assigns message parameters, and actually sends out the message on the selected ip:

```
{
msg*m;
m = mk_msg(MessageSize);
    m    FormalParameter₁ = ActualParameter₁;
                ...
    m    FormalParameterₙ = ActualParameterₙ;
send_msg(ipDescriptor,m);
}
```

To. This instruction allows to modify the main state of the automaton. It is translated to a straight assignment on a local variable of the task called State, whose type is enum.

All. The instruction all i: LowBound...UpperBound do < instruction > is a non-directivist loop, without previous declaration of the loop index. We implement it with a classical C loop.

Trace. This instruction is our only extension to the Estelle language (which does not own input/output instructions). Its syntax is the Pascal written one, but its semantic is specially designed within the experimentation context (Adam et al. (1988)).

6.2. THE GENERATED CODE STRUCTURE

The code generated by our compiler has the following form:

```
# include < echidnak.h > /* External declarations from the
DRTK */
# define (list of constants declared with Estelle keyword const)
typedef (list of types declared with Estelle keyword type)
typedef struct {
    msg_type msg_kind;
    union {
        /*on the parameters of each possible message type*/
            } u;
} msg;

typedef union s_context {
    ker_workspace kw; /*private space for the DRTK (invisible)*/
    union for all modules type of {
        list of (ip*) lip;
        union for all the possible bodies of each module of {
            list of (struct context *) lt;
            list of (local variables) lv;
            list of (parameters) lpar;
        }
    }
} context;

/*Here is the code for meta-transitions, for i: = 1 to n*/
int guard_i(a,p)
    int a;
    context *p;
{
    /*a is used to set up ANY-clause variables*/
    /*test to perform guard evaluation*/
    if fireable return (priority) else return (-1);
}
int action_i(a,p)
    int a;
    context *p;
{
    /*a is used to set up ANY-clause variables*/
    /*code to fire the transition*/
}

/*Definition of variables to be exported to the DRTK*/
/*The array transition[] gives the correspondence between a*/
```

```
/*meta-transition text and its absolute number for the DRTK*/
int(*transition[])() = {
    guard_1,action_1,
    ...
    guard_n,action_n
};
/*The array transany[] gives the variation bound for the */
/*any key for each transition*/
int transany[n] = {nany_1,...nany_n};

void configuration()
{
    /*realise the nesting module creation (the specification)*/
    /*and call its initialisation transition*/
}
```

6.3. PASCAL TRANSLATION

On the syntactic level, the Pascal and C languages only differ in minor ways. The situation is worse on the semantic level.

Our translation is very similar to the public program PtoC written by Per Bergsten of the university of Gothenburg in Sweden.

Here is a list of the main problems we have encountered and their solutions:

- Constants:number aliases are simply defined but string constants are converted to static character arrays, in order to avoid unnecessary duplication of strings in the object code.
- Types and variables: integer subranges are mapped onto standard C arithmetic types according to a short table in the translator (scanned topdown until an enclosing subrange is found).

  C-arrays have peculiar semantics. Pascal arrays are encapsulated in a struct with a single member named a.

  Records and their variants are translated into C struct and union definitions. Artificial names (u and v_xxx) must be supplied for all record variants.

  The problem of recursive types as pointer types is solved by introducing a name (s_xxx) for the record type.

  Set types are translated in arrays of words. The first member gives the size of the set and the others hold the bits.

- Statements: the only parts that require special care are with and for statements. The with-statement is translated into nested compound statements, where pointer variables, referencing the corresponding records are declared and initialized. In order to evaluate once the record address, the accessible record fields are renamed within the scope of the with-statement.

  The for-statement requires that the loop boundaries are evaluated exactly once and must be exited when the upper bound has been reached. For that reason, the upper/lower bounds are held in local variables and a conditional break statement is added to the end of the loop.

- Expression: when the operands are sets, the expression is converted into a function call.

The lower bound of the index type must be substracted when indexing.

Pointer references and var parameters are handled by prefixing the expression with an asterisk. The special case of dereferencing followed by selection is also recognized.

6.4. VARIABLES ACCESSES AND RENAMING

In order to generate reentrant code for transitions, the variables of Estelle bodies must be accesses through references to a process context. We have chosen a simple way to do this using the C-preprocessor: before entering the generation of the transitions of the considered body, the variables strings are defined to be references through a context pointer to the union structure coding all the Estelle bodies. They are undefined when the transitions are generated.

Renaming is necessary since the block structure of the Estelle description is partially destroyed in the generated code. We chose to rename an user identifier only if its string is declared several times in the source text. In that case, it is prefixed by a unique number identifying its scope.

To prevent clashes of identifiers with the DRTK, the user identifiers are written with an initial uppercase letter, while the C-identifiers begin by a lower case character.

7. Implementation of the Compiler

The compiler is written in Pascal and is seven thousand lines long. Parsing is performed using a left recursive descent of procedures. It consists of three major procedures that performs successively the conversion of the Estelle source program into a parse tree, some necessary transformations to prepare C generation, and the final traversal of the tree that prints the corresponding C constructs.

They are augmented by a set of procedures that maintain internal data structures (table for identifiers and strings, a multi-level symbol table, the parse tree, ...).

Full Estelle is parsed: the considered subset is defined by filtering. The most of semantics checks are performed, either statically during parsing, either dynamically during execution.

8. Conclusion

The experience of using Echidna is still not very large, as it is available for only two years. However, we can see that there are some real needs that it addresses.

First, Echidna is used as an high level programming environment for DM-PCs, featuring a windowed interactive visual debugger and full portability of an Estelle application across parallel machines as different as an iPSC and a Transputer network. This is the very important issue we contributed since DMPCs come usually without any decent software environment. Moreover, debugging an Estelle program is a lot easier than debugging C or Fortran parallel ones, and once it runs fine on a centralized machine, it usually runs directly on any parallel machine.

Echidna has been also used for prototyping activities, in order to compare various versions of an algorithm - in terms of efficiency, resource management, etc. -, or to measure real time related performances. It can also be used to discover unexpected situations, like macro effects of suitable perturbations.

Furthermore, as users always find applications that were not initially expected by designers, we saw echidna being used for classical simulation, demonstration and teaching purposes (for example with one protocol entity on different Sun stations, the users playing the role of upper layers of the protocol, thus issuing requests and receiving indications on an interactive way). The Echidna relevant features were here its openness (interfacing with Unix is buit-in) and its relative efficiency, which allows students to compile an Estelle program as often as they wish.

9. References

Adam, M., Ingels, Ph., Jard, C., Jézéquel, J.M. and Raynal, M. (1988), Experimentation on parallel machines is helpful to analyse distributed algorithms. In Proceedings of the Workshop on Parallel and Distributed Algorithms, Bonas, France, North Holland, September 1988.

Bochmann, G.V. (1987), Usage of protocol development tools: the results of a survey. In 7th IFIP International Workshop on Protocol Specification, Testing and Verification, Zurich, Suisse, North Holland, May 1987.

Budkowski, S. and Dembinski, P. (1987), An introduction to Estelle: a specification language for distributed systems. Computer Networks and ISDN Systems, 14:3-23, 1987.

Courtiat, J.P., Dembinski, P., Groz, R. and Jard, C. (1987), Un langage ISO pour les algorithmes distribués et les protocoles. Technique et Science Informatique, 6(2), 1987.

Diaz, C., Vissers, M. and Ansart (1985), Sedos: software environment for the design of open distributed systems. In Proceedings of the Esprit '85 week, North Holland.

ISO (1986), Estelle: a Formal Description technique based on an Extended State Transition Model. ISO TC97/SC21/WG 6.1, (1986).

Jard, C., Groz, R. and Monin, J.F. (1988), Development of VEDA: a prototyping tool for distributed algorithms. In IEEE Trans. on Software Engin., March 1988.

Jard, C. and Jézéquel, J.M. (1989), A multi-processor Estelle to C compiler to experiment distributed algorithms on parallel machines. In Proc. of the 9th IFIP International Workshop on Protocol Specification, Testing, and Verification, University of Twente, The Netherlands, North Holland.

Richard, J.L. and Claes, T. (1989), A generator of C-code for Estelle. In M. Diaz, J.P. Ansart, J.P. Courtiat, P. Azéma and V. Chiari, editors, The Formal Description Technique Estelle, results of the ESPRIT Sedos Project., North Holland.

Richier, J.L., Rodriguez, C., Sifakis, J. and Voiron, J. (1987), Verification in XESAR of the sliding window protocol. In 7th IFIP International Workshop on Protocol Specification, Testing and Verification, Zurich, Suisse, North Holland, May 1987.

Vuong, S., Lau, A. and Chan, R. (1988), Semi-automatic implementation of protocols using an Estelle-C compiler. IEEE Transactions on Software Engineering, SE-14(3):384-393, March 1988.

A PETRI NET TOOL FOR DESIGNING TRANSPUTER NETWORK APPLICATIONS

F. BEAUFILS, C. REZE
IBSI Electronique
2, rue Maurice Hartmann
92130 ISSY les Moulineaux - France

ABSTRACT. ELSIR, a simulation tool based on distributed systems modelling by extended Petri Nets (the ELSIR language) is presented. Its application to the design and code generation of transputer network applications is described. Two major approaches are distinguished. The first one, the Petri Net virtual machine approach consists of the interpretation of the ELSIR language. The second one consists of the identification of the processes of the application and of the generation of a resource manager which will be responsible for communication and synchronization between processes.

1. Introduction

The subject of this paper is the code generation for a transputer network from a specification written in an extended Petri Net language. This work is done in cooperation with IMAG/LGI (Grenoble) and LRI (Université Paris Sud Centre d'Orsay).

IBSI Electronique has developed and commercializes a tool, ELSIR, for the modelling of distributed systems. ELSIR is a discrete-event simulation tool based on an extended Petri Net formalism (the ELSIR language).

The functions of this tool are the followings:
- specification of distributed systems, using the ELSIR language;
- validation of the dynamic behaviour of such systems (no deadlock, no lack of resources, invariant, ...);
- performance evaluation.

ELSIR has been initially developed for the need of and in cooperation with the French Navy (CPM/ST). It is commercially available since 1989 on the following workstations: SUN3, SUN4, DN4000 (APOLLO), UNIGRAPH (CETIA). The present work is supported by the French ministry of Industry.

The areas of application of ELSIR are mainly:
- Combat systems, command and control systems, weapon systems, ...;
- networks and protocols;
- computer integrated manufacturing systems (CIMS);
- computer architecture;
- computer aided software engineering (CASE).

D. Gassilloud and J. C. Grossetie (eds.), Computing with Parallel Architectures: T.Node, 79–100.
© 1991 *ECSC, EEC, EAEC, Brussels and Luxembourg. Printed in the Netherlands.*

We wish to complete the capabilities of ELSIR in the CASE area. Presently, there is a gap between the specification and the production of software. The specification can be validated but if the software is produced independently of the specification or if there is no conformance test afterwards, validation of a specification is not as useful as it could be.

If fact, three different methods allow for the conformance verification of a software to its specification:
- Observation;
- code generation;
- a posteriori proof.

Observation consists in observing the external behaviour of a software component, i.e. its reaction to external events, and to check if the occurrence of observed events is in conformance with the specification and shows no ambiguity (software testability notion).

Code generation consists in automatically, or semi-automatically, producing the source code or its skeleton, from the specification of the software. The fact that the generation process is automatic insure the conformity of the software to its specification.

A posteriori proof consists in generating a formal model of a software from its source code, and in validating the extracted formal model, e.g. the LRI has worked at the extraction of Petri Nets from OCCAM code and at the validation of these Petri Nets.

We choosed code generation because it seemed us the easiest and more practical way.

Why do we choose transputer networks as the target machine?

Transputer networks are distributed systems, so are they ideal targets for a distributed system specification tool. Nevertheless, the communication scheme of transputers and ELSIR are different: synchronous for one, asynchronous for the other. From a short experience of transputer programming, reinforced by widespread comments on this subject, the debugging of software on transputer networks is a very hard task. So having a tool to help producing correct programs would be very convenient, and save a lot of time.

As to the target language, two major languages are widely used for transputer programming: OCCAM and C. We choosed C as the language that will be used to complete the automatically generated skeleton. The reason is that OCCAM is not a high-level programming language, its use is reserved to transputer and is not straightforward. Instead, a majority of programmers knows C.

What will be target configuration?

We can distinguish two types of configuration:
- Massively parallel configuration well-adapted to micro-parallelism (operations on vector, matrix, parallelization of loop, ...);
- application dedicated configuration dealing with macro-parallelism (distributed tasks).

As ELSIR is employed for the design of embedded software, the target configuration will be the second one.

Mapping is another important problem when you program transputer networks. The load of each transputer and of each link has to be balanced in order to optimize the use of the resources and, as a consequence, to minimize the reaction delay of the application.

The simulation capacities of ELSIR could be used to evaluate the need of each task of a distributed application in CPU resources and in communication resources and therefore to provide some guidance for a mapping algorithm.

This paper only deals with the problem of code generation from the ELSIR language and presents an overview of the different methods that could be experimented.

Chapter 2 will introduce you to the ELSIR language. Chapter 3 will discuss different styles of programming in ELSIR. Chapter 4 will describe the virtual machine approach and Chapter 5 the resource manager approach.

2. The ELSIR Language and its Environment

2.1. OVERVIEW

ELSIR is a distributed data processing system evaluation tool.

ELSIR is:
- a method of analysis;
- a graphic language;
- a set of tools.

The ELSIR method of analysis is based on a hierarchical breakdown of systems into components of ever decreasing size.

The ELSIR language enables:
- systems to be modelled in the form of component networks interlinked by connections on which messages transit;
- components to be modelled in the form of place-transition graphs (Petri Nets) provided with the following devices: structured tokens, timed transitions, firing conditions, actions, ...

The structure of the model is static.

Each component evolves in a parallel and asynchronous way (random choice of the transition fired amongst the enabled transitions at a given time).

The ELSIR tools are made up of:
- a graphics editor to key in graphs and networks;
- an analyzer (or compiler);
- a constructor (or link editor);
- an interactive interpreter;
- an observer to analyze results (curves, histograms).

You can execute your specification or model, debug it using an interactive interpreter and thereby validate your system. The approach adopted for the exploitation of ELSIR models is that of interpretation.

You can evaluate the performances of your system (number of messages processed, processing time, throughput, ...). These results can be printed in table, histogram or curve form.

ELSIR is a user-friendly tool, animed at system designers.

The ELSIR methodologies based on four concepts:
- the token;
- the process;
- the network;
- the graph.

82

A token is a typed, structured message.

An elementary typed token is a piece of information made up of a type indicating the nature of the information and a value (the information).

A typed structured token is a token made up of several fields, each field being itself an elementary or structured token (tree form structure).

A process externally appears as a "box" with input and output gates and assigned a given state. It receives tokens on the input gates and, depending on its state, generates tokens on its output gates.

A network is a network of components linked together by connections from output gates to input gates. A component is a process instantiation, where process is a generic term.

The components are executed in parallel and they exchange tokens via the connections. In the example given in Figure 2.1, process PR1 is a network made up of components PR2 and PR3.

It receives tokens of the token type on input A and generates tokens of the token 4 type on output D.

A graph is a place-transition graph similar to Petri predicate-transition Nets. It enables the behaviour of the elementary processes (which cannot be broken down into other processes) to be modelled.

The graph is a Petri Net with the following extensions (see Figure 2.3):
- typed tokens;
- local memory;
- inhibitive firing rules (test for the lack of a token of a given type and given value in a place, test whether a place is empty);
- enabling conditions concerning the configuration of tokens in input for a transition or the state of the local memory;

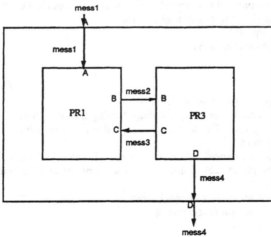

Figure 2.1. Network.

- actions (creation of produced tokens in terms of the consumed tokens, writing in memory);
- timed transition (estimation of the execution time of a transition).

The fact that each token has a type which enables its structure to be known, allows implicit operations to be performed on these tokens (splitting, concatenation).

The use of local memory locations allows the graphic representation to be simplified.

2.2. TYPES

We have seen that all tokens are characterized by a type identifying the nature and structure of the token.

There are two main type categories:
- elementary types;
- structured types.

The category of a type indicates the type constructor.

The elementary type categories are as follows:
- Interval:
Eg: a = 1...10;
A type "a" token can have integer values between 1 and 10.
- Integer:
Eg: a = ENTER;
A type "a" token can have positive or negative integer values. This type is similar to an interval type, the limits of which are defined as the maximum and the minimum values that can be represented on the machine.
- Enumeration:
Eg: colour = ENUM red, green, blue;
A type "colour" token can have the values red, green or blue. Red, green and blue are marks.
- Boolean:
Eg: a = BOOLEEN;
A type "a" token can have the values TRUE or FALSE.
- Signal:
Eg: a = SIGNAL;
A type "a" token does not have any specific value; only its presence is significant.

The structured type categories are as follows:
- Concatenation;
Eg: a = [b,c,d];
A type "a" token is a token made up of a type "b" token, a type "c" token and a type "d" token.
- Selection:
Eg: a = [b|c|d];
Type "a" is the union of types "b", "c" and "d";
A token cannot be of the selection type.
- Segment:
Eg: a = SEG X;

84

a token of this type is a list of type "x" tokens.

Moreover, the methodology defines two special types:
- TOKEN
A TOKEN type token corresponds to a simple mark on generalized Petri Nets.
- ANY
This type is the union of all types.

2.3. SPECIFICATION

The description of a process includes:
- its specification;
- its realization.

The specification of a process describes:
- the process interface;
- the process parameters either functional (constant) or timing laws.

The specification of a process describes the external aspect of the process. It describes the way the process must be used. The process is considered to be a black box with input gates, on which tokens are deposited, and output gates on which tokens are received. The behaviour of the process can be modified by modifying its parameters.

A component can receive tokens from another component on an input gate and it can send tokens to another component via its output gate.

All the input and output gates of a process make up its interface.

Each process gate is assigned:
- an identifier (the name of the gate);
- a type indicating the type (or types, if of the selection category) of the tokens which can transit through this gate;
- the direction (input or output).

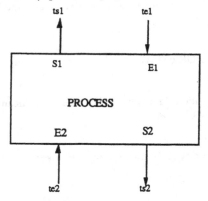

PARAMETRES
PTEMPO = EXPO(15)MS;
pfonc1 : t1 := 5;
pfonc2 : t2 := 1;

Figure 2.2. Specification.

2.4. GRAPH

Any elementary process, that is any process which cannot be broken down into a network of components, is represented by a place-transition graph.

This graph is a model similar to that of Petri predicate-transitions nets.

The following extensions have been added to generalized Petri Nets:
- Tokens are typed tokens.
- Places are queues containing tokens, and managed as FIFO.
- Inhibitive arcs (to be compared with enabling arcs) are defined (test whether the place is empty).
- Predicates (conditions) concerning the token configuration present in the input places condition transition enabling.
- Actions allow for tokens to be generated in output places in terms of the tokens removed from the input places.
- Output arcs indicate the number of tokens added to output places.
- Execution times are assigned to transitions.
  The tokens produced are only produced after a given time.
  This time can be defined by probability laws (exponential, normal, ...).
- Memories are also defined.
  A memory can be assigned a single value (it only contains one token).
  It is read and/or written by actions.
  It is tested by conditions.

The graph representation conventions are as follows:
- A place is represented by a circle.
- The places can have names, in which case the name is written inside the circle.
- Places with the same name represent the same place.
  This enables simple graphs to be created:
- A gate with the same name as a place is equivalent to this place. If it is an input gate, the tokens arriving on this gate will be deposited in the input place.
  If it is an output gate, as soon as a token is deposited in the output place, it will be immediately transferred to an input place, in accordance with the connections existing between the components.
- A memory can also be represented by a circle, its name being written inside the circle.
- A transition is represented by a rectangle.
- A transition can have a name, in which case the name is written inside the rectangle or to the left of the border.
- Input and output arcs are represented by an arc terminated by an arrow.
- An inhibitive arc is represented by an arc terminated by a ring.

In the example in Figure 2.3:
- P1, P2, P3 and P4 are four places;
- T1 is a transition;
- arcs P1 + > T1 and P2 + > T1 are input arcs;
- arc P3 -> T1 is an inhibitive arc;
- arc T1 = > P4 is an output arc;
- t = ENTIER (french for integer) is an integer type declaration;
- x = [a,b]; is a concatenated type declaration made up of two fields of types a and b;

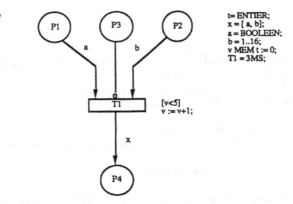

Figure 2.3. Place-transition graph.

- v MEM t: = 0; is a memory declaration of type t, initialized with the value zero;
- T1 = 3 MS; is the timing declaration associated with T1;
- [v < 5] is the enabling condition;
- v: v + 1; is the action.

    To fire T1, the following conditions must be true:
- a type a token must be present in P1;
- a type b token must be present in P2;
- no token must be present in P3;
- v must be less than 5.

    If such is the case, then:
- a type a token is removed from P1;
- a type b token is removed from P2;
- memory v is incremented;
- the execution of the transition lasts three milliseconds;
- a token x is produced by concatenation of tokens a and b removed from P1 and P2, and deposited in P4.

2.5. NETWORK

2.5.1. *Presentation.* A network is a network of components, the gates of which are inter-connected via connections (see Figure 2.4).

    This concept allows a system to be broken down into less complex sub-systems. The last breakdown level is the breaking down into elementary components which can be modelled in graph form.

    A network is fully defined by:
- its components;
- its inter-component connections.

    A network component is then called the father component and the components making up this component, the child components.

2.5.2. Component. A component is a process instantiation, the process being a generic model. For example, in order to create the model of a communication system, we can define a Subscriber process. The system will be broken down unto n Subscriber components (Subscriber 1, Subscriber 2, ...) and a network.

During process instantiation, the name of a component can be defined; otherwise, its default name is that of the process.

Parameters are passed using their names; that is the association between the formal parameter and the effective parameter is based on the name and not on the location. If no new value is assigned to the parameter during the instantiation, the default value is used.

Note:

The parameter notion, such as it is used, does not correspond to the parameter notion used in a programming language for procedures. A procedure parameter can be compared with a token deposited on a gate. A process parameter can be compared with a constant definition.

2.5.3. Connections. The connections on a network allow the various components of the network to communicate. A message received by the father component is redirected to the child component(s) connected to the input gate of the father component. The messages sent by the child components are collected by the output gates of the father component.

For two gates to be connected, the type of one of them must be included in the type of the other one, in terms of selection. For example, if A is an input gate of the type $a = [m1|m2|m3]$ and B is an output gate of the type $b = [m1|m2]$, then b is included in a. A and B can therefore be connected.

The rules determining the connection of process are defined below:

a) *Connections between child components:*
   - an input gate can be connected to one or more output gates (one consumer, n producers). The type of input gate must include the types of the output gates;
   - an output gate can be connected to one or more input gates (distribution). The type of the output gate must be included in the types of the input gates.

b) *Connections between the father component and child components:*
   - an input gate of the father component can be connected to one or more input gates of the child components (orientation, distribution). The type of the input gate of the father component must include the types of the input gates of the child components to which it is connected.
   - an output gate of a father component can be connected to one or more output gates of the child components. The type of the output gate of the father component must include the types of the output gates of the child components to which it is connected.

Figure 2.4 gives two examples of a network, one with message orientation to child components and one with distribution.

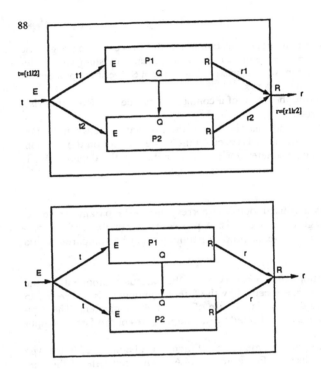

Figure 2.4. Network.

2.6. TOOLS

The graphical ELSIR set of tools includes:
- a graphics editor enabling the specifications, networks and graphs to be entered in graphic form;
- a compiler to compile the model;
- a constructor;
- a graphical interpreter;
- a data analyzer enabling the results to be presented in curve, histogram and pie chart form.

The interpreter provides the following capabilities:
- system configuration (modification of the values of the component parameters);
- choice of the simulation mode.

You can choose between:
- the step by step mode (firing transition by transition);
- execution at a given speed;
- breakpoint.

You can set breakpoints for:

- transition firing;
- production of tokens in a place;
- removal of tokens from a place;
- crossing of a connection.

You can also select the number of simulation steps to execute or an halt date.

You can stop the interpretation at any time in asynchronous mode (keyboard interrupt).

- Modification of the state of the system.

Dynamically, you can:
- remove a token from a place;
- add a token to a place;
- modify a token.

- Printing

At any time you can list traces (in direct or batch mode) for debug sequences delimited in time.

- Extraction

You can extract results in order to create statistics for the following variables:
- number of tokens in a place;
- length of time the tokens stay in a place;
- time between two firings of the same transition;
- time between two crossings of a connection.

Moreover, you can extract the tokens produced or consumed in a place and the tokens transiting through a connection. The data can then be analyzed directly by the user.

The graphical data analyzer allows for the following diagrams to be drawn:

- For transitions:
- the time interval between two transition firings, in function of time;
- the statistical distribution (histogram) of the time interval between two transition firings.

- For places:
- the number of tokens in a place in function of time;
- the statistical distribution of the number of tokens in a place in function of time;
- the length of time tokens stay in a place;
- statistical distribution on the time tokens stay in a place.

- For connections:
- time interval between two connection crossing;
- statistical distribution of the time interval between two connection crossing.

3. Different Styles of Programming

ELSIR encourages two different styles of programming:
- state automata like programming;
- data-flow programming.

State automata like programming is illustrated by the model, Figure 3.1. The semantic of the places SO, S1, S2 is "state". The semantic of the places I1, I2 is "event". The semantic of the place O1 is "generated event". The semantic of the transitions T1, T2 is "state transition".

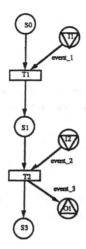

Figure 3.1. State automata like programming.

Data-flow programming is illustrated by the models, Figure 3.2. The first one allows for parallel processing of each field of a data structure. T2, T3, T4 can be executed in parallel. The second one allows for parallel processing of each element of a segment. T2 is a re-enterable transition i.e. as many transition as tokens in P2 can be executed simultaneously.

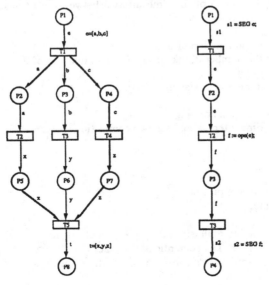

Figure 3.2. Data flow programming.

The first style is mainly used for system specification, the second one for algorithm specification, therefore in a more advanced step in the design of the system. The first style will be used to deal with macro-parallelism, the second one will be used to deal with micro-parallelism. We will see that the programming style have some influence on the most appropriate method for code generation.

4. Petri Net Virtual Machine

4.1. PRESENTATION

The problem of code generation is the problem of the transition of a language, ELSIR, into another, C or OCCAM. It is the problem of the translation of one concept in another concept. It is not very difficult to translate Pascal code into C code because the semantics of these two languages are quite similar. We cannot say that of the semantic of ELSIR and the semantic of OCCAM or C.

Communications are asynchronous in ELSIR but synchronous in OCCAM and they do not even exist in C (run-time primitives are used instead). In ELSIR, communication and synchronization are two different concepts. Communication is expressed by connections between components, synchronization by transition. In OCCAM, communication and synchronization are bound. Communication can only take place when both the sending and the receiving processes are ready to communicate on the same channel (c!v and c?v).

When the concepts of two languages are so different, there are two alternatives:
- try to simplify the concepts of the source language in order to be able to translate them, but it will be less powerful;
- Build a virtual machine implementing the concept of the source language which cannot be translated in the target language (i.e. build a Petri Net interpreter).

We will describe in this chapter the second approach i.e. the ELSIR virtual machine approach.

Some research works has already been led in this field. We can quote the work concerning the generation of ADA, Pascal or C code from a language, PROTOB, based on PROTnet (Bruno (1989)) and the work concerning the implementation of Petri Nets and coloured Petri Nets using high-level concurrent languages (Colom (1988)).

The ELSIR Virtual machine will be composed of two modules:
- the mailer in charge of the asynchronous communications between ELSIR graphs;
- the coordinator, an inferential engine which will iteratively select the transitions of a graph to fire.

4.2. THE MAILER

Communication in ELSIR is asynchronous. When a process producers a message on an output gate, it continues its processing without being blocked, independently of the state of the receiving process. A receiving process is not interrupted when a message is transmitted to one of its input gate. The receiving process will examine the contents of the input gate at its convenience. If it was waiting on this input gate, it will be nevertheless waken up.

92

A message type is associated to each gate i.e. only messages of the specified type can transit through a gate. As a consequence, connection between gates are also typed.

An ELSIR model of a system is a hierarchical model, but this hierarchical model can be translated into a flat model (Figure 4.1), composed of ELSIR graphs connected via a net of typed connections. When a message is produced on an output gate, depending on its type, it is routed to the associated input gate. Multicasting is possible. In this case, the message is replicated and one copy is delivered to each input gate in destination.

So the function of the mailer will be to route messages from output gates according to the type of the messages and according to the net of connections between output and input gates.

It is well-know that for most applications running on a transputer networks such a function has to be developed all the way. Transputers have only four physical links, each supporting a channel in each way. Transputers have only four physical links, each supporting a channel in each way. So, when OCCAM processes are not allocated in neighbouring transputer (i.e. connected by a link), they need a relay to communicate and if too many channels are used between two transputers you have to multiplex them on the links (4 maximum) between these two transputers. So a lot of different routers have already been developed, many of them specific to an application, some of them in a more general purpose but they will differ by the kind of communications they implement (synchronous, asynchronous, ...) and by their routing algorithm.

Therefore, the mailer will be no more than a router, but an asynchronous one. Due to this fact, at each gate, input or output, will be associated a queue for the buffering of the messages between the sending and the receiving processes.

The mailer is distributed i.e. a process will represent the mailer in each transputer and have the exclusive use of the links of the transputer. When an ELSIR process will produce a message on an output gate, it will send the message to the local mailer process,

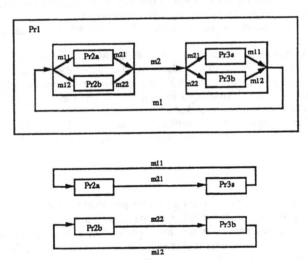

Figure 4.1. Hierarchical and flat model.

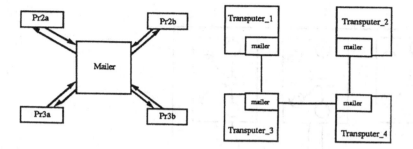

Figure 4.2. A distributed mailer.

through a local channel. The mailer process must always be ready to accept a message on such a channel (send is non-blocking) that means all communications between the mailer processes must be non-blocking. It will buffer it and then route it i.e. determine which link to use for sending the message to its destination. The mailer process will also receive messages on links and then according to the routing table, retransmit the message to another transputer or put the message into an input gate if the destination of the message is a local input gate.

The mailer will be implemented over SCK, the router developed by the IMAG/LGI (Gonzales (1990)).

4.3. THE COORDINATOR

The coordinator is in charge of the selection of the transitions to be fired. For a transition to be enabled, the following conditions must be fulfilled:
- the enabling rules must be matched;
- the predicate associated to the transition must be true.

If the transition is enabled, it will be fired that is, messages will be removed from the input places, the action will be executed, and new messages generated and put in the output places.

The conditions and actions will be translated in the target language as there is no difficulty for that. So the coordinator will just have to issue a call to a Boolean function, to evaluate the predicate, and then to some procedure, to execute the action. But the evaluation of the rules i.e. the selection of tokens that match the rules will be let to the coordinator. To translate them would involved the generation of an average of 30 lines of code for each transition.

The coordinator is also distributed that is there will be in each transputer a process (or a set of processes) carrying out the functions of the coordinator. The ELSIR graphs will be dispatched between the transputers. A coordinator will manage all ELSIR graphs located on its transputer, and fire the transitions of these graphs, one per one.

There will be at most one coordinator (and also one transputer) per ELSIR graph. That are the limits of macro-parallelism. There is no true parallelism inside of a graph because all transitions of a graph are associated to the same transputer.

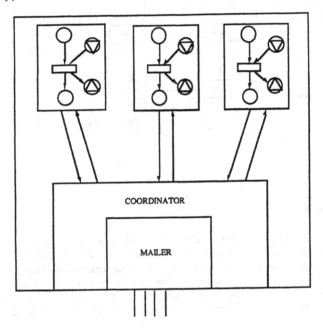

Figure 4.3. The coordinator.

The coordinator will used the mailer. When a message is provided on an output gate, it will send the message to the mailer. Before evaluating the enabling rules and conditions of a transition, it will ask the mailer to update the contents of the input gates associated to the transitions.

The drawback of such a method is its relative inefficiency due to time involved to select an enabled transition. You have a lot of transitions to evaluate each time (all transitions for which an input place, or a memory implicated in the condition have been modified) and the evaluation time is not negligible. For example, in the ELSIR interpreter used for simulation (but for which actions and conditions are not compiled), 300 Transitions are fired per second, in an average, on a 68030 UNIX workstation. When implementing this solution, a reasonably good level of performance would be to fire 10000 transitions per second (not taking into account the processing time due to the actions).

However you have to consider that only the skeleton of the application will suffer from this drawback. We can expect than the part of the skeleton, accounting for the performance of an application, will be no more than ten percent.

Another shortcoming resides in the fact there is no parallelism inside of a graph. Only one transition of a graph can be fired at once. So this translation scheme is well adapted to macro-parallelism i.e. when ELSIR processes do execute simultaneously, but not well-adapted to micro-parallelism i.e. when transition of a process can execute simultaneously.

4.4. REMOTE PROCEDURE CALL

Can we extend the ELSIR virtual machine to also implement micro-parallelism, in order to efficiently execute graphs in which transitions are re-enterable, such as the one described Figure 3.2.

A way to do it, is, once a transition is declared as enabled by the coordinator, to have it executed on another transputer i.e. to place a call to a remote procedure to execute the action.

We can compare this approach to the one of RPC for dealing with parallelism in a UNIX environment. In a Remote Procedure Call, a procedure is identified by:
- a remote server machine name;
- a program number;
- a version number;
- a procedure number.

The input arguments and the results are transmitted according to the External Data Representation (XDR) standard.

In our case, we will only have to transmit the transputer server number, the procedure number and the input arguments in internal representation since we are supposed to work in an homogeneous environment.

The crucial point is how to dispatch these remote procedures. In the case of operations on each element of a segment, you must have several copies of the same procedures dispatched on different computers. Do you allow procedure to be dispatched on transputers already supporting the execution of a coordinator and is associated ELSIR graphs? Do you have a set of transputers dedicated to the execution of the actions of the graphs associated to a specific coordinator? Do you have a pool of transputers devoted to remote procedure call service? The responses to these questions depend on the application considered. In doubt, we will consider only the first solution that is general.

This RPC mechanism will be supported by the coordinator and the mailer. To execute an action, the coordinator will issue a remote procedure call i.e. it will first choose a free server to execute the procedure (if there is multiple servers implementing this procedure) and send a remote procedure call message to the mailer.

At the other end, a mailer will receive the message and direct it to the coordinator via a specific mailbox. The coordinator will then issue a call to the server and wait for the result and then back the result to the calling coordinator.

The efficiencies of this RPC mechanism will depend on the performance of the mailer. It is clear you will not issue a remote procedure call to execute and addition. It is also clear than before to begin a remote execution, the coordinator has to check if it can or not fire another transition.

Our feeling is that an RPC implementation will be only useful with the next generation of transputers, when integrated routing will be achieved.

96

5. Process Identification

5.1. PRESENTATION

An another approach to code generation from Petri Net is the characterization of the places and transitions of a Petri Net in order to associate a semantic to them which will help for code generation. This characterization is obtained by an analysis of the Petri Net (linear invariant). This method leads to the identification of processes in Petri Net. In the Petri Net, Figure 5.1, we can identify three processes.

To a place can be associated the following semantics:
- The place is a state of a process. The sum of tokens of the state places of process must always be equal to one. In Figure 5.1, the places P1x, P2x, P3x represent the states of the processes P1, P2, P3..
- The place can be a local resource (as RL).
- The place can be a global resource i.e. shared by at least two processes (R1, R2, R3, R4, X).
- The place can be an event (I1, I2, I3).

To a transition can be associated the following semantics:
- Action executed by a processes (T1a, T2x, T3x).
- Synchronization (join) between processes (T1b).
- Fork (T1a).

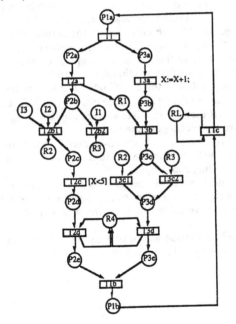

Figure 5.1. Three processes in an ELSIR graph.

Some works have been led by research centres following these principles: (Cousin (1988)), (Bréant (1990)), (Colom (1988)).

Our approach will be very practical. In a first step, we will assume that the semantic of the Petri Nets objects will not be deduced from an analysis of the Petri Net but just indicated by the users.

5.2. FINITE STATE MACHINE

To simplify the semantic of the ELSIR graph to be translated, we will consider first the sub-class of ELSIR graphs which are equivalent to finite-state machines (state-automata), see Figure 3.1. Then all resources are local resources. For efficient programming, we will had other restrictions such as:
- All resources places are bounded by 1 (no more than one token in a resource).
- Or even, the marking of each resource is always one (like a memory). This allows to omit the test for the presence or not of a resource.

The translation of events i.e. access to input gates, requires some attention. Unlike finite state machine, the enabling rule of a transition can depend on more than one event and can be mixed with alternative between events, like in OCCAM (see Figure 5.2).

First, we have to assume, that like for an ELSIR virtual machine, there will be a mailer that will be in charge of the communications between components, from input gates to output gates. When a process is waiting for an event, it will transmit a request to the mailer. This request will specified the characteristics of the event it is waiting for. For example, in state SO of Figure 5.2, the process will ask for reception of (event I1 and event I2) or even I3. This can be expressed as follows, OC and IC being two channels, one in each way, between the process and the mailer:
- OC!START_REQ   : starts the request.
- OC!I1;type-x   : token of type x on gate I1.
- OC!AND   : AND.
- OC!I2;type-y   : token of type y on gate I2.
- OC!OR   : OR.
- OC!I3;type-z   : token of type z on gate I3.
- OC!EOR   : End of Request.
- IC?id-gate   : waiting for event.
- if id_gate == I3 : event I3.
- iC?z   : token reception.
- elseif...   : else reception of I1 and I2.

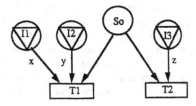

Figure 5.2. Alternative between events.

5.3. THE RESOURCE MANAGER

The drawback of the preceding method is that it applies only to the sub-class of Petri Nets that is equivalent to finite state machine, using the principles described in Par. 5.1. This kind of formalism is less powerful than Petri Nets and we choosed Petri Nets instead of finite-state machines to model distributed systems precisely because of their powerfulness. For example, Petri Nets allow you to express synchronization between processes, sharing of resources. Synchronization, resources sharing are a major concern when designing distributed systems. It is the reason why code generation from Petri Nets is more attractive than code generation from finite-state machines.

We can often identify more than one process in an ELSIR graph (see Figure 5.1). When you introduce multiple processes on an ELSIR graph, you also alternatives on shared resources (i.e. a process can need either resources R1 and R2 or resource R3). It can be compared with Figure 5.2, replacing event by resources.

The idea is to introduce a distributed resource manager, that would be a generalization of the mechanism employ to manage events as described in Par. 5.2. The distributed resource manager will be in charge of the allocation of the resources to the processes which need them, when they need them. The resource manager will maintain a distributed allocation table indicating, for each resource, whether the resource is free or not, the process it is allocated to and the process that is waiting for it.

The resource manager is distributed i.e., in each transputer, a resource manager process will allow to carry out this function. The allocation table is a small distributed data base. It will be managed in "pull mode". For each resource will be associated a resource manager process in charge of the management of the resource, called the "owner" of the resource. When another resource manager needs the resource for one of its processes, it will issue an allocation request to the owner of the resource.

Each resource manager will know, for each ELSIR process it is in charge of, and according to the current state of the process, what resources are needed for him for its next execution step. In fact, by communicating its state to the resource manager, the process issues a multiple request for resources (either this set of resources or this other one set ...). In function of the state of the resources and events produced, and of the state of the process, the resource manager will decide which transition the process may fire.

At code generation time will be generated for the resource manager, a table of resource requests indicating for each process, for each state of a process, for each transition allowed from this state, the set of resources and events needed to enable this transition.

Figure 5.3 illustrated the principles of the resource manager. Each time a process will need some resources or events, it will issue a request to the resource manager. The request will specify the state in which is the process. The resource manager will send back the number of the transition to fire and all the resources and events necessary. After the transition has been fired, the process will send back to the resource manager, the resource generated or release and the events generated together with its new state.

Such a translation scheme can be applied either to shared memory or non shared memory architecture. If shared memory is used, request and release of a shared resource will be implemented more or less like semaphore. So the code generation will depend on the mapping of processes to transputers.

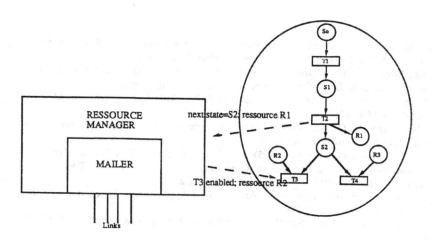

Figure 5.3. The resource manager.

For this translation scheme to be applicable, the following restriction to ELSIR still have to be applied:
- No valued input arcs.
- No enabling or inhibitive conditions involving tokens coming from global resources. Condition like the one associated to transition T2c of Figure 5.1 will be forbidden because the resource manager is only concern with the presence or absence of a resource, not with its value.

6. Conclusion

Both the Petri Net virtual machine approach and the resource manager will be implemented in the next months on a T.Node (TELMAT). We expect that, after experimentation on a transputer network application, we will be able to make a choice between these two approaches, to prove the efficiency of the choosen approach, to improve the specification language and the transition scheme. The next step will be the development of the final product.

Another field that could be explored in a next future is distributed simulation.

7. References

Brams, G.W., Réseaux de Petri: Théorie et pratique. MASSON 83.

Bréant, F., Estrailler and P., Leroch, M.F. (1990) Génération automatique de code OCCAM à partir d'un réseau de Petri. Laboratoire MASI.

Bruno, G. and Marchetto, G. (1985) Process translatable Petri-Nets for the rapid prototyping of control system. IEEE Trans. on Software Engineering Vol. SE-12 N° 2. February 1986, pp. 346-357.

Baldassari, M. and Bruno, G. (1989) An Environment for Operational Software Engineering in ADA. TRI-ADA Conference, Pittsburgh USA, October 1989.

Colom, J.M., Silva, M. and Villaroed, J.L. (1988) On Software Implementation of Petri Nets and Coloured Petri Nets using high-level concurrent languages.

Cousin, B. and Estrailler, P. (1988) Generation of ADA Code from Petri Nets Models. Laboratoire MASI N° 256.

Gonzales, N., Muntean, T. and Waille, P. (1990) A correct communication kernel for networks of transputers. IMAG/LGI.

Groz, R., Jard, C. and Lassudrie, C. (1985) Attacking a Complex Distributed Algorithm from Different Sides: an Experience with Complementary Validation Tools. Computer Networks, Vol. 10 Nb 5, December 1985, pp. 245-257.

Murata, T. (1989) Petri Nets: Properties, Analysis and Applications. Proceedings of the IEEE, Vol. 77, No. 4, April 1989.

Peterson, James L. (1981) Petri Net theory and the modelling of system. Prentice Hall 1981.

Rukoz, M. and Sandoval, R. (1988) Specification and Correctness of Distributed Algorithms by coloured Petri Nets. Laboratoire MASI. N° 257.

SOFTWARE TOOLS FOR DEVELOPING PROGRAMS ON A RECONFIGURABLE PARALLEL ARCHITECTURE

Ch. FRABOUL, J.Y. ROUSSELOT, P. SIRON
ONERA-CERT, Département d'Informatique
2, Avenue Edouard Belin
31055 Toulouse Cedex - France

ABSTRACT. Performance of a parallel program on a computer network architecture strongly depends on the underlying interconnection topology. A reconfigurable architecture whose interconnection topology can be modified to match the communication characteristics of an algorithm provides flexibility for efficient execution of various applications. But tools are still needed to exploit dynamic reconfiguration of the architecture.

This paper presents the software tools for developing programs on a reconfigurable architecture which have been studied in the context of a research project named MODULOR. We briefly describe main characteristics of the assumed modular reconfigurable architecture context. Then we explain how we choose to describe a reconfigurable parallel application before presenting main steps of such an application's development.

MODULOR project is supported by French Ministry of Defense under DRET (Direction des Recherches, Etudes et Techniques) contract. Study undertaken in SUPERNODE context is supported by a CEE PCA (Parallel Computing Action) contract.

1. Reconfigurable Architecture Context

Processors network allow the connection of a large number of processors. Such distributed memory architectures avoid classical bottle-neck when accessing a shared common memory. Each processor has only access to its local memory (where program code and data are stored) but it can communicate with other processors through communication links. Message based communication and synchronization mechanisms are generally handled in such a context.

But the performance of a parallel program on a processors network strongly depends on the underlying interconnection topology. As each processor has a limited number of links, it can directly communicate with few neighbours. Thus, due to classical integration constraints (pin limitations, wiring problems, communications capabilities, ...), most of highly parallel architectures are based on a fixed interconnection topology:
- For specialized architectures the interconnection topology is chosen in order to match communication requirements of a given (class of) application(s).

D. Gassilloud and J. C. Grossetie (eds.), Computing with Parallel Architectures: T.Node, 101–110.
© 1991 *ECSC, EEC, EAEC, Brussels and Luxembourg. Printed in the Netherlands.*

- For more general purpose architectures, the processing elements are connected according to a regular pattern. But routing mechanisms must be implemented to allow a processor to communicate with a not neighbouring processor. Such routing mechanisms may introduce unacceptable delays.

A reconfigurable processors network, whose interconnection topology can be dynamically configured in order to match communication needs of an algorithm, presents interesting features (Wang and Xu (1985), Murakami et al. (1988), Harp (1987)):

- It provides flexibility required for efficient execution of various applications. The processing elements can be interconnected using direct point to point communications. Moreover an optimal topology can be chosen for each application or each application's phase.
- Programming of a parallel application becomes more independent of the target architecture in the sense that it is the architecture that adapts to the application.
- Classical mapping problem (such that neigh neighbouring processes are assigned to neighbouring processors) becomes easier to manage in such a reconfiguration context. As processors are identical, the solution of this problem is strongly connected to the possibility of setting up the needed communication links.

2. Architectural Model

Main problem encountered when designing a highly parallel reconfigurable architecture deals with the connection of a large number of processors on a programmable interconnection topology. Such an architecture must be able to allow the connection of additional processors. Moreover architectural features have to be, as far as possible, consistent with potential processor design evolution (such as the number of available communication links).

Due to technological constraints, the connection of all the links of all the processing elements on a single communication links switch is impossible. MODULOR project's architectural context relies on two main assumptions (Boniol et al. (1990), Comte et al. (1989)):

- A first idea deals with needed limitation of communication possibilities. Communication constraints are introduced: in the case of a four links processor only North/South and East/West links can be established. If the number of links increases, additional links would be allowed (North-East/South-West and North-West/South-East for a eight links processor). As we will explain a little later such an assumption doesn't limit mapping potentialities of the architecture. In fact switching element complexity can be divided by the number of communication links available on each processor.
- When connecting a large number of processors, a second assumption is needed to take into account switching elements size constraints. The design of a modular architecture can benefit from communications locality. A module is defined as the connection of a limited number of processors on a reconfigurable interconnection structure. According to the previous assumption such an intra-module interconnection structure is composed of four communication switches (for a few links processor). As explained on Figure 1, a second level of interconnection switches is needed for inter-module communication.

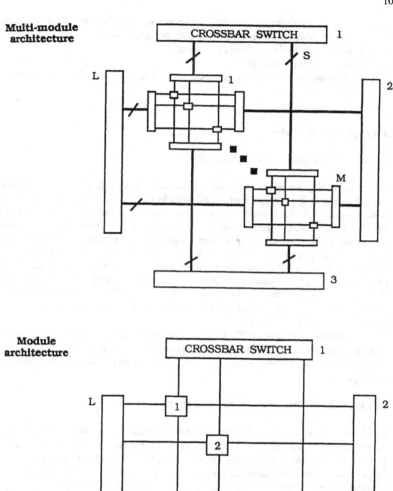

Figure 1. MODULOR Architecture.

Such an architectural context can be summarized by the following parameters:
- L : the number of communication links per processor.
- N : the number of processors per module.
- M: the number of modules.
- S : the number of external links connected to each communication switch of a module.

3. Programming Model

3.1 EXPLICIT PARALLELISM EXPRESSION

When executing an application on a processors network, parallelization techniques are essential. Explicit expression of parallelism is handled by message based communicating processes model. This model, chosen by languages such as CSP (Hoare (1985)) and OCCAM (TELMAT (1990)), allows a communication oriented parallelism expression. Moreover it offers needed parallelism granularity for execution on a highly parallel architecture. Main problem encountered when developing a parallel application in OCCAM for execution on a TRANSPUTER based architecture, is static allocation of processes on processors and of processes communication channels on processors communication ports. This allocation is described in the allocation part of the OCCAM program (PLACED PAR). This description corresponds to a given interconnection topology (wiring table given by OCCAM compiler).

We choose to use OCCAM language for explicit description of parallelism of a reconfigurable application. But the allocation part of such an OCCAM program becomes inadequate in a reconfiguration context which needs different successive configuration descriptions.

3.2 EXPLICIT RECONFIGURATION EXPRESSION

Up to now, it seems irrealistic to aim an automatic detection of the application's points where the interconnection topology has to be modified. We propose to offer the programmer the possibility to explicitly describe at which stages of a given application, reconfiguration of the interconnection topology may occur. Different kinds of reconfiguration strategies can be handled. We limit, in a first step, our objectives to quasi-dynamic reconfiguration: all the processors must be synchronized before each modification of the interconnection topology.

We ask the programmer to decompose his application into algorithmic phases. After completion of a given phase, the interconnection topology can be modified before beginning the execution of the following phase. Thus an optimal topology can be automatically associated to each algorithmic phase. So a reconfigurable application can be described as a set of algorithmic phases separated by predetermined reconfiguration points. When reaching a reconfiguration point a processors synchronization procedure and a switches setting sequence will be initiated.

Each algorithmic phase can be coded in classical communicating processes context. For execution on a Transputer based architecture, OCCAM will be used for coding all algorithmic processes. It can also be used as a hardness to other sequential programming languages. In order to benefit from locality of distributed memory, the programmer must be able to express that data can be left in a processor's memory by a process of a given phase for a process of a following phase.

3.3 RECONFIGURABLE APPLICATION'S DESCRIPTION

A reconfiguration application is seen by the programmer as a set of algorithmic phases (Boniol et al. (1990)). Each phase can be described as processes communicating and synchronizing through messages sent on communication channels. Each process corresponds to an algorithmic entity that can be executed on a processor (a second level of parallelism can be expressed within such an algorithmic entity for exploitation of quasi-parallelism on a processor). A communication graph, where nodes represent processes and edges represent communication channels linking two processes, can be associated to each algorithmic phase. Figure 2 illustrates a three phases application's example.

Thus the global description of a reconfigurable application requires three aspects:
- The description of the various communication graphs of the application (a graph for each algorithmic phase).
- The description of algorithmic code of various processes of the application (a process for each node of each communication graph).
- The description of the host program which indicates where are the synchronisation points and in which way the various phases have to be chained. These phases can be executed in sequence but more complex structure can be handled (conditional execution, iterative execution, ...).

4. Reconfigurable Application Development

4.1 APPLICATION'S GRAPHS DESCRIPTION

A graphical interface has been chosen for description of the communication graphs of a reconfigurable application (Boniol et al. (1990)).

In a first step a set of nodes is entered for a given application. This set corresponds to the level of parallelism decided by the programmer. A node is associated to a processing element. So global variables located in local memory of processors, can be defined for each node.

Description of a given phase leads to the specification of the following items:
- Each node receives a procedure reference. This procedure code can use global data associated to this node. A node without procedure reference doesn't belong to this phase.
- Edges linking nodes which represent communication channel needed between two procedures are then built. These edges are oriented and thus can be mono or bidirectional.

An example of a complete application's graph description is given Figure 3.

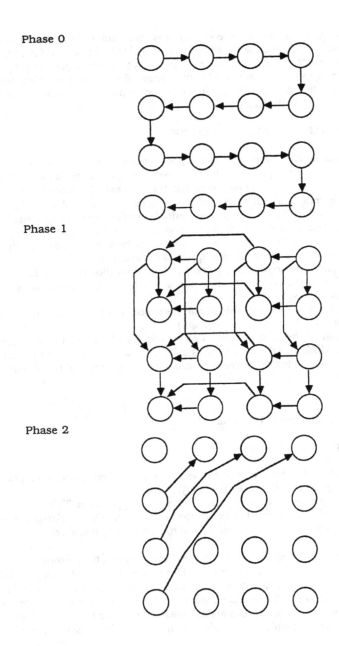

Figure 2. Application's phases description.

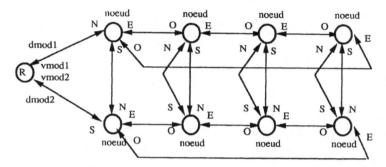

Figure 3. Application's graph description.

4.2 APPLICATION'S GRAPHS MAPPING

A second step of a reconfigurable application development deals with application graphs mapping on a given reconfigurable network (Boniol et al. (1990)). This mapping phase leads to the determination of needed communication links and switches setting control. In a first step, we made following simplifying assumption:
- The number of nodes of an application is less or equal to the number of available processors.
- The number of edges per node (processes connectivity degree) is less or equal to the number of available links on each processor.
     Two levels of problems must be handled by such a mapping software:
- Mapping a communicating processes graph on a module of the reconfigurable architecture can be easily done. All the processors are identical so we only have to determine which links must be set up in order to program the communication links switches. It has been demonstrated that, in spite of communication constraints (North South and East/West), all graphs verifying the previous properties can be implemented (size and connectivity degree) (Lloyd et al. (1988), Boniol et al. (1989)).
- Mapping a communication graph on a multi-module architecture, leads to more complex problems. They mainly consist in partitioning a graph into loosely interconnected subgraphs. Each obtained subgraph has to be allocatable to a module of the reconfigurable architecture. Different constraints have to be verified:
  . number of subgraphs/number of modules (M parameters);
  . number of processes of each subgraph/number of processors per module (N parameter);
  . number of inter-subgraphs communication channel/number of available external communication links on a module (L * S parameter);
  . compatibility of inter subgraphs communication channels with North/South and East/West communication constraints (S parameter).
     Application's graphs mapping on a module and switch setting determination is illustrated on Figure 4.

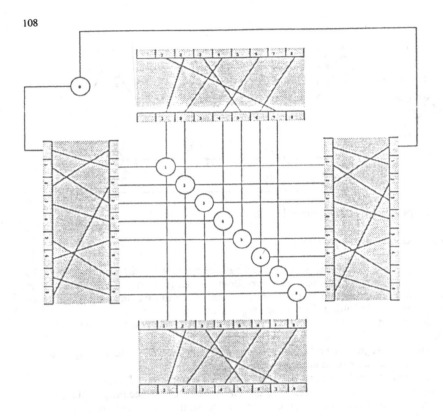

Figure 4. Application's graph mapping.

4.3 APPLICATION'S CODE GENERATION

The last step of a reconfigurable application development consists in generating executable code for a transputer based architecture (Boniol et al. (1990)). We choose to generate OCCAM code compatible with existing development software: a PROGRAM code is generated for execution on the process network and an EXE code corresponds to the algorithm executed on the host processor.

As various configurations are needed for a given application, the configuration part of the OCCAM PROGRAM (PLACED PAR) is only used for allocating a channel name to each communication port of each processor.

The generated code for each processor of the network includes procedure codes of the various phases. Execution of a given procedure will be initiated according to synchronization messages. Thus the way of chaining the various phases has to be explicited only in host code.

All the processors have to be synchronized with the host processor at each reconfiguration point. A minimal tree is automatically determined for each configuration for synchronization message exchange (phase initialization and completion).

Needed switches setting messagesare automatically generated in host processor's code.

5. Conclusion

Given the need for evaluation and experimentation of the proposed software tools on reconfigurable applications, a first version of a complete reconfigurable application development software has been implemented. These tools allow the development of reconfigurable parallel applications on an experimental module of the proposed architecture:
- This module is composed of 32 INMOS T800 TRANSPUTERS connected through 4 INMOS C004 switching elements driven by 2 INMOS T414 TRANSPUTERS.
- The reconfigurable application development software (graphical interface, mapper and switches configurer, code generator) has been implemented on an Apollo DN 3500 workstation connected to the experimental module via an ARCHIPEL VOLVOX interface.
- Applications have been firstly studied in numerical context: linear systems solvers (GAUSS method, cyclic reduction, ...) and level 3 BLAS (Basic Linear Algebra Subprograms) have been coded. New applications under development deal with neural networks methods and image and signal processing algorithms (FFT, ...).

Research underway concerns the generalization of the proposed software tools in a multi-module architectural context. A multi-module prototype will be realized soon.

The reconfigurable application development software is also being adapted to SUPERNODE (Harp (1987)) architecture's specific aspects. An implementation is underway in the context of a 48 processors TELMAT Tandem TNode machine (TELMAT (1990)).

6. References

Wang, K.H. and Xu, Z. (1985), "Remps: a reconfigurable multi-processor for scientific computing", Parallel processing, Sept. 85.

Murakami, K., Akira, F., Toshinori, S. and Shinji, T. (1988), "An overview of the Kyushu University reconfigurable parallel processor", Computer Architecture News, Sept. 88.

Harp, J.P. (1987), Phase 2 of the Reconfigurable Transputer Project, HMSO London 87.

Lloyd, E.D., Nicole, D.A. and Ward, J.S. (1988), Switching networks for transputer links, 8th OCCAM User Group, March 88.

Boniol, F., Fraboul, Ch., Rousselot, J.Y. and Siron, P. (1990), Etude d'architectures reconfigurables: project MODULOR, Rapport CERT/DERI No. 3/3344, Jan. 90.

Boniol, F., Fraboul, Ch., Rousselot, P. and Siron, P. (1989), Etude du problème de placement d'une application répartie, Internal Report CERT/DERI, Sept. 89.

Comte, D., Fraboul, Ch, Rousselot, J.Y. and Siron, P. (1989), MODULAR: a modular reconfigurable parallel architecture, 1st European Workshop on Hypercube and Distributed computers, Oct. 89.

110

Hoare, C.A.R. (1985), CSP: Communicating Sequential Processes, Prentice Hall Publication 85.

Pountain, D. and May, D. (1988), A tutorial introduction to OCCAM programming, Document INMOS, March 88.

TELMAT Informatique (1990), Tnode presentation, Tnode Tools, Document TELMAT, Feb, 90.

THE PAC SYSTEM AND ITS IMPLEMENTATION ON DISTRIBUTED ARCHITECTURES

J.L. ROCH [1]
Laboratoire LMC-IMAG INPG- CNRS
46, Avenue Félix Viallet
38031 Grenoble Cedex - France

Abstract :

PAC is a parallel environment, based on a MIMD distributed model, aimed at development of computer algebra algorithms. It uses parallelism as a tool for processing large size problems. In a first part the relation between computer algebra and parallelism is discussed. Then, the general features of the project are described, and some of the obtained results are presented.
PAC has been implemented on the FPS Tseries hypercube, and an implementation on the TELMAT Meganode is in progress.

1. A PARALLEL ENVIRONMENT FOR COMPUTATION

1.1. MATHEMATICAL FIELDS AND ALGORITHMS

The final purpose of most mathematical computations is to give a canonical (normal) representation of an element in a given set.
Namely, to compute $2+3$ in $\mathbb{Z}/4\mathbb{Z}$ consists in associating to this expression the element 1.

Considering a given problem with a mathematical point of view brings often new algorithms.

For example, let us consider the problem of string matching (i.e. looking for a given substring in a string). This problem is defined in the non-commutative multiplicative group $S=(\{0,1\}^*, \wedge)$, where $\wedge$ denotes the concatenation law. The best algorithm for this problem is due to R.Boyer and S.Moore [BOY77].
To allow powerfull manipulations in this set, the idea proposed by M.Karp and O.Rabin [KARP87] is to dig this problem in a group that as more properties. $E=(M_{2,2}(\mathbb{Z}), o)$ is a non-commutative multiplicative group too. So, by choosing a good homomorphism from S to E, a powerful arithmetic is obtained, including, for example, fast multiplication or inverse computation. In this way, new good algorithms may be found - like probabilistic algorithms -, and an efficient parallelization, based on a parallel prefix computation, may be defined.

───────────────
1   This work is supported by the *PRC Mathématiques et Informatique* and by the *GRECO Calcul Formel* of the french *Centre National de la Recherche Scientifique (CNRS)*.

D. Gassilloud and J. C. Grossetie (eds.), Computing with Parallel Architectures: T.Node, 111–122.
© 1991 *ECSC, EEC, EAEC, Brussels and Luxembourg. Printed in the Netherlands.*

One of the aim of PAC is thus to provide a friendly environment for computing in mathematical fields.

1.2.   WHAT ARE THE BEST SUITED FIELDS FOR COMPUTATION ?

The duality between approximated and exact computations leads two different approaches of a same problem : the choice of the best approach is often difficult.

Let us consider three examples.

Ex 1 :   matrix inversion using Gaussian elimination
If the entry matrix A is stable, then an approximated resolution (in f=floatting point numbers set, or $f[X]$...) is convenient. However, if A is non-stable (eighenvalues of A are far one from the others) than the approximated resolution is no more valid : one has to turn to an exact resolution. When the stability of A is not known, or if a general inversion algorithm for any matrix is to be defined, then the problem seems much more complex : the choice of the good approach may not be done without considering the matrix in entry.

Ex 2 :   Jordan form computation
This problem, like most of the problems based on eighenvalues, is intrisically non-stable, and needs exact algorithms to be solved .

Ex 3 :   matrix product
Here, the standard algorithm is numerically stable whatever the matrices in entry are, in the sense that the error on the result is directly related to the approximations made on the entries and on the computations.

Thus, both computation frameworks (exact or approximated) are necessary. The choice of the good approach for a given problem depends on mainly three parameters : the problem itself, its entries, and the means of computations that are to be used.

1.3.   PAC : A PARALLEL SYSTEM DEDICATED TO COMPUTATION

One of the major problems brought by exact computation is the increase in complexity. This problem resticts the use of exact computations to small size problems. For instance, under Macsyma, it is quasi-impossible to invert a linear system with rational coefficients of size 100x100 [VIL88]. However, on the practical point of view, the ability of a computation system to solve such large problems should be one of its credibility criteria.

For those large problems, time spent in symbolic manipulations is neglectible in respect with time spent in mathematical calculus. Thus, it seems interesting to turn to parallelism, because it allows to consider many problems under a new approach, decreasing in most cases their complexity.

2.   RELATION BETWEEN COMPUTER ALGEBRA AND PARALLELISM

FROM COMUTER ALGEBRA TO PARALLELISM

The two control primitives (AND-Parallel and OR-Parallel) for parallelism appear inherently in many computer algebra algorithms.

2.1.   AND-PARALLELISM IN COMPUTER ALGEBRA

Let us consider a problem P given in a space E. One of the methods often used to solve P consists in projecting it onto sub-spaces $E_1,....,E_n$ so as to obtain sub-problems $P_1,....,P_n$. Then the solutions $s_1,....,s_n$ of $P_1,....,P_n$ may be computed independently. Finally, using a lifting process, the solution s in E may be computed.

Ex. 1 :   A problem P in the rationals, where numerators and denominators of solution coefficients are bounded depending on the entries, may be computed modulo several prime numbers p_i (here $E_i = \mathbb{Z}/p_i\mathbb{Z}$). The solution in $\mathbb{Q}$ may then be found using the chineese remainder theorem.
This leads often to good solutions : for instance, if P is the matrix inversion problem, this method applied on Gaussian elimination, instead of appliyng the same algorithm in $\mathbb{Q}$, leads to a better solution.

Ex. 2 : manipulation of algebraic extensions is a basic problem in computer algebra. D. Duval [DUV88] gives a nice approachto this problem, using a special strategy.
Let μ be defined as a root of a given polynomial P. During the execution of a program where μ is manipulated, some problems may appear, depending on values of the different roots of P.
For example, let us suppose $P = \mu^3 - 2.\mu^2 + \mu - 2$ (i.e. $\mu \in \{-i, i, 2\}$).
If the instruction : $if (\mu == 2)$ then (I) else (J) is to be executed then two cases are to be considered.
If μ corresponds to roots of $P(\mu)/(\mu^2+1)$ the instruction (I) has to be executed, else, μ corresponds to a root of $P(\mu)/(\mu-2)$, and (J) has to be executed.
So, the ring E where the problem has been defined ($E = \mathbb{Q}[\mu]/(\mu^3 - 2.\mu^2 + \mu - 2)$) has to be split in two sub-rings : $E_1 = \mathbb{Q}[\mu]/(\mu - 2)$ and $E_2 = \mathbb{Q}[\mu]/(\mu^2 + 1)$.
Thus, the solution of the algorithm in E is the union of both solutions found respectively in E_1 and E_2.

2.2.   OR-PARALLELISM IN COMPUTER ALGEBRA

We have already pointed out the importance of probabilistic methods in Computer Algebra : they allow to compute efficiently solutions of a problem, but with a probability of chess, that is those solutions are not always solutions of the inner problem, and so have to be verified.

So, a good way of computing a problem for which it exists both a deterministic algorithm and an efficient probabilistic one, consists in computing both algorithms in parallel, and taking the first good solution that has been computed.

This way of computing corresponds obviously to OR-Parallelism approach. Applications may be found for computation of polynomials gcd (probabilistic and deterministic algorithms), or to compute the standard basis with the Buchberger algorithm (using different strategies in parallel [SEN90]).

2.3.   FROM PARALLELISM TO COMPUTER ALGEBRA

Let us consider the NC classification [COO85][PIP79] on uniform boolean circuit families [RUZ83] [BOR77]. NC^k is the class of functions computable in polylog time on a boolean circuit with a polynomial number of nodes .
On the boolean model, a parallel algorithm for a given problem corresponds to a well-balanced algebraic expression of the solution. As an example, a good way for computing matrix inverse is to use Cayley-Hamilton identity [CSA76] : thus, the problem remains to compute the powers of the entry matrix .

3. ADEQUATION BETWEEN COMPUTER ALGEBRA AND PARALLELISM

The intrinsically large complexity of computer algebra algorithms comes mainly from two facts :

♦ many elementary operations are performed : obviously, this is not typical of non-numeric problems. However, even small size problems, but badly conditionned, may let appear a large swelling of intermediary coefficients, which increases the number of elementary machine operations performed.
Thus, MIMD machines, that allow to perform different tasks in parallel seems well-suited to computer algebra algorithms.

♦ handled objects have a complex structure, and need a large memory space to be stored. Namely, Hermite normal form computation [SIE90] is typical of this problem : even if coefficients of the solutions are bounded, the bound on intermediate coefficients is enormous : thus, space needed for computation is very large compared with space needed for storing the result.
The genericity of distributed machines seems attractive, as it allows to increase the local memory space needed for nodal computations.

3.1. TARGET ARCHITECTURES

A first version of PAC has been implemented on the hypercube FPS-T40 (32 processors T414). On this machine, different algorithms, with static distribution of tasks, have been studied. In this paper, we present some of the obtained results.

A second version is being implemented on the TELMAT Meganode (128 processors T800) : this new version allows dynamic distribution of tasks, with different levels of parallelism for a problem. This approach is based on the reconfiguration ability of this machine.

4. GENERAL PRESENTATION OF PAC

PAC is an environment for development of parallel computer algebra applications.

Pac includes :
- nodal primitives : on each node, several primitives are provided, that allows to handle symbols and complex algebraic expressions.
- parallel primitives : suited to some expensive problems, they allow to reduce their cost by using parallelism.

There are two ways of using PAC :
- as a basic library for development of parallel applications.
- PAC is interfaced with classical computer algebra systems (ex. Reduce). Thus, it may be easily used to solve some specific problems (polynomial arithmetic, linear system solving, normal form computations...). Namely, from Reduce, commands may be forked to PAC, and the result of the parallel evaluation of the commands may be handled symbolically, until it has been computed.

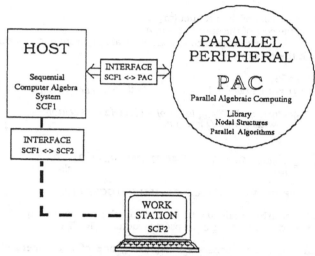

General Organization of PAC

5.   A DIDACTIC STUDY : THE PRODUCT OF TWO POLYNOMIALS

The product of sparse polynomials is a typical example of non-numeric problems depending on entry data : it mixed symbols handling and computations (sums and products of coefficients).

We consider here a sparse representation of polynomials of $\mathbb{Z}[X]$. The method presented is however directly suited to the multivariate case. The parallel resolution involves methods generally used in parallelism : partition of the problem, broadcast of data, lifting process to the global solution.

Let $m = a.X^n$ be a monomial of $\mathbb{Z}[X]$, with $a \in \mathbb{Z}$ and P be a polynomial of $\mathbb{Z}[X]$. In the following, we denote :

- ♦ $Size(m)$ the numbers of digits of a (i.e. $\lfloor Log_\beta |a| + 1 \rfloor$)
- ♦ $d(P)$ the degree of P
- ♦ $N_{mon}(P)$ the numbers of non-zero monomials in P

We restrict the study to sparse polynomials [ROC89] : P and Q are *sparse each other* iff $N_{mon}(P).N_{mon}(Q) = N_{mon}(P.Q)$

Ex. : $P = \sum_{i=0}^{n-1} X^{n.i}$ and $Q = \sum_{i=0}^{n-1} x^i$

MODEL OF COMPUTATION

Let $m_1 = a_1.X^{n_1}$ and $m_2 = a_2.X^{n_2}$ be two monomials of $\mathbb{Z}[X]$, with $(a_1, a_2) \in \mathbb{Z}^2$.

We denote :

$T_{mul}(m_1, m_2)$: the cost of the product $(m_1.m_2)$

$T_{add}(m_1, m_2)$: the cost of the sum $(m_1 + m_2)$

$T_{com}(m_1)$: the cost needed to communicate m_1 from one processor to one of its neighbours in the network

Axiom 1   [SAA88].

$$T_{com}(m_1) = \alpha + taille(m_1).\tau_{com} = \alpha + taille(a_1).\tau_{com} \quad (\tau_{com} > 0, \; \alpha > 0)$$

Axiom 2 $T_{mul}(m_1, m_2) = T_{mul}(a_1, a_2) = g(Size(a_1)+Size(a_2))$
with $g(n) = \Omega(n.\log n)$

Axiom 3

$$T_{add}(m_1, m_2) = \begin{cases} T_{add}(a_1, a_2) = O(Size(a_1)+Size(a_2)) & \text{if } n_1 = n_2 \\ 0 & \text{else} \end{cases}$$

5.1. ANALYSIS OF THE PROBLEM AND PARALLEL ALGORITHMS

The sequential algorithm consists in generating the monomials of the product by decreasing order in degrees -using a heapsort structure -[JOH74] .

A direct parallel approach consists in splitting one of both operands; then two balanced products may be obtained [RSS86].

Let $P = \sum_{i=0}^{p} a_i.x^{\alpha_i}$ and $Q = \sum_{i=0}^{q} b_i.x^{\beta_i}$ be two polynomials.

The computation scheme is the following :

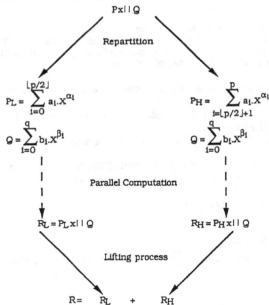

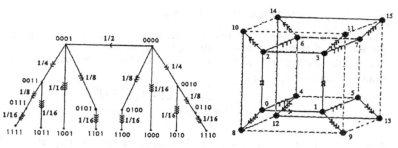

Graph of repartition on the 4-cube

This parallelization is well-suited to hypercube topology. At step i, the processors in dimension lower than i split their operands, and distribute half of their tasks to their neighbour in dimension $i+1$.

5.2. CHOICE OF THE POLYNOMIAL TO SPLIT

This choice is related to two constraints. On one hand, by splitting the smaller polynomial, less arithmetic operations have to be computed. On the other hand, so as to minimize length of communicated data, it is better to split the larger polynomial.

5.3. COMPLEXITY STUDY

Coefficients of polynomials are assumed to be bounded by B, and polynomials are sparse each other.

With the previous conventions, times needed for the sequential and parallel algorithms are [ROC89] :

$$T_{seq}(P,Q) = p.q.T_{mul}[B(P),B(Q)] + (p.q - 1).T_{add}[B(P)+B(Q)]$$

$$T_{par}(P,Q) = p.q.\left(\frac{T_{mul}(B,B)}{2^N} + T_{add}(B,B) + T_{com}(B) \right) \quad (1)$$

If p and q are small compared to 2^N, the parallelization is unefficient. Let us consider the computation of a large product, assuming that p and q are very large compared to 2^N.

Then, the corresponding efficiency is :

$$e = \frac{T_{seq}}{2^N.T_{par}} \approx \frac{T_{mul}(B,B) + T_{add}(B,B)}{T_{mul}(B,B) + 2^N.(T_{add}(B,B) + T_{com}(B))} \quad (2)$$

So, if B is large enough, communication times become neglectible, and coefficients multiplication times (that are non-linear) are the largest : then efficiency is close to one.

118

5.4.   THE BEST NUMBER OF PROCESSORS

The compromise between number of processors and size of the problem for which parallelism is of interest ,may be here precisely studied.

The parallelization is of no benefit as soon as the number of processors 2^N is larger than 2^{N_0}, where N_0 is defined by :

$$\begin{cases} T_{Par}^{(N_0-1)}(P,Q) > T_{Par}^{(N_0)}(P,Q) \\ T_{Par}^{(N_0)}(P,Q) \le T_{Par}^{(N_0+1)}(P,Q) \end{cases}$$

Assuming N_0 is large enough ($2^{N_0} \gg 1$), from (1) we may obtain the following approximation of N_0 :

$$N_0 \ge Log_2\left(1 + \frac{2.p.(B_p+B_q).g(B_p+B_q)}{\tau.B_q + \alpha} \right) \qquad (3)$$

5.5.   EXPERIMENTATIONS AND CONCLUSION

Other algorithms for this problem have been studied, nothingly Karatsuba splitting [ROC89] : we compare here the experimentalobtained results .

For both algorithms, implementation shows that the best choice is to split the larger polynomial, so as to decrease communication times : this is justified by the ratio (communication time)/(computation time) on the FPS-T40. This conclusion should be yet valid on the Meganode.

It is very difficult to study practically efficiency : by increasing the number of processors, larger problems may be solved (mainly because of the corresponding memory extension). However, speed-up are good, even if, in the benchmark used here, parallel tasks are unbalanced (middle coefficients are much larger than extremal ones). So as to take in account this increase in the size of the treated problems, an extension of Gustafson' speed-up has be studied [SIE89].

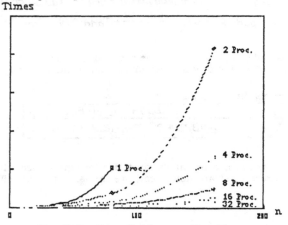

Parallelization of Johnson Algorithm
$$P = Q = (x+y)^{5.n}$$

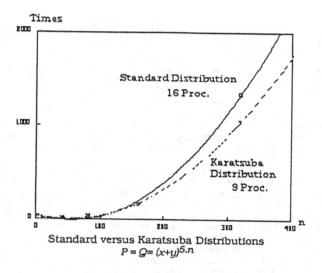

Standard versus Karatsuba Distributions
$$P = Q = (x+y)^{5.n}$$

6. THE BASIC PARALLEL ARITHMETIC MODULE OF PAC

One of the basic principles of a computer algebra system is to allow the building of embedded domains. Thus, once the integer group $\mathbb{Z}$ has been built, the rational field $\mathbb{Q}$ or the integer polynomial ring $\mathbb{Z}[X]$ may be constructed.

The rational arithmetic is a very important basic set, and its implementation has been carefully studied. Different algorithms have been studied and implemented, depending on the size of the operands [ROC89].

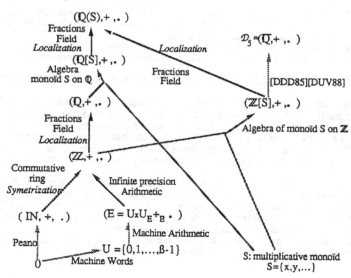

Those basic extensions lead us to define bigger and bigger domains, whose elements have complex structures, built from already defined structures. For each set, defined operations have their own level of parallelism, but may involve other operations in lower level sets. Thus, two levels of parallelization are distinguished :

- low level parallelization : the problem is split into elementary concurrent tasks, that handle basic elements (string, machine integers...). This corresponds to a very fine grain description of the problem : so, this parallelization is suited only to problems that handle no complex structures.

- high level parallelization : the problem is split into tasks that handle objects of other complex sets. This allows to take benefit of the intrinsic parallelism of the problem. For instance, the previous parallelization of polynomial product, without taking care of the coefficient multiplications, is in this framework

The new version of PAC, on the Telmat Meganode, includes primitives to exploit dynamically this high level of parallelism. Two approaches are considered :

- "static" : the expression to evaluate is given as a graph, and algorithms are implemented to evaluate this graph in parallel with algorithms dedicated to the distributed model. Some theoretical results have been studied in the shared memory model [KOS88][COL88]. Extensions and adaptations of those algorithms are in progress in the framework of PAC [REV90].

- "dynamic" : to each parallel operation corresponds a parallel cost, related to the size of the operands. When this operation is to be computed, this cost is evaluated so as to eventually assign tasks to other processors, depending on this cost and the occupation of the network [YEH90]

7. SOME APPLICATIONS IN PAC

We present here some results obtained within the PAC project on the FPS T20 and T40 [RSS88].

7.1. EXACT SOLUTION OF LINEAR SYSTEMS WITH RATIONAL COEFFICIENTS

This problem has been studied by Gilles Villard [VIL88]. Different algorithms have been implemented : standard Gauss inversion, Gaussian elimination using p-adic developments or modular arithmetic.
The implementation allows to solve 700x700 dense system -with integral coefficient in entry bounded by 100- in 3 hours 35 minutes on 16 processors.

7.2. HERMITE NORMAL FORM COMPUTATION ON INTEGERS AND POLYNOMIALS

This problem has been studied by Françoise Siebert-Roch [SIE90]. This problem has the particularity that it needs a large memory space to be computed.
Two cases are distinguished. In the integral case, the Ilopoulos algorithm gives the best results : two ways of distributing data have been studied (by rows and columns [SIE89]). The implementation allows to compute Hermite form of a 160x160 matrix in 3 hours on 32 processors : for this computation, 5 Gbytes of memory have been allocated.
In the polynomial case, a parallelization of Kannan algorithm has been proposed. However, the obtained speed-up is not as good as in the integral case, because of the inherent unbalancing of the tasks : only a dynamic approach would bring efficiency on this peculiar problem, as it is impossible to balance statically the elementary tasks because of the intermediate coefficients swelling.
The Hermite normal form of matrix computation in PAC is interfaced with Reduce system, and so may be called directly from the host.

8. CONCLUSION

The obtained results show the interest of parallelism to computer algebra. The validation of theoretical algorithms with the implementation on a dedicated model is very important.

The implementation in progress on the Telmat-Meganode makes possible the use of a pretty large number of processors : then, the use of different levels of parallelization becomes interesting as it allows to dynamically take advantage of parallelism.

Parallelism and computer algebra seem to be strongly related. On one hand, the modelization of parallel And and Or mechanisms in an algebraic point of view should bring powerful tools for description of computer algebra algorithms. On the other hand, different applications of computer algebra give a new sight in parallelism : one of the most important is the straight-line program parallel evaluation [MIL88].

BIBLIOGRAPHY

[BOR77]   A. Borodin, "On relating Time and Space to Size and Depth", SIAM Journal of computing, 5, pp 733-744, 1977
(1977)

[BOY77]   R.S. Boyer, J.S. Moore, "A Fast String Searching Algorithm3, Comm. of the ACM. vol. 20, n°10, Oct.77
(1977)

[COL88]   R. Cole, U. Vishkin, "Optimal Parallel Algorithms for Expression Tree Evaluation and List Raking", Proc. AWOC 88, Springer Verlag Lectures Notes Computer Science, 319, pp 91-100
(1988)

[COO85]   S.A. Cook, "A Taxonomy of Problems that have Fast Parallel Algorithms", Information andControl, vol. 64, pp2-22, 1985
(1985)

[CSA76]   L. Csanky, "Fast Parallel Matrix Inversion Algorithms", SIAM Journal of Computing, 5/4, pp. 618-623, 1976
(1976)

[JOH74]   S. Johnson "Sparse Polynomial Arithmetic", Bell Labs research report   (1974)

[KAO62]   A. Karatsuba, Y. Ofman "Multiplication of multidigit numbers on automata", Dok. Akad. Nauk. SSSR vol.145 (p. 293-294)
(1962)

[KARP87]   R.M. Karp, M.O. Rabin, "Efficient Randomized Pattern-Matching Algorithms", IBM Journal of Research and Development, vol.31, n°2, Mar. 87
(1987)

[KOS88]   S.R. Kosaraju, V. Ramachandran, "Optimal Parallel Evaluation of Tree-Structured Computations by Raking", Proc. AWOC 88, Springer Verlag Lectures Notes Computer Science, 319, pp 101-110
(1988)

[MIL88]   G.L. Miller, E. Kaltofen, V. Ramachandran, "Efficient Parallel Evaluation of Straight-Line Code and Arithmetic Circuits", SIAM Journal of Computing, 17 / 4 pp. 687-695   (1988)

[PIP79]   N. Pippenger, "On Simultaneous Ressource Bounded", Proc. 20th Ann. IEEE Symp. on Fundations of Computer Science, pp 307-311, Oct. 79
(1979)

[REV90]   N. Revol, "Evaluation Parallèle d'Arborescences", Rapport de fin d'études, Inst. Nat. Polytechnique de Grenoble"
(1990)

[ROC89]   J.L. Roch, "Calcul Formel et Parallélisme : Le système PAC et son arithmétique nodale", Ph.D. Thesis "Inst. Nat. Polytechnique de Grenoble"
(1989)

[RSS88]   J.L. Roch, P. Sénéchaud, F. Siebert, G. Villard, "Computer Algebra on MIMD machine", SIGSAM Bulletin, 23 / 1, Janv 89
(1989)

[RUZ81]   W.L. Ruzzo, "On Uniform Circuit Complexity", Journal of Computer and System Sciences, 22, 3, pp 365-383, Jun 81
(1981)

122

[SAA88]   Y. Saad, M.H. Schultz, "Topological Properties of Hypercubes", IEEE Transactions on Computers, 37 / 7 - 1988   (1988)

[SEN90]   P. Sénéchaud,"Calcul Formel et Parallélisme : Bases de Gröbner Booléennes - Méthodes de Calcul - Applications - Parallélisation", Ph.D. Thesis "Inst. Nat. Polytechnique de Grenoble"   (1990)

[SIE90]   F. Siebert-Roch, "Calcul Formel et Parallélisme : Forme Normale d'Hermite - Méthodes de Calcul et Parallélisation", Ph.D. Thesis "Inst. Nat. Polytechnique de Grenoble"(1990)

[VIL88]   G. Villard,"Calcul Formel et Parallélisme : Résolution de systèmes linéaires ", Ph.D. Thesis "Inst. Nat. Polytechnique de Grenoble"   (1988)

[YEH90]   H.J. Yeh, "L'intepréteur PAC, et l'évaluation parallèle dynamique", Rapport de fin d'études, Inst. Nat. Polytechnique de Grenoble"   (1990)

IMAGE SYNTHESIS ON T.NODE

DENIS GASSILLOUD(*), BERNARD MIGNOT(**)

(*) Joint Research Centre - Ispra Site - I-21020 Ispra, Italy
(**) TELMAT Informatique - Z.I.rte d'Issenheim - BP12 - 68360 Soultz

ABSTRACT. Ray-tracing is an efficient method for realistic picture synthesis. This method encloses the necessary effects for realism synthesis (shadow casting, multiple reflections, transparency with refraction), by use of light illumination models as near as physical laws. As this method necessitates prohibitive computation time, parallel machines offer an interesting performance improvement.

A ray-tracing implementation has been developed in an application work package of Supernode I Esprit project. Parallelism is exploited at the highest level of the algorithm. Each transputer of the network computes one part of the picture, a square composed of 16 x 16 pixels. Data base is all distributed in the processors. The geometric model used is CSG (constructive solid geometry), with primitives as spheres, cubes, splines). The communication volume is minimal: only parameters of the area to compute and pixels are transferred. An implementation has been realized on a T.Node machines, from 16 to 256 transputers. The network is composed of parallel pipes with 16 processors each one. The performances depend on the capability of the communication model to solve the bottle-neck with the graphic resource. Efficiencies reached are more than 90% in comparison with one transputer. Computation time depends extremely on the picture and data base complexity. For a scenary composed with around 200 primitive objects, and picture resolution 1024x1024, times are around 1 minute computation on Mega.Node.

0. Presentation

Ray-casting is a powerful method of synthesis to produce realistic images. It allows the rendering of reflections, transparency, casted shadows, specular lights, using illuminations model very near actual optical laws. Its draw-back is the use of huge means of computation and drives to drastic run-times. So many algorithms have been proposed to reduce the computation time. A lot of them deal to reduce the combinatory aspect of the calculus, a few of them lead to exploit the parallelism of the method.

TELMAT participates in an ESPRIT project to construct a multiprocessor machine easily reconfigurable. To prove and demonstrate the power of this machine we have studied and implemented a parallelized ray-tracing. This implementation is presented in this paper.

D. Gassilloud and J. C. Grossetie (eds.), Computing with Parallel Architectures: T.Node, 123–136.

124

First the main hardware and software features of the machine developed in the Esprit project 1085 are presented. In a second paragraph the principles of ray-tracing and the algorithms used are exposed. Then the implementation itself is explained, including the exploited concurrency, tests and a global scheme of the software.

1. The ESPRIT project 1085: T.Node

The goal of this project is the development and application of a high performance, low cost multiprocessor machine (Harp et al. (1987)). This machine is mainly based on the transputer T800 of INMOS (the T800 is partially funded by the project).

The IMS T800 is a 64 bit floating point unit. It has a full 32 bit transputer architecture, with four 10/20 Mbits/sec INMOS serial links. A T800 transputer is a RISC processor allowing a fast execution of program written in Occam.

The basic module of the machine is called T.Node. It contains 16 or 32 transputers with 256 Kbytes or 4 Mbytes of memory local to each processor. A dedicated processor acts as a master to control a switch than can dynamically configure any kind of network allowed by the four links of each transputer. One T.Node develops a peak rate of 48 Mflops. This power was benchmarked on the computation of the Mandelbrot set. T.Nodes can be connected together in the same way at an upper level to make a machine containing up to 1024 T800 and keeping the reconfiguration capabilities.

As the basic component of the T.Node is the T800, OCCAM is used as the basic programming language for the machine. Upper software tools are developed mainly to exploit the reconfiguration possibilities of the machine and to ease the mapping of a logical parallel architecture to a physical machine. T.Node is programmed from a UNIX host machine running the Transputer Development System (TDS) from INMOS, and using software tools including C and Fortran compilers for the T800 target, and a linker to Occam code.

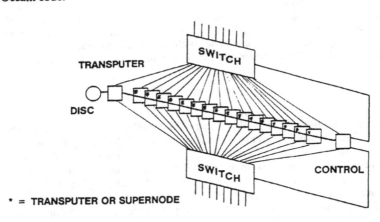

* = TRANSPUTER OR SUPERNODE

The T.Node

2. Ray-tracing: presentation

Because of its analogy with reality, ray-tracing is a computer method able to synthetize very realistic images.

The idea is to analyse the way covered by light rays passing through the space from their source and reaching the observation point. The study comes off in fact in the opposite direction of the light, that is to say from the observer to the infinite. To obtain a numeric picture, it will be enough to cast the ray passing by each pixel and compute its colour. The first met object will be the visible object, and will give part of the colour to the pixel from where the ray is born. Indeed, from initial ray going through the screen, we can build all light rays that it creates taking into account optic properties of the met object (reflexion, transparency) and light sources disposed in the space. This set of rays is called ray tree. Colour computation of the pixel is achieved using all the physical parameters of the scene interfering with the ray tree (Roth (1982)).

Generally, ray-tracing programs are relatively simple in their presentation. However, most ray-tracing implementations are heavy users of floating point arithmetic. Even a simple illumination function called Phong shading (Phong 1975)) uses additions, multiplications, a power operation, it is called more than a million times. It is the law used to recombine secondary rays energy at an impact point. These functions can be more computational expensive if we use laws closer to actual physic such as Snell Law or Fresnel laws (Cook and Torrance (1982), Whitted (1980)). The most time consuming process remains the computation of the intersection between a ray and the objects of the scenary.

3. Ray-tracing parallelisation on T.Node

The implementation of ray-tracing on T.Node was conduced in successive phases. The first phase consisted in reviewing improved methods saving computation time. Then we have worked up the geometric parallelism of the application. The main tasks of the ray-tracing process are considered, the communications between them defined. We have deepen our analyse of the independencies between these internal processes. Using these independencies, we have defined diverse strategies for a parallel implementation. The entity-relation model of our analyse is easily mapped to the process-communication model of Occam. Each of these main processes is then refined, and can be considered as a virtual machine having and managing its own computing power. As much as possible,

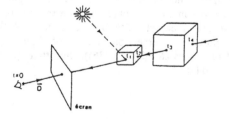

A ray, short through a pixel, intersects objects in scenary.

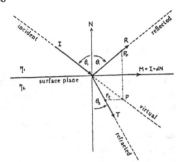

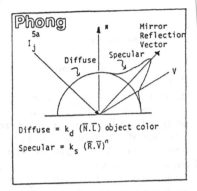

$$\text{Diffuse} = k_d \ (\bar{N}.\bar{L}) \ object \ color$$

$$\text{Specular} = k_s \ (\bar{R}.\bar{V})^n$$

Phong shading model.

improved sequential algorithms are included in this frame of parallel execution. But it is relatively difficult to find a solution valid in all cases of picture, and effective in computation time: algorithm execution conjures an aleatory working with frequent sequences ruptures.

3.1. ALGORITHMS

The first phase consisted in reviewing suitable algorithms for an implementation on T.Node. We have gathered improved methods saving computation time.

A CSG representation is used to modelize the scenary (Roth (1982)). Objects are modelized in their modeling coordinate system then put together in a world coordinate system. A transformation is made depending on the parameters of observation to a viewing coordinate system that we call a virtual screen and then mapped to the actual frame buffer. The ratio between the virtual screen and the actual frame buffer determine the level of sampling (over, normal and subsampling are possible). To reduce the number of computed pixels, grid refinement is used. The virtual screen is split in grids whose corners are computed. Depending either on the presence of an object in the grid, either on the level of sampling of the process, either on the difference between the corners; the grid is recursively split (Jansen and Van Wijk (1983)). To reduce the number of rays, an adaptative ray tree is used. We do not compute all branches of the tree but only those significant (Hall and Greenberg (1983)). To reduce the number of object to intersect we use improvement methods such as filtering the set of objects with box enclosures (Roth (1982)). Two improvement methods to compute the intersection of a set of objects by rays were studied. One uses a pipe-line of processes (Madani (1986)), the other space coherence (Coquillart (1985)). They are detailed later.

3.2. PARALLELISM

We have worked up the geometric parallelism of the application, using pixels, rays and objects independency. These levels of indepency between tasks are of main importance to construct an execution graph and detect all possible parallelisms. In the case of ray tracing these levels are detailed below.

3.2.1. *Level 1: pixels.*

$$\text{PIXEL: pixel} \hookrightarrow \text{colour}$$
$$(X,Y) \mapsto (R,V,B,Z)$$

X,Y are the coordinate of a pixel in the virtual screen, R,V,B are the components of its colour, Z is its depth in the world coordinate. This Z is anecdotic, we compute it because we use a huge frame-buffer containing a Z-buffer (CUBI9000 of CAPTION) and we mix ray-traced images and B-rep synthetized pictures.

In fact as we take into account the level of sampling to compute a pixel, the pixels under the sampling level are not independent so it is better to consider a grid of pixel as the unit of calculus.

$$\text{GRID: pixel X pixel} \rightarrow \text{colour X colour}$$
$$(X,Y,T) \mapsto (R,V,B,Z)$$

T is the side tail of the grid, R,V,B are now square arrays of colour of size T*T.

3.2.2. *Level 2: rays.*

For one impact point of a father ray on an object many sons rays will be casted. These rays are the rays directed to light sources (one ray for each) and secondary reflected and refracted rays. Each of these rays are independent. But the existence of these rays depends on physical properties of the scenary. The children rays are composed to give the colour of the father ray. The root ray gives is colour to the pixel from which it is issued.

$$\text{RAY: ray} \rightarrow \text{energy}$$
$$(Ox,Oy,Oz,Dx,Dy,Dz) \mapsto (R,V,B)$$

Ox,Oy,Oz are the coordinate of the ray origin in the world coordinate. Dx,Dy,Dz is the director vector of the ray. R,V,B are the components of the colour brought back by the ray.

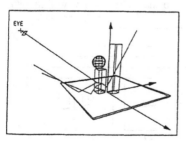

Multiple reflections/refractions: the ray tree.

3.2.3. *Level 3: objects.* For one ray, achievements of exclusion tests, intersection calculations and impact parameters are own to each objects.

OBJECT: ray → object intersected
(Ox,Oy,Oz,Dx,Dy,Dz) ↦ (T1,T2,P1,P2,I1,I2)

Ox,Oy,Oz are the coordinate of the ray origin in the modeling coordinate system of the object, Dx,Dy,Dz is the director vector of the ray. A Ti is the parameter of an impact point to the object, this parameter is independent of the coordinate system used, P,I are the type of primitive intersected and the indexes to physical properties of this primitive.

3.2.4. *Level 4: operations.* Most calculation are vectorial arithmetic operations with matrixes and vectors of dimension 3 or 4: products, scalar products, normalization. This vectors are space coordinates but also colour coordinates. This level was not explored because it is not peculiar to ray-tracing and work is done on it elsewhere in the project. This is the task of a good compiler or at least of an already parallelized library.

3.2.5. *Algorithmic level.* We notice that the previous levels of independencies define a "geometric" parallelism intrinsic to the application. An other level was studied and was called algorithmic level. The goal of it was to break big functions in small one that can be executed in pipe-line.

An example of it can be found in (Madani (1986)). A ray is given and we wish to compute its first impact with an object of the scene. The algorithm is composed of three phases. P0 is the selection of objects which have a good probability to be intersected, P1 the calculs of the intersections of the ray with these selected objects, P2 the sort of all actual impacts taking in account the structure of the scenary (CSG tree).

- P0: ray   set of CSG nodes possibly intersected.
- P1: ..   set of CSG actually intersected.
- P2: ..   the intersections with the CSG tree.

4. Experimentation

We have driven many experiments, to have a good idea of the deportment of the numerous modules in various conditions. The behaviour of the basic tasks are now well known

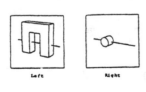

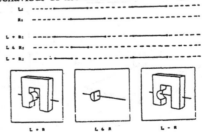

Combining ray classifications.

(time to compute, memory space required). The first three high levels were tested separately and performances mesured. The performance is for us the "efficiency" of the parallel implementation, in respect to the sequential implementation. The efficiency of the network is given by the formula:

$$E = tl/(N * tN)$$

where tl is the computation time on one processor, N the number of processors and tN the computation time on N processors.

4.1 LEVEL 1: GRIDS OF PIXELS

As all the grids are fully independent, a process is associated to the computation of each grid. A process called WINDOW makes the preprocessing and manages the parameters, a process called BUFFER collect the pixels in the frame buffer.

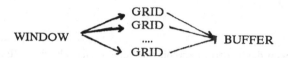

Several mapping of this scheme to the real machine have been done.

3 communication protocols were studied:
- a protocol with request between processors.
- a protocol without request, and without buffering one task in each grid processor.
- a protocol without request, with buffering one task in each grid processor.

For the ray-tracing application, there is no differences in the performances of these models. The application results in a very large computation time, in comparison with communication time.

In a first study, we determined an optimal size for the grid entity. The following computation times are given in function of the grid size:

grid (pixels)	time (ms)
1	6784
4	6659
16	6628
64	6599
256	6598

The time quickly reaches an asymptotic limit and it does not seem necessary to take a grid greater than 256 pixels (16x16).

Here is the result for a part of one picture (the ant), composed with 161 CSG nodes, and 83 primitives. The computed picture size is 512x512 pixels, either 4096 grids in totally.

processors	1	4	16	32	96	
th time (s)		1045	522	261	131	55
time (s)	4179	1045	523	263	138	46
E (%)		100	100	99	95	95

The efficiency is very good for these implementation of high level parallelism. The efficiency decreases as the number of processor is growing because more communications are needed. Nevertheless a good load balancing of each processor is done.

4.2. LEVEL 2: RAYS

The use of an adaptative ray-tree needs the use of a linear composition of the secondary rays in the illumination function. In this case the tree is tracked down and the root is directly updated when a leaf is reached. It is unnecessary to exploit the independence of the rays of a same generation.

4.3. LEVEL 3: OBJECTS

Some algorithms have been developed to exploit the dependencies between the objects: they are said to exploit space coherence (Dippe and Swensen (1984)). Bouatouch and all (Bouatouch et al. (1987)) have summed up the main methods and proposed a space tracing. We have implemented such an algorithm using a regular space subdivision. Our method uses an extension of the Bresenham algorithm to the third dimension to pass the ray from one cell to another instead of a volumnic index. This was simulated on one processor. The results were very encouraging when using a prototype of T.Node with T400 (without floating point unit) but not with the real T.Node: the preprocessing time has become prohibitive in respect to the run time. A good reason to use this level of parallelism remains that this is a method to distribute the data-base among the network. A processor processes a certain number of space cells not necessary adjacent and contains only the pruned CSG tree corresponding to this cell. The fact that the run time is quasi independent of the scenary has to be considered with the major draw-back introduced by the huge preprocessing time. An effort must be made to parallelize this preprocessing.

4.4. ALGORITHMIC LEVEL

The three processes explained in 3.2.5. have been implemented using groups of three processors.

```
WINDOW    = =    GRID     ←····→     GRID
BUFFER           P0                  P0
                 ↕                   ↕
                 P1                  P1
                 ↕                   ↕
                 P2                  P2
```

The efficiency obtained varies from 30% to 40% depending of the scenary. This is very low. The results given by many tries on diverse data bases show that a good efficiency at this level is hard to obtain as it depends too much on the data. The load balancing between the three processors is weak.

5. Final implementation

5.1. SOFTWARE MODEL

According to the different experimentations, an optimal solution has been found for the computing. The software model is a processor farm, in which each module correspond to a grid level computing.

In fact, the software of one processor is organized in several processus, each corresponding to a geometric level. All runs in parallel.

Logical representation of the worker processus in each processor.

Occam implementation of worker process:

```
PROCESS worker (CHAN OF ANY from.prev, to.pre, from.next, to.next,
                VAL INT nb.worker.following)

    ... variable declarations
    CHAN OF ANY c.g,g.c,g.p,p.g,p.r,r.p:
    WHILE TRUE
        SEQ
            ... receive data base
            PRI PAR
```

```
comm (from.prev, to.prev, from.next, to.next, c.g, g.c)
PAR
    grid (c.g,g.c,g.p,p.g)
    pixel (g.p,p.g,p.r,r.p)
    ray (p.r,r.p)
```

5.2. PERFORMANCES

5.2.1. *Data base volume.* The data base is compacted before it is sent to the network. It principally depends on the geometry description. Here are some examples of scenaries:

Picture 1 (rings)   :   6   CSG trees
                            116   CSG nodes
                             61   primitives
                              4   primitive aspects
                      data base size: 27,301 bytes

Picture 2 (ant)   :   5   CSG trees
                            161   CSG nodes
                             83   primitives
                              9   primitive aspects
                      data base size: 37,561 bytes

Picture 3 (network) :   9   CSG trees
                            219   CSG nodes
                            114   primitives
                             15   primitive aspects
                      data base size: 51,273 bytes.

On 256 Kbytes can be coded a data base with more than 400 primitives and 800 CSG modes.

5.2.2. *Computation times.* The selected software model is very well adapted to a parallel architecture, such as T.Node. The performance does not depends on the contents of the picture, neither on the architecture. With the communication protocol we have written, the processors are always saturated with a 16x16 pixels grid to compute. Unit about 100 processors, the efficiency of the network reaches 100%. Complex pictures with around 200 CSG objects are computed in less than 5 minutes on a single node configuration (32 processors T800), for a definition 512x512.

Picture 1: the blue ant   1024 x 1024 pixels
Picture 2: T.Node logo with mirrors   1024 x 1204 pixels
Picture 3: the mirror room   512 x 512

Computation times in seconds

	T800	16	32	64	96	128	256
Picture							
1		436	219	110	75	60	36
2		478	242	122	82	63	35
3		492	257	130	92	76	40

For a 256 transputers machine, the used configuration is a matrix network organized in 16 parallel pipes, with 16 workers each one. The performance depends on the calculation definition. In definition 512x512, only 1024 grids have to be computed, and 4096 grids for the definition 1024x1024. If the last grids necessitates a long time for computation, the efficiency decreases. For different complex pictures, the efficiency varies from 70 to 90%. Pictures as the ant or the mirror room are computed in less than one minute in definition 1024x1024.

5.2.3. *Antialiasing.* Antialiasing is realised during the computation, with the variation of the ganularity of grid level. The 16x16 computed grid can correspond to a 16x16 pixels grid (normal computation), or to 8x8 pixels (first antialiasing level), or to 4x4 pixels (second antialiasing level). A test is made on colour of neighbour pixels to evaluate the necessity of pixel oversample.

Acceleration factor = Ta/Tna

$$gain = \frac{Tth - Ta}{Tth - Tna}$$

Tna: time for non aliased picture
Ta : time for aliased picture
Tth : theoretical time for aliased picture.

Picture 1 (rings), computed on 32 transputers

definition	time	factor	gain
512	0' 27"		
1024	0' 48"	1.8	74%
2048	1' 30"	3.3	84%

Picture 2 (ant), computed on 32 transputers

definition	time	factor	gain
512	1' 00"		
1024	1' 49"	1.8	73%
2048	3' 20"	3.3	84%

6. Evolutions and perspectives

The program can evaluate on two ways. First, the quality of computed pictures can be improved, according to more sophisticated computation methods: new primitives, other illumination models (diffused sources, radiosity), new textures. These evolutions can be realised without changing the modular constitution of the present program. The parallel model has to be conserved, only software subroutines have to be upgrated. More, some modules can be written in other languages as occam, using the evolution of the development environments (toolset, helios).

Secondly, the environment of the program has to be adapted. Presently, the data base and rendering parameters are edited on ASCII files. An interactive editor to modelize data base, aspects, animation, can be easily interfaced on the simple data format used by the rendering program. The choice of the models and developments are not in progress, but the modularity of the computation program offers this possibility. This part of development concerns only the host user interface, without influence on the parallel implementation of the ray-tracing software.

7. Conclusions

The task distribution is a fundamental factor for the good efficiency of a network. For a given distribution, efficiency does not depend on the volume of calculation but on the class or level of the calculation. In the case of the T.Node the power of the T800 needs a good load balancing that can be achieved only at upper level. A great number of processors is not sufficient to have a good efficiency, even if it decreases computation time. The higher the level of parallelism is, the best the load balancing can be. It is very difficult to achieve a good task balancing at low level.

When a great number of processors is available then low level parallelism becomes useful. Rather than space subdivision algorithms that needs a too great preprocessing an effort must be made on general parallel execution models. In the case of ray-tracing the tree processing has a great importance. The data are structured in a CSG tree, the execution model uses a ray tree. One can notice that the three processes described in 3.2.5. are: P0 a tracking down the tree, P1 a treatment at the leaf or at the lowest useful level, P2 a tracking up. This is not peculiar to ray-tracing, an expression evaluation tree, a LISP evaluation function or the PROLOG AND/OR trees are under the same constraints. A systematic programmation of the tree has been made in (School (1979)), the problem of systematic parallel tree processing is open.

These conclusions lead a strategy for the implementation on a T.Node. All processors perform the same high level task (compute a grid) on the same data base of scenary. Remember that on a T.Node we can have up to 4 Mbytes of memory for one processor. One master processor is nevertheless dedicated to drive hard devices and to make the task management. When the computation is almost finished and that some processors become lazy, they run lower level tasks and become servers for other processors. In fact the granularity of the implementation is changed at run time. This change uses a dynamic reconfiguration of the T.Node.

This work was helped by the facility of using the reconfiguration features of the T.Node.

8. References

Harp, J.G., Jesshope, C.R., Muntean, T., Whitby-Strevens, C., Phase 1 of the development and application of a low cost high performance multi-processor machine, ESPRIT 86: Results and achievements, Elsevier Science, (1987), pp. 551-562.

Roth, S.D., Ray-casting for modeling solids. Computer Graphics and Image Processing, Vol. 18, No. 2, Feb. 1982, pp. 109-144.

Phong, B.T., Illumination for Computer Generated Pictures, Comm ACM, Vol. 18, No. 6, June 1975, pp. 311-317.

Cook, R.L., and Torrance, K.L., A reflectance model for computer graphics, ACM Trans. Graphics, Vol. 1, No. 1, Jan. 1982, pp. 7-24.

Whitted, T., An improved illumination model for shaded display, Comm ACM, Vol. 23, No. 6, Jun 1980, pp. 343-349.

Jansen, F.W., Van Wijk, J.J., Fast previewing techniques in raster graphics, Eurographics '83, pp. 195-202.

Hall, R.A., Greenberg, D.P., A testbed for realistic image synthesis, IEEE Computer Graphics and Applications, Nov. 83, pp. 10-20.

Madani, M.O., Etude d'architecture de calculateur parallele adaptee a la synthese d'images 3D par lancer de rayon, These ENST 86.

Coquillart, S., An improvement of the ray-tracing algorithm, Eurographics '85, pp. 77-88.

Dippe, M., Swensen, J., An adaptive subdivision algorithm and parallel architecture for realistic image synthesis, ACM SIGGRAPH '84, pp. 149-158.

Bouatouch, K., Madani, M.O., Priol, T., Arnaldi, B., A new algorithm of space tracing using a CSG model, EUROGRAPHICS '87, pp. 65-78.

Clark, J.H., The geometry engine: a VLSI oriented design for a raster graphics engine, ACM SIGGRAPH '82, pp. 127-133.

Scholl, P.C., Vers une programmation systematique: etude de quelques methodes et outils, (These d'etat, Grenoble 1979).

Brusq, R., Synthese d'image par lancer de rayons: la machine cristal - resultats et perspectives, CESTA '86, pp. 404-410.

9. Comments to the pictures

The hardware used is a T.Node with 64 T800, a STE30 under UNIX as host computer, the frame buffer of a CUBI9000.

Photo 1: The blue ant.

```
CSG trees      :   5   (2 transparent)
CSG nodes      : 161
primitives     :  83   (8 transparent)
aspects        :   9
ligths         :   3
ray tree depth :   6
definition/time
2048 x 1532  3 mn 00 s
4096 x 3064  4 mn 40 s
```

Photo 2: The mirror room

CSG trees	:	4	(1 transparent)
CSG nodes	:	126	
primitives	:	65	(1 transparent)
aspects	:	8	
ligths	:	3	
ray tree depth	:	6	

definition/time
2048 x 1532 5 mn 01 s
4096 x 3064 8 mn 51 s

This work is partially funded by CEC under contract P1085.
T.Node is a registered trade mark of TELMAT.
CUBI9000 is a registered trade mark of CAPTION.
Transputer, T400, T800, TDS are registered trade marks of IMNOS.
UNIX is a registered trade mark of ATT.

PORTING SIMULATION OF PHYSICS PARTICLES EXPERIMENTS ON
TRANSPUTERS

C. FRITSCH, A. JEJCIC, J. MAILLARD, J. SILVA
Collège de France - IN2P3
11, Place Marcellin Berthelot, 75231 Paris
Cedex 05, France

1. Introduction

This article relates the experiment in installing large simulation programs, by the group of
parallel computing of the Laboratoire de Physique Corpusculaire (College de France).

We shall first explain why and in what context our group began and developed this
activity.

We shall in a second part describe the installation of GEANT and other programs
on T.Node, and the difficulties of this work.

The last part shall give a more prospective view and review the changes in algorithms and applications, that parallel architectures will bring. It shall also indicate what
has to be done in order to have more operational computers.

2. Why a Group of Parallel Computing in a Particle Physics Laboratory?

Particle Physics research is grounded on experiments, each experiment is a collaboration
lasting a few years, and at which participate between a few dozen of physicists and a few
hundred.

Generally, these experiments are made in the framework of an accelerator complex
which furnishes particles of high energy (from a few billion electron-volts, GeV, to a few
thousand billion electron-volts, TeV).

On Figure 1 is the LEP, an electron-positron collider, on which are installed four
great experiments (Delphi, Aleph, L3, Opal).

The LEP is a ring of 21 kilometers, at 100 meters underground, and there are 4
zones where the beams collide. In these zones are installed the four experiments, which a
few hundred physicists participate in. The 4 electron beams and the 4 positron beams run
in opposite direction, in the same vacuum tube, and see the same fields (magnetic fields
of curvature and focalisation, electric fields of acceleration). Each beam has about 100
billion particles. These fields are produced by magnets and cavities situated around the
vacuum tube. The energy of each particle (positrons and electrons) in 45 GeV.

The beams collide together in the interaction zone, and around these zone is

137

D. Gassilloud and J. C. Grossetie (eds.), Computing with Parallel Architectures: T.Node, 137–152.
© 1991 ECSC, EEC, EAEC, Brussels and Luxembourg. Printed in the Netherlands.

138

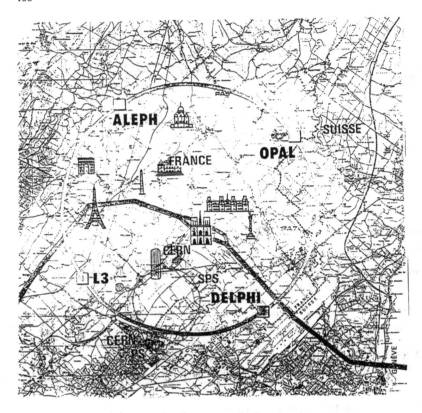

Figure 1. The LEP collider.

installed an experiment.

In the LEP the collision rate is about of a few per second in each interaction zone, at the maximum intensity.

This gives a few million of good signal events per working year (maximum) and about the same number for background events (collision of the beam on the residual gas, on the material, cosmics rays).

But in the future, experiment are programmed on an accelerator, built in the same tunnel, but with an intensity 100 times greater, and an energy of 7000 Gev per beam (LHC).

In this case the price of the experiment, on which 1000 physicists should have to work, is of a few billion ECUs...

The events happen all the 15 ns and each of them represents a few million kbytes of data.

For the moment experiments can be simulated in the LEP. The problem of simulation on the LHC will be immense.

Each experiment is built from a detector, one is represent in Figure 2.

The detector are modular, and each module correspond to a given way of particle detection.

Figure 2 represents the Delphi experiment detector. In this detector 16 kinds of modules exist, each of them represented in a given number in the detector. Each module is often called a detector, but in fact there is only one part.

Al the center one finds the vacuum chamber of the accelerator where the beams collide.

The first module around the vacuum chamber reconstructs the beginning of the track.

Then some modules reconstruct the charged tracks in the magnetic field.

One also finds a cerenkov-effect detector able to identify the masses of particles.

One other way to measure this mass is to measure the time of flight on a counter. This is also useful to reject background.

A superconducting magnet provides the constant high field necessary to get enough curvature and therefore enough precision on energy.

Outside of this magnet we find two kinds of calorimeters, which are detectors able to measure the energy of particles, the electromagnetic calorimeters and the hadronic calorimeters.

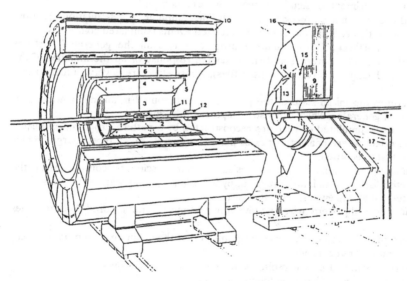

Figure 2. The DELPHI detector. 1: Vertex detector (Si-strips), 2: Inner Drift chamber (ID), 3: Time Projection Chamber (TPC), 4,13: Ring Imaging Cherenkov counter (RICH), 5: Outer Drift chamber (OD), 6,12,15: electromagnetic calorimeters (High density Projection Chamber HPC; luminosity monitor SAT; lead-glass counters (FEMC)), 7: superconducting solenoid, 8,17: scintillators, 9: hadron calorimeters, 10,16: muon counters, 11,14: forward drift chambers.

Around all the detectors there are muon chambers.

This structure is general to particle physics experiments, with configurations where one or several modules are present, or with linear developments in case of fixed targets.

Each of these modules analyses with different techniques the interaction of the particles with the materials.

An analogical electronic device amplifies the signal, and a digital electronic device makes a numerical storage of this signal.

A trigger electronic device is able to make a decision, on the basis of the different signals received by the detector modules.

A sophisticated acquisition electronic device transmits to a central computer all the numerical information stored by the modules. This is necessary to reconstruct the events, this means the data.

Each event is a collision of two particles which has to be recorded on magnetic tape in order to be analysed off-line in all the different laboratories participating in the collaboration.

Figure 3 shows data flow in such an experiment.

Each @ represents a data set.

Two sources of data exist:
- data really taken by the experiment which are collected on tape by the on-line computer of the experiment, or sent by network on permanent disks;
- simulated data which are produced on an off-line computer by a simulation program, on the basis of theoretical models giving simulated events (simulated collision with initial state of particles). The simulation program tracks all the generated particles through the different materials and simulates the response of all the modules of the detector, producing tapes (or permanent files), whose structure is very similar to that of real data.

Sometimes the initial state of the particles are computed in an independent program, the event generator, which can also be a part of the program.

These data, simulated or real, are reconstructed by a pattern program, producing reconstructed data where characteristics of particles (energy, mass, type, charge, impulsion) are explicitly recorded.

An analysis program allows the physicist to extract scientific conclusions on the theory injected for the simulation program, by a statistical, comparative and sometimes graphical study of all the events, simulated or real.

Simulation and pattern are programs of more than several hundred thousand lines of code.

An essential feature of all these programs is that they contain a loop on independent events, this means collisions.

Each event can be treated absolutely independently of the others.

Simulation programs have the following properties:
- very extensive code, several hundred thousand lines,
- standardised program, because physical phenomena described do not depend on the experiment,
- important memories, several mega-bytes,
- huge consumptions of computing time, days, weeks or months of running on an IBM 3090 to get the 100000 simulated events necessary to the statistics of a consider

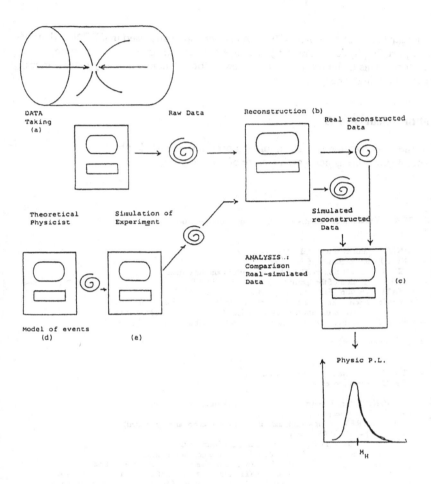

Figure 3. Data flow in particle physics experiments.

able experiment (300 seconds per event).

Simulation algorithms have been the target of numerous studies to increase the computing velocity of the program (vectorisation was a failure), and to increase the computing power of the laboratories (building of farms of processors).

The simulation program is used at the step of elaboration and realisation of an experiment:
- to design the detector,
- to design and test the analysis programs,
- to simulate the events during the analysis period.

We have seen that these programs produce data similar to those obtained by the real experiment.

A standard form of data bank (ZEBRA) is developed and used in CERN and more generally in particle physics, permitting exchange between programs and computers in a normalised form. This is done within the framework of a dynamic memory management, necessary to all the high energy programs.

3. Generalities about GEANT

GEANT is the most frequently used simulation program of particle physics.
Figure 4 shows the general architecture of the program.

```
MAIN (user)

  — GZEBRA  initialisation of ZEBRA system, dynamic core allocation
  — UGINIT  (user)

        — GINIT    initialisation of GEANT3 variables
        — GFFGO    interpretation of data cards
        — GZINIT   initialisation of ZEBRA core divisions and link areas
        — GPART    creation of the 'particle' data structure JPART
        — GMATE    creation of the 'material' data structure JMATE
        — 'user code' description of the geometrical setup, of the sensitive detectors
                     creation of data structures JVOLUM, JTMED, JROTM, JSETS
        — GPHYSI   preparation of cross-section and energy loss tables for all used materials

  — GRUN  loop over events

        — GTRIGI   initialisation for event processing
        — GTRIG    event processing

              — GUKINE (user)  generation (or input) of event initial kinematics
              — GUTREV (user)
                    |— GTREVE (loop over tracks, including any secondaries generated)
                         |— GUTRAK (user)
                              |— GTRACK  control tracking of current track
                                   |— GMEDIA  find current volume/tracking medium
                                   |— GTVOL   loop over successive media seen by the particle
                                        |— GTGAMA/GTELEC/.... tracking of particle according to type
                                             |—GUSTEP (user) recording of hits in data structure JHITS
                                                            and of space points in data structure JXYZ
              — GUDIGI  computation of digitisations and recording in data structure JDIGI
              — GUOUT   output of current event

        — GTRIGC  clearing of memory for next event

  — UGLAST (user)

        |— GLAST    standard GEANT3 termination.

stop
```

Figure 4. GEANT flow diagram.

The program begins with a general initialisation of common and variables, which are used in physics, in the tracking of particles in the volumes, and in the simulation of the detectors.

Then comes the big loop on the events (collisions), whose number is fixed by the user.

For each event, complete treatment can be described in four steps:
- the generation of the collision products, their computation is done according to the formulas of a theoretical model,
- the tracking of the particles through material and fields,
- the simulation of the analogical response of the detectors and the treatment of the non-line electronic device (digitalisation),
- the filtering and storage of the data on files or magnetic tape (they can be also be displayed on graphics).

Each step can be replaced by the lecture of a file where the stored information was processed by a previous program on another computer, saving the information at a previous step.

Tracking is usually the more consuming computing time. We simulate the trajectory of the particles step by step. For each step we begin to compute the length of tracking (about a fraction of centimeter), taking in account all the different physical possibilities, and deciding randomly the one which happens if necessary, taking also into account the magnetic field, media borders, places of detectors. Then we compute the step, with all the different process which happen. This part of the code has a lot of IF and a lot of indirections in calling up the memory, killing the efficiency of any vectorisation.

Only for certain kinds of particle (neutrons and muons) and in certain media (not too heavy) vectorisation can be useful. But computation is local and independent (each particle has no interaction with the other, in our order of magnitude), which allows other kinds of parallelisation.

At the end of the loop on the events, histograms can be final product of the program (if we have not saved the digitalized event).

The installation of a simulation program has 4 steps:
- The installation on a single node of the entire code. The transputer must have the memory necessary to run the job (at least 2 megabytes), and the input-output of the histograms or the digitalised event on other computer.
- The installation of a "farm". This means the installation of the event loop on "worker" transputers and the installation of the input-output, of the initialisation phases and the supervision of the loop on the "master" transputer. The memory necessary for the worker is the one to run the loop, and this can decrease up till 1 megabyte for GEANT. The master has to concentrate the information, and to save the event if necessary.
- The internal parallelisation of event. This can be done by "particle" parallelisation or by "geometrical" parallelisation. The memory now necessary is the one necessary only to describe the particle or the geometrical zone which is treated in the transputer. The exchanges via the links increase, and we have to know pretty well the program in order to make the changes. This is possible because the code is very well structured and can be cut in some natural places. This approach permits a more rational use of the memory.

An exemple of application used as benchmark exists for GEANT: "GEXAM1".

This need about 200000 lines of code (Table 1).

GEXAM1 simulates the development of an electromagnetic shower in a calorimeter like the one mentioned in section 1.

4. Running GEANT on a single node

The wide spread of GEANT as a tool for HEP event and detector simulation justifies the choice we have made to port it on a parallel computer. Through benchmarks running for different parallelisation schemes significant information was expected on the computing potential of the operated computer.

The preliminary step, required as a reference for performance evaluation, consisted in running GEANT on a single node.

4.1 PORTING PROGRAMS

In the table below are recollected the codes and their dimensions, in number of instructions, forming the software environment which was ported on the T.Node.

TABLE 1. The list of codes ported on the T.Node.

FFREAD	2800	lines
HBOOK4	16000	lines
KERNGEN	5500	lines
KERNNUM	9400	lines
ZEBRA	33200	lines
GEANT	25000	lines
GEANG	51500	lines
GEANH	41500	lines
GEXAM1	600	lines
Total	185500	lines

The implementation was carried carefully, all the test programs provided were executed and the results verified. Nevertheless some unsolved problems could be quoted; the ZEBRA structure exchange between VAX 6210 and the T.Node is not yet possible (Storr (1989)).

A number of bugs were discovered in the compiler and in the associated FORTRAN library. Some problems resulted also from the fact that the compiler did not provide all the standard extensions (Jejcic et al.).

4.2 RANDOM NUMBER GENERATION

The program for random number generation was carefully examined. The identity of the sequence produced by the VAX and the transputer T800 was verified for 10^6 drawings and the seeds stored in a data file.

4.3 PERFORMANCES

GEXAM1, the code used as benchmark, is a program simulating an electromagnetic shower for sufficiently complex material and geometric conditions and requiring significant processing power. It was run at the same time on a VAX 6210 and on an IBM 3090, as results had to be verified and performances compared.

The results delivered by the three machines were different, it was necessary to evaluate its importance. If it was possible to establish differences even in the topology of shower for identical initial conditions in turn the distributions of energy deposits were observed to become closer to one another as the number of processed events was increasing. In any case the differences found between the results furnished by the VAX and the T800 were of the same order of magnitude of those observed between the IBM and the VAX, two computers which are usually running GEANT.

In Table 2 the processing time obtained are given. Two figures are given for the transputer T800, they correspond to two processing configurations. One was obtained by operating the transputer of the memory server module running with 5 cycle memory access, the other with the worker which has 3 cycle memory access. Two figures, obtained with transputers T800, are added for the sake of performance comparison (Booth et al. (1989), Badize et al. (1990)).

TABLE 2. GEXAM1 processing time [s] per event.

T.Node ITFTP32 T800	50.18
T. Node Worker T800	30.79
MEIKO T800 (CERN)	36.3
VOLVOX-1/v T800	30.7
VAX 6210	23.81
IBM 3090	3.86

The performances of the node processing unit appeared to be sufficient, and even promising, compared to the figures encountered by operating other computers. GEANT parallel operation therefore could be experimented on the T.Node with a reasonable likelihood of obtaining valuable good cost/performance conditions.

5. GEANT Farming on the T.Node

Bringing in operation the event parallelisation scheme is almost straightforward on the T.Node. The only problem lies in the process initialisation and results gathering, for which many different solutions are possible. We tried two types of networks to ensure communications between host computer and workers: they are displayed on the Figures 5 and 6.

The GEANT farm operation, i.e. running GEXAM1, was worked out on the basis

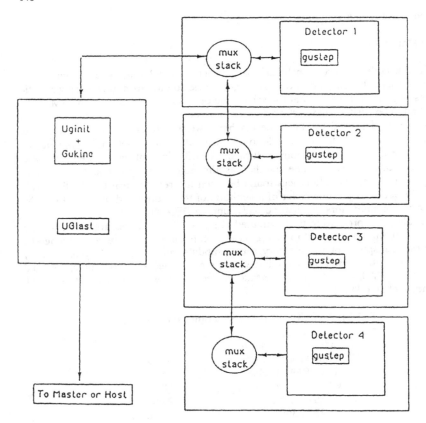

Figure 5. Pipeline farm block diagram.

of code division into two parts. According to this division initialisation, mainly input of data card and seed initialisation for random number generation, and final data processing, i.e. the histogram build up, were imparted to the root transputer. Event processing, in the literal sense, was done by the workers. There was a supplementary process implemented on workers in order to broadcast the simulation results to the root processor. The same process was put into operation for initialisation.

The results in term of processing time (in seconds) per event are gathered in Table 3. They were obtained by processing 100 events on each operated worker.

The dependence of processing time per event on the number of operated workers as expressed by the figures hereabove does not show any saturation effect which could be connected to the communication charges. Indeed the data transfer charge is small and the number of workers is not sufficient to constrain substantially the computing process by the communications.

The farming in these two approaches gives two problems on T.Node:

TABLE 3. T.Node GEXAM1 farm processing time [s] per event.

Number of workers	Processing time per event
1	30.79
2	15.63
4	7.94
16	1.96

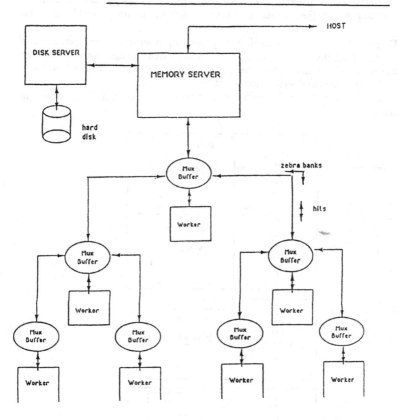

Figure 6. Tree farm block diagram.

- the time to load the program (1 hour with 256 processor?),
- the huge memory taken on the disk (16 by 2 megabytes).

6. Operation of Inside-event Parallelisation Schemes

Parallelisation schemes worked out inside the process of one event simulation are important, it was estimated that their operation on tightly coupled machine might represent a valuable alternative to emulator "farms" from the economic view point (cost/performance criteria) (Jejcic et al. (1989)). It is believed that their impact will be growing. When HEP will have to come to grips with the software crisis they will probably reach their full importance (Nash (1989)).

Many different parallelisation schemes are possible. The choice depends on the application considered and is usually made as a compromise by taking into account different factors, among which the needed software modifications are probably the most important.

GEANT's modular structure, allowing easy steering operation, represents a real advantage for working out distributed processing. It was chosen to conceived various parallelisation schemes on the basis of user supplied subroutine only. Thus, the software modifications were restricted and strictly localised.

To test this approach an implementation was made, one version is which is displayed on Figure 7.

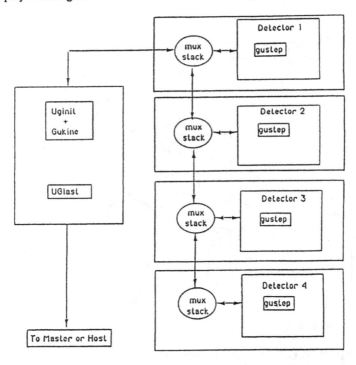

Figure 7. Block diagram for inside-event parallelisation.

The root transputer assumes all the initialisation tasks and final processing. The simulation is scattered over several workers, subroutines GUSKIP and GUSTEP are used to manage the interprocessor exchanges. For this purpose a specific process, handling a local stack, is implemented on each worker. Two versions are being experimented.

The efficiency of the parallelisation depends of several factors.

The memory can not be equally scattered on all the transputers, this gives loss of (unused) memory and also duplication of information.

The timing of different processes is different for each volume, each particle, each detector. We shall have to optimize later this repartition.

But the memory repartition can be as different as the one for the time.

Synchronisation points can give deadtime in the transputer, waiting to send or to receive information.

The network is now not dynamically reconfigurable. This means that during the execution of a job we cannot change the network configuration.

The group has made experimentation of such problems on the OPSILA prototype. This was a 16 processor SPMD machine allowing reconfiguration of networks during execution of programs.

We used a concentrated benchmark of GEANT, the heart of this program, short enough to be translated in assembler (300 lines of codes).

We have seen that for an optimised run of the parallel computer, an intensive job has to be done, to study the operational repartition of both the memory, that is the description of the experiment, and the computing time.

This avoids any scheme of automatic parallelisation for this kind of program, because the optimised repartition depends too much of the used configuration.

7. Other Programs

In the DELPHI experiment we use another program called DELSIM to simulate the experiment. Its structure is the same as for GEANT. But we get the following problems:
- Theoretical generation of collission products need double complex precision, a fortran extension which is non standard but usual in scientific computers (IBM, VAX).
- The standard program is huge, needing 16 megabytes of memory. We have to cut it because we have up to now only 2 megabytes maximum by transputer.
- This huge program is written by several physicists. Bugs in coding sometimes appears, fatal in 31-fortran. It is sometimes difficult to rewrite the code.
- Huge data basis is necessary to run the program, 12 megabytes. This has to be transferred correctly into ASCII mode from one computer to another.
- Output events must be filtered by another filter program. This program has to be put on the machine and needs 4 megabytes of data.
- Output events have to be send to another computer by a standard CERN-Package called ZEBRA. We got some problems (now solved) in exchanging the bank of data between VAX and T.Node in ASCII mode.

We have succeeded in running a shorter version of this program, on the transputer. This version has a simple model to generate an initial particle and no detector representation. This program was used to simulate the development of particle showers coming from cosmic rays in the atmosphere.

8. Prospective

Why should physicist be interested by these study?

Today the parallel computer should offer computing time at low cost. This is an urgent problem concerning the huge experiments, but also for a lot of physicists, interested in the simulation of various phenomena.

On a long range basis parallel architecture will bring 3 kinds of changes in the work procedures.

First, the great memory capacity and the fine coupling between processors allow us to have at the same time more than one program in the machine, for example the simulation, the pattern, and the analysis programs. So the simulation can produce only filtered and condensed data. This can avoid manipulating huge data bases: 1 million simulation events for the DELPHI experiment represent more than 100 gigabytes of data. For specific physics only a few megawords, sometimes less, are necessary.

This is a great progress, not only in price but also in facility and reliability.

Second, new parallel architecture shall allow a new approach to problems.

The huge memory that exists in a Meganode (up to 500 megawords) gives new perspectives for imagining programs. What now is analytically computed can easily be put in a huge table, reducing the computing time. Description of the problems can be more simpler and more general.

In simulation cases the precision depends on computation founded on tables.

This table can take a huge place if one wants to avoid computation (for exemple the fit of a magnetic field).

The network (and specially if it can be reconfigurated during the execution of programs), can be a kind of computation. In Jejcic et al. (1990) we have simulated an accelerator by tracking the beam on a parallel computer (Jejcic et al. (1988)). The parallel program was 16 times faster than the sequential one.

The computation of the address was avoided by the information exchanged by the network.

The same algorithm can be put without difficulties in T.Node. But in more complicated configuration the processor and the link can also transmit information.

The localisation of the algorithms in the processors is also a way to avoid bugs, because the self-running programs can directly be put into the processor. The general communication with the rest of the program is only the compatibility of the exchanged information and not the internal common and subroutines names.

Third, parallel computers can be a way to approach new problems that are not now studied, by lack of computing power, of memory capacity, of input-output, and by excess of complexity.

A gain of 100 (tomorrow of 1000 with H1?) in memory capacity, in computing power, and in the number of processors, allows for exemple micro-tracking, multicorps-tracking, and multiconfiguration-tracking, that push our imagination farther than all today Monte-Carlo programs. Today's programs (GEANT) can be a general scheme of such development, but special applications are under study.

I hope that they shall not be monsters, but comprehensive codes, where the memory and the computing power are used to simplify the problems.

9. Conclusions

1. The T.Node parallel computer appears to be a valuable farming facility for GEANT. In its basic configuration comprising 16 workers, the computer power obtained is comparable to 2 IBM 3090 processors.
2. Taking advantage on the transputer architecture one could provide solutions for GEANT applications with important data flow.
3. The T.Node architecture appears promising for operation of GEANT with more sophisticated parallelisation schemes.
4. Parallel computers are a means to anticipate and imagine the algorithms and the applications of the future.

This work was supported by the Direction des Recherches et Etudes Techniques (DRET), contract 89/197. Professor M. Froissart is gratefully aknowledged for help and support. The present work was done at TELMAT. We express our gratitude to Mr. G. Dudckiewicz for hospitality and support.

10. References

Nash, T. (1989), Event parallelism; distributed memory parallel computing for high energy physics experiments. Proceedings of the International Conference on Computing in HEP, Oxford 10-14 April 1989. Computer Physics Communications 57, 47-58.

Poutain, D. and May D. (1988), A tutorial Introduction to OCCAM programming. Blackwell Scientific Publications, London.

Flieller, S. (1989), T.Node, industrial version of supernode. Proceedings of the International Conference on Computing in HEP, Oxford 10-14 April 1989. Computer Physics Communications 57, 492-494.

Storr, M. (1989), Porting GEANT to the MEIKO Computing Surface. CERN/DD AC Group Note, 21/2/1989.

Jejcic, A., Maillard, J., Silva, J. and Boun, K.K., Portage de GEANT sur une carte Transputer T800. College de France, LPC 89-28.

Booth, S.P., Dobinson, R.W., Jefery, D.R.N., Lu, W., Storr, K.M. and Thornton, A. (1989), An evaluation of the MEIKO computing surface for HEP FORTRAN farming. Proceedings of the International Conference on Computing in HEP, Oxford 10-14 April 1989. Computer Physics Communications 57, 486-491.

Badize, J.F., Bazan, A., Lecoq, J., Rosset, A., Thenard, J.M., Tricot, C., Ungerer, A. and Vialle, J.P. (1990), A Multi-Transputer Environment for GEANT3. Report presented at the Workshop on On-line Application of Transputers at CERN 2 March 1990.

152

Jejcic, A., Maillard, J., Silva, J., Auguin, M. and Boeri, F. (1989), Could running experience on SPMD computers contribute to the architectural choices for future dedicated computers for HEP simulation. Proceedings of the International Conference on Computing in HEP, Oxford 10-14 April 1989. Computer Physics Communications 57, 507-511.

Jejcic, A., Maillard, J., Silva, J. and Mignot, B. (1990), Running GEANT on T.Node parallel computer. Contributed report to the Conference on Computing in High Energy Physics, Santa Fe, USA, 9-13 April 1990.

Jejcic, A., Maillard, J. and Silva, J. (1988), Accelerator simulation on a parallel computer. European Particle Accelerator Conference, Rome, 7-11 June 1988.

PARALLEL IMAGE PROCESSING ALGORITHMS AND ARCHITECTURES

I. PITAS
Department of Electrical Engineering
University of Thessaloniki
Thessaloniki 54006, Greece

ABSTRACT. Digital image processing usually involves computationally intensive operations and handling of large amounts of image data. In many cases real-time performance is expected. Therefore the only solution in such a situation is parallel computation. This paper provides a description of the basic image processing architectures and the implementation of some basic image processing algorithms on these architectures. These algorithms represent well both digital image processing and computer vision.

1. Introduction

Digital image processing has had a tremendous growth in the past twenty years. Its applications range from telecommunications (ISDN and HDTV) to medical imaging and remote sensing (Gonzales and Wintz (1987), Jain (1989)). In almost all applications, a vast amount of data must be handled. The typical size of a digital image is 512x512 pixel. The typical pixel is one byte (8 bits) long. Thus, in most cases the processing of 256 Kbytes per image frame is required. If colour images are processed, the frame size is 768 Kbytes per image frame. In HDTV applications the size of the image frames is even larger and the total data rate is of the order of 80 Mbytes/sec. A requirement in many digital image processing applications namely, HDTV, ISDN, remote sensing and surveillance, digital video, quality control and robotic vision, real-time performance is expected. In several other applications, e.g. image retrieval from data bases, medical imaging, fast digital image processing is a must. The image processing operations are usually computationally intensive, as it will be seen later on. Their order is at least $0(KN^2)$ for image dimensions NxN and for relatively simple operations (e.g. point operations, local operations). The computational complexity is much higher for complex computer vision tasks (e.g. shape description and recognition, motion estimation, stereo matching) and for certain advanced digital image processing tasks (e.g. image restoration, image compression). Based on the speed requirements, the computational complexity and the data volume, it can be seen that the limit of general purpose computers can be easily reached in digital image processing applications. The solutions to this problem are the following:
1) Subsampling
2) Fast algorithms

D. Gassilloud and J. C. Grossetie (eds.), Computing with Parallel Architectures: T.Node, 153–172.
© *1991 ECSC, EEC, EAEC, Brussels and Luxembourg. Printed in the Netherlands.*

3) Fast specialised processors
4) Parallel processing

The first solution is trivial and usually results in low image quality. Therefore it is unacceptable in most applications (e.g. in medical imaging). However, it is a viable solution in other areas, e.g. in HDTV, where downward compatibility with previous standards (PAL, SECAM, NTSC) is desirable (Chiariglione (1988)).

The second approach has produced numerous fast digital signal and image processing algorithms in the past three decades. The best example of this approach is the Fast Fourier Transform (FFT) and the related algorithms (Gonzales and Wintz (1987), Burrus and Parks, Elliot and Rao (1983)). Such algorithms reduce the computational complexity for the calculation of the Fourier Transform of an NxN image from $O(N^3)$ to $O(N^2\log_2 N)$. The area that has profited a lot from the construction of fast algorithms is digital image processing in its narrow sense (transforms, encoding, filtering, restoration). Many fast algorithms have also been constructed for computer vision applications (e.g. for shape description and recognition, connected component analysis, region growing) (Pavlidis (1982)). However the nature of computer vision tasks leads to rather fragmented and scattered clusters of fast algorithms. In general, the development of fast algorithms is a hot research area both in digital image processing and in computer vision. Most of the fast algorithms developed has an inherent parallelism that can be exploited for parallel computation.

The third approach (fast specialised processors) has had an impressive development in the past decade with the development of specialised VLSI chips. Several chips have been developed primarily for digital signal processing and they are called Digital Signal Processors (DSPs). The most prominent DSP families are the TMS320 (Texas Instruments), DSP56000 (Motorola) and DSP32 (AT&T) (Lee (1988)). Their use has been spread to digital image processing applications in the form of fast image coprocessors on specialised boards or in the form of parallel machines having DSPs as processing elements (e.g. image processing systems by AT&T and ANDROX). A second class of VLSI chips or boards have also been constructed for specialised low-level image processing operations, namely edge detectors, convolvers, median filters, histogram calculation (IC handbook (1988)). Such boards can be used either as specialised coprocessors or in pipelined image processing systems to be described later on. The highly non-standard nature of high-level vision algorithms has slowed down the development of specialised processors for such applications. However, there exist two notable exceptions: neutral networks and LISP machines (Wasserman (1989), Myers (1982)). Both neural networks and Lisp machines have emerged from other research areas, i.e. from pattern recognition and artificial intelligence respectively, where they still have their main applications.

The fourth approach (parallel processing) provides the mainstream solutions to fast digital image processing and computer vision. Its origins can be traced back to the work of Golay (1965) and Unger (1958). A large amount of literature has been published in this area (Golay (1965), Proceedings of the IEEE (Dec. 1989)), especially in the form of edited books. There are very good reasons for using parallel digital image processing.

The following types of parallelism can be categorised in digital image processing (Danielsson and Levialdi (1981)):
1) Pixel-bit parallelism
2) Geometrical parallelism
3) Neighborhood parallelism
4) Operator parallelism.

Pixel-bit parallelism exploits the fact that an image can be decomposed in b bit planes, where b is the number of bits in the image pixel (usually b=1 or 8). Several image processing operators, notable the linear operators can be performed to each bit plane independently. Let x_{ij} be an image pixel, $x_{ij}^{(k)}$, k=0,..,b-1 its pixels and L a linear operator. In this case:

$$L(x_{ij}) = L(\sum_{k=0}^{b-1} x_{ij}^{(k)} 2^k) = \sum_{k=0}^{b-1} L(x_{ij}^{(k)}) 2^k \tag{1}$$

The arithmetic that is performed at a bit plane is called distributed arithmetic. One-bit Processing Elements (PE) have been constructed to exploit bit-plane parallelism (Duff (1978), Reddaway (1979), Batcher (1980)).

Image data are usually sampled on a rectangular grid (Gonzales and Wintz (1987), Jain (1989)) and are stored on a two-dimensional array. Therefore they possess an inherent geometrical parallelism. This parallelism can be exploited by using a large two-dimensional array of PEs, possible one per image pixel. However, this is not possible for image sizes greater than 128x128 approximately. In this case the image is segmented in square MxM (M<N) sub-regions and each region is assigned to a specific processor. The only problem that is encountered in such a solution is the border effects that are created in many image processing applications.

Many digital image processing algorithms are essentially local neighborhood operations of the form:

$$Y_{ij} = F(x_{i+r, j+s}) \quad (r,s) \quad A \tag{2}$$

where A is the operator window. Such windows are shown in Figure 1.

CROSS   **SQUARE**   **CIRCLE**

Figure 1: Image processing windows.

The most frequently used window is the 3x3 rectangular window. It contains the pixels having city block distance 1,2 from the central pixels, as it can be seen in Figure 2.

The pixels having distance 1 from the central pixel are also called 4-connected neighbors, whereas the pixels having distance 1 or 2 are called 8-connected neighbors. Neighborhood parallelism denotes the parallel execution of local neighborhood operations. In this case a local processor must have access or communication to its neighbor data or processors.

Two types of operator parallelism exist in digital image processing operations: pipelining and parallel decomposition. Pipelining is the most commonly used and can be expressed by:

$$Y = F(X) = F_n(F_{n-1}(..F_2(F_1(X))..)) \qquad (3)$$

where X is the input image or image subregion, Y is the output image, F is an operator and F_i, $i = 1,..,n$ is its cascade decomposition. Typical example of such a decomposition is the cascade realisation of a linear digital filter (Dudgeon and Mersereau (1983)) shown in Figure 3.

Another example of a digital image processing pipeline is the computation of morphological operations, namely erosion and dilation (Serra (1982), Pitas and Venetsanopoulos (1990)):

$$Y = X \oplus B = (..(X \oplus B_1) \oplus B_2) \oplus ..) \oplus B_n \qquad (4)$$

An example of intermediate-level vision pipeline can be the one involving preprocessing and particle counting in a image shown in Figure 4.

The difference between the pipelines of Figure 3, 4 is the structure of the pipeline stages. Low-level digital image processing usually involves homogeneous pipelines, whereas intermediate and high-level digital image processing involves heterogeneous pipelines in most cases. The parallel decomposition form involves operators of the form:

$$Y = F(X) = F_1(X) \; || \; F_2(X) \; || \; ... \; || \; F_n(X) \qquad (5)$$

where $||$ denotes parallel execution. A typical example of this type of parallelism for low-level vision is the parallel realisation of two-dimensional digital filters (Dudgeon and Mersereau (1983)) shown in Figure 5.

Another typical example for high-level vision and pattern recognition is statistical decision making of the form shown in Figure 6. $\underline{x}$ denotes the feature vector, $\underline{x}_i$, $i = 1,..,n$ denote the reference vectors and $d(\underline{x},\underline{x}_i)$ denotes the distance between $\underline{x},\underline{x}_i$.

Based on the discussion of the possible parallelization forms in digital image processing, it can be seen that a variety of parallel digital image processing architectures and algorithms can be built. The most commonly used parallel architectures will be reviewed in the next section.

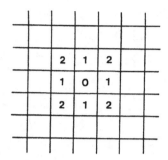

Figure 2: 3x3 square window.

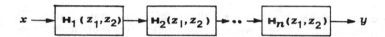

Figure 3: Cascade realisation of a digital filter.

Figure 4: Object counting in an image.

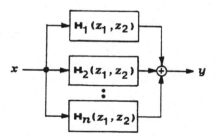

Figure 5: Parallel realisation of a digital filter.

158

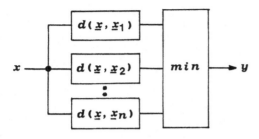

Figure 6: Statistical decision making.

2. Parallel Architectures for Digital Image Processing

Bit-plane parallelism is exploited by using the so-called cellular logic arrays (Duff (1978), Reddaway (1979), Batcher (1980)). Such systems consist of large arrays of simple one-bit processing elements (PE). A typical example of such a system is CLIP4 which consists of an array having 96x96 processing elements (Duff (1978)). The MPP system has an array of 128x128 bit-serial processors (Batcher (1980)). The processing elements of a cellular logic array are connected to their immediate neighbors and form a processor grid of the form of Figure 7. Local neighborhood operations can be easily performed by using local data transfers. Thus, cellular logic arrays exploit at the same time both geometrical and neighborhood parallelism.

Each cell has a register for storing the state of the cell and a logic module which calculates the new state of the cell as a function of its current state and the state of the neighboring cell (Sterberg (1983)). Such a structure is shown in Figure 8.

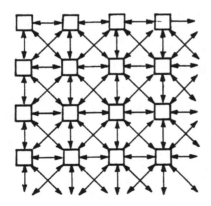

Figure 7: Cellular array architecture.

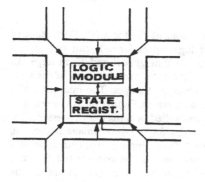

Figure 8: Structure of a cell.

Instructions are broadcasted to all PEs. Therefore cellular logic arrays are essential SIMD (Single Instruction Multiple Data) machines. The main problem of cellular arrays is their small size compared to the image size (512x512 or 1024x1024). Thus, image must be segmented and each segment must be processed independently. This approach causes border effects that become serious when multiple local operations must be applied in pipeline. It also introduces heavy IO load to the system. Another disadvantage of cellular arrays is their limited use in high-level vision applications. In this case the nature of the tasks is not well suited for such an architecture. Conventional serial languages (like FORTRAN) are out of question the case of cellular arrays. Array-based high level languages must be constructed (Reeves (1988)). Such a language is Parallel Pascal developed for MPP (Reeves (1984)).

An alternative approach is pipelining. A primary example of an image processing pipeline system is the Cytocomputer (Sternberg (1983)). Its structure is shown in Figure 9.

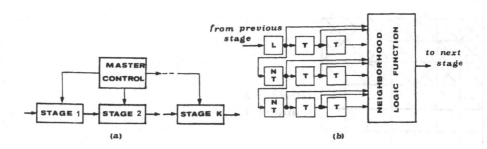

Figure 9: Structure of Cytocomputer. T denotes delay. L denotes point to point logical operation.

It has been developed for morphological operations of the form (4). Each stage of the pipeline performs pointwise or neighborhood logic operations. It can operate on either a 3x3 square neighborhood or in a 7 pixel hexagonal neighborhood. Each stage can store two lines of N pixels each for an NxN image. These data form the input of the logic function. The output of each stage is input to the subsequent stages. The operation of a two stage pipeline working in a 3x3 neighborhood is shown in Figure 10. All operations are performed in one step. The whole operation is controlled by a master processor. Processor pipelines can also be composed from DSP chips for low-level image processing applications (e.g. linear filtering and FFT calculation). Such pipelines are extremely efficient for low-level imaging. Heterogeneous pipelines can also be constructed by using special purpose boards operating on a high-speed image bus. Such processors can be optimised for certain tasks each (e.g. histogram, linear FIR filtering, nonlinear filtering). The routing of the image bus can be easily reconfigured.

The performance of the system can be controlled from a host (usually a Unix workstation) by using board drivers. The overall system is hosted on a VME bus. A primary example of such an approach is the MAXbus pipeline by DATACUBE (Datacube (1990)).

A conceptually simpler approach that matches parallelism of the form (5) is to use independent processors that are interconnected by a high speed bus. Such processors are usually MIMD (Multiple Instruction Multiple Data). Such a parallel architecture is shown in Figure 11 (Edwards).

The processors may share common memory that can be accessed through the bus or may have local memory as well. An example of such a system is PICAP II (Kruse et al. (1982)). It has up to 15 special purpose PEs connected through a 40 Mbyte/s, 32 bit bus and controlled by a host processor. A global memory of 4 Mbytes is used. PEs are specialised either in display or in filtering or in IO. The major hazard in such a topology is bus contention, when many PEs try to communicate to each other and/or to the global memory. Another problem is global memory conflicts, when more than one PE tries to access the same location. These two problems limit the system performance. Thus the speed-up is not linearly related to the number of the PEs.

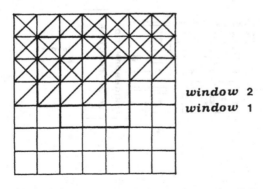

window 2
window 1

Figure 10: Operation of a two stage pipeline.

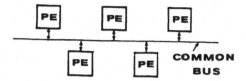

Figure 11: Common bus architecture.

Another MIMD image processing architecture is the loop shown in Figure 12 (Edwards). They are suitable for operation pipelining.

ZMOB (Krusner et al. (1982)) and PX-1 (Sato et al. (1982) are such loop architectures.

Finally a common memory MIMD architecture can be used similar to that shown in Figure 13.

FLIP (Gemmar (1982)), CYBA-M (Dagless et al., (1983)) and NYU ultracomputer (Gottlieb et al. (1983)) fall in this class of MIMD image processing machines.

With the advent of transputers, a hard push towards reconfigurable MIMD machines has been made. Image processing libraries have appeared for transputers based systems. Such systems have definite advantages for high-level vision tasks. However, their performance in low-level digital image processing tasks and in digital signal processing seems to be inferior to that of the DSPs (Sandler (1989)). Their main competitors seem to be parallel machines using DSPs in their PEs. Another limitation for image processing applications is the relatively slow transmission speed in the serial communication ports of the transputers. Perhaps a good compromise could be the use of both DSPs and transputers in the same PE. DSPs can be used for number crunching and transputers for communication purposes. Another approach could be to use heterogeneous structures (pyramids) with cellular arrays or DSPs at the lowest level and transputers in the inter-mediate or high levels. The Warwick pyramid is such an example (Nudd (1989)). It con-sists of four levels as it is shown in Figure 14. Its lowest level consists of a 256x256 SIMD bit-serial PEs. The intermediate level has 16x16 MIMD microprogrammable PEs. The third level consists of an 8x8 transputer array used for symbolic processing. Thus the structure of the pyramid corresponds directly to the low-level, intermediate-level and high-level vision tasks.

Typical programming environment on current MIMD machines consists of conven-tional languages (FORTAN,C) plus message and data passing mechanisms.

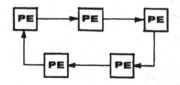

Figure 12: Loop architecture.

162

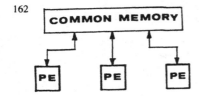

Figure 13: Common memory architecture.

Typically the user writes a single program which runs on every processor. A unique processor identifier is used to determine message destinations. Thus the program organisation is quite complex, despite its user friendly appearance. Despite the MIMD capabilities, SIMD operation is used for several digital image processing operations. In this case, each node (PE) runs the same code with the other PEs but processes its own image segment. Subroutine libraries have been constructed for such operations (e.g. FFT, matrix transposition).

3. Processing Element Complexity

One of the most important issues in parallel image processing systems is processing element complexity. There exist two extreme approaches in this case. The first approach is to use single-bit bit-serial PEs in cellular logic arrays. The opposite approach is to use 32-bit microprocessors (e.g. T800) or floating point DSPs. With the current advances of VLSI technology, the issue of constructing specialised Digital Image Processors (DIPs) becomes of crucial importance. Such a processor must have all the capabilities of a DSP plus capabilities for edge detection, nonlinear image processing operations, statistical operations etc (Pitas and Venetsanopoulos (1990)). Such a DIP can cover at least basic low-level digital image processing operations. It is highly improbable to construct a DIP specialised in high-level vision applications. A proposed structure for a DIP is shown in Figure 15.

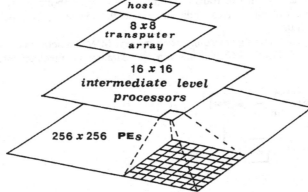

Figure 14: Warwick Pyramid Machine.

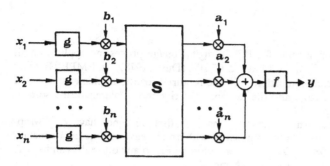

Figure 15: Structure of a DIP module. S denotes sorting.

Its basic blocks consist of two pointwise nonlinearities, an array of multipliers, a sorting network and a linear FIR filter (Pitas and Venetsanopoulos (1990), Pitas and Venetsanopoulos (1988)). Several classes of image processing operations can be performed by this module by choosing its coefficients appropriately, as it can be seen in (Pitas and Venetsanopoulos (1990)).

Among others are linear FIR filters, homomorphic filters, order statistic filters, morphological operations and edge detectors.

Another basic processing structure that can be used as a building block in massive parallel systems for high-level vision and object recognition are the neural networks whose structure is shown in Figure 16 (Rumelhardt (1986)). Note the this structure is a special case of the module of Figure 15. Therefore this module can be used not only in low-level vision but also in high-level vision applications.

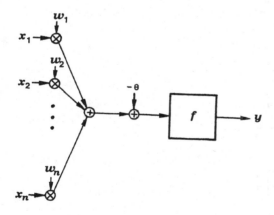

Figure 16: Model of a neuron.

164

4. Connection Schemes

The natural interconnection scheme for PEs in digital image processing applications is the two dimensional mesh. Examples include CLIP4 (Duff (1978)) and MPP (Batcher (1980)). PEs having four communication links are required for the implementation of a mesh. The top and bottom rows and the leftmost and rightmost columns are also connected, as it is shown in Figure 17.

This interconnection forms a torus. A machine that does not have the "wraparound" connection can simulate a torus machine with an increase in time by a constant factor (Cypher and Sanz (1989)). Data transfer from one PE to any other PE can be performed in no more than N-1 moves in an NxN mesh.

Another interconnection scheme that is used in digital image processing is the pyramid shown in Figure 18. It consists of a base of NxN PEs and $\log_2 N + 1$ levels. Each level $0 \le i \le \log_2 N$ is a mesh having $(N/2^i)\times(N/2^i)$ PEs. Such a pyramid has $(4N^2-1)/3$ processors. Each processor (except for the root) must have 9 links: 4 for its children PEs, 4 for its neighbor PEs and one for its parent PE. Any two nodes can communicate by using at most $2\log_2 N$ links. Examples of image processing pyramids are the HCL Pyramid (Tanimoto et al. (1987)), the MPP pyramid (Pitas and Venetsanopoulos (1988)), SPHINX (Merigot et al. (1985)), PAPIA (Cantoni et al. (1985)) and Warwick pyramid (Nudd et al. (1989)). HCL pyramid has 4 levels and a total of 85 bit-serial processors. Pyramids are very well suited for multiresolution image processing, due to their structure.

Mesh connected computers have many local links and are well suited for local operations. However, in certain cases in digital image processing (e.g. in the FFT) and in computer vision (e.g. in connected component analysis) long distance data transfer is required. Mesh computers are not the best architecture in this case.

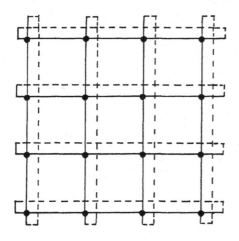

Figure 17: Mesh interconnection.

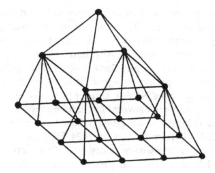

Figure 18: Pyramid interconnection.

Other connection schemes providing fast communications between long-distance PEs must be explored. Such an interconnection is the hypercube shown in Figure 19. A hypercube of dimension n has $N = 2^n$ PEs. The interconnections form an n-dimensional hypercube whose corners are the PEs. A hypercube of order $N = 2^n$ can be constructed from two hypercubes having 2^{n-1} PEs each by connecting their corresponding corners. Each PE is assigned a number from 0 to N-1 in binary notation. Two PEs are connected if and only if the binary representations of their indices differ in one bit only. Thus processor 0000 is connected to the processors 0001, 0010, 0100 and 1000. Each node has n links. Thus the overall number of links in nN/2. Any two PEs are at most n links a part. Thus far data transfer can be easily performed. No edge or boundary PEs exist that need special treatment. Mesh interconnection can be embedded in hypercube interconnection so that adjacent nodes in the original structure are mapped on adjacent nodes in the hypercube. However, there exist problems in simulating mesh computers on hypercubes.

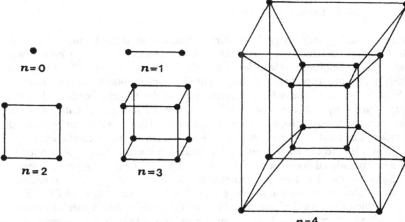

Figure 19: Hypercube interconnection.

A right shift operation on a $N^{1/2}xN^{1/2}$ mesh computer requires log_2N operations on the hypercube of order N and vice-versa (Cypher and Sanz (1989)). An image of dimensions $N^{1/2}xN^{1/2}$ can be stored in several ways on a hypercube of order N. The easiest way is to store pixel (i,j) in the PE having order $iN^{1/2}+j$ (row-wise storage). Alternatively, both row and column numbers can be coded by the Gray code (Cypher and Sanz (1989)). This code is a list of integers $0 \leq i \leq N^{1/2} - 1$ arranged so that consecutive integers differ in exactly 1 bit position. The pixel (i,j) is stored on the PE having order $N^{1/2}$ (i_label)+(j_label). Such an image storage has advantages on hypercubes. There exist several hypercube machines, namely Cosmic Cube (Seitz (1985)), NCUBE (Hayes et al. (1986)) and Connection Machine (Hillis (1985)). NCUBE/ten is an MIMD hypercube having 1024 PEs. Each of them has a 32-bit floating point processor and 128 Kbytes of memory. The Connection Machine has up to 65536 SIMD PEs. Each PE is a bit-serial processor with 4 Kbits memory.

5. Parallel digital image processing algorithms

A vast number of digital image processing algorithms exist. Therefore their parallel implementation can not be described or even reviewed in a single paper. In the following we shall try to review same basic low-level and high-level digital image processing algorithms implemented on mesh, pyramid and hypercube architectures. An excellent review in this area is (Cypher and Sanz (1989)). Several algorithms can also be found in (Stout (1986), Guerra e Levialdi (1989), Tanimoto (1983), Pitas (1989)).

5.1. MxM CONVOLUTION

An MxM convolution is defined by (Gonzales and Wintz (1987), Jain (1989)):

$$Y_{ij} = \sum_{k=-m}^{m} \sum_{1=-m}^{m} h_{kl}x_{i-k, j-1} \tag{6}$$

where $M=2m+1$ and h_{kl}, $-m \leq k,1 \leq m$ is the convolution kernel. If the kernel size is relatively small $(M < < N)$, definition (6) is used for its direct computation, otherwise the two-dimensional FFT is employed (Gonzales and Wintz (1987), Jain (1989), Pitas and Strintzis (1986)). A brute force approach for its parallel implementation on a mesh computer will involve almost M shifts for the pixels lying at the window border. Thus the computational complexity is of the order $0(M^3)$. However, by shifting the entire array in unit steps horizontally or vertically, all data pixels within the filter window can be reached in a spiral order. The total steps required are M^2-1. At each step one coefficient h_{kl} is transmitted to all PEs and the corresponding multiplication and addition is performed in (6). Thus the computational complexity is reduced to $0(M^2)$ (Lee and Aggarwal (1986)). The same algorithm can be used for convolution calculation on pyramid machines. However, only the PEs at the bottom of the pyramid are active, thus reducing PE utilisation. The convolution can be calculated on a hypercube by embedding a mesh computer in it. Since a single operation on a mesh can be implemented on a hypercube in a

$0(\log_2 N)$ time, the convolution algorithm can be computed in $0(M^2\log_2 N)$ time. Convolution algorithm can be computed in $0(M^2\log_2 N)$ for hypercubes having $0(M)$ words of memory per PE are reported in (Fang and Li (1986), Prasanna Kumar and Eshaghian (1987)).

5.2. HISTOGRAM

The histogram is the experimental probability density function of an image (Gonzales and Wintz (1987), Jain (1989)). Let us suppose that an image has $V < N$ gray levels and that it is stored on an NxN mesh. Its histogram can be calculated as follows. The column histograms are calculated by shifting down the image N times and by incrementing the counter of a PE whenever a pixel value equals the row number of the PE. The column histograms can be added by shifting them to the left once and adding them, by shifting them twice to the left and adding and so on. After N-1 shifts to the left, the (scaled) histogram values are found at the leftmost column. Thus the entire algorithm has complexity of the order $0(2N)$ (Kushner et al. (1982).

A different algorithm can be devised for pyramid machines. The bottom PEs count the pixels having values 0,1,...,V-1 (one at each step) and forward the number to their parents. This process can be pipelined for i=0,1,...,V-1. Thus the total computation time is of the order $0(V+\log_2 N)$. The term $\log_2 N$ comes from the propagation delay from the bottom PEs to the root PE (Reeves (1980)).

Let us suppose that a hypercube can store V numbers at each node and that V = N. An algorithm for histogram calculation on the hypercube is the following. At the first step the arrays are initialised to zero. Only the array position corresponding to the pixel value at a PE is set to 1. At the second step the PEs that differ in the most significant bit (MSB) exchange data. The PE with the higher index receives the V/2 highest elements from the array of the other PE and transmits the V/2 lowest elements of its own array. At the end of this step each PE contains an array of V/2 elements. This procedure is repeated at the second step with the PEs differing in the next MSB. At the end of this step each PE contains an array of V/4 elements. After $\log_2 N$ such steps each PE contains only one element that is equal to a value of the desired histogram. Similar algorithms can be written for the case $V < N$ (Siegel et al. (1984)). The computational complexity of this method is $0(V+\log_2 N)$.

5.3. LABELING CONNECTED COMPONENTS

A connected component in a binary image is the maximal region of pixels having value 1, such that any two pixels in the region can be connected by a path of pixels having value 1. Labeling connected components is a classical example of a computer vision algorithm that requires global information. Several algorithms appeared for labeling connected components on a mesh computer (Rosenfeld (1983), Cypher et al. (1987), Nassimi and Sahni (1980). A relatively simple algorithm is the following. Each pixel having value 1 is labeled by the concatenation of its column and row coordinates. Then an iterative scheme is used. Each PE calculates the minimum of its current label and of the labels of its neighbors that have pixel value 1. The time complexity of the algorithm depends on the size and shape of the connected components. If the components are small and convex, the algorithm converges very fast. If they are very long the algorithm will require $O(N^2)$ in the worst case for an NxN mesh. Other faster algorithms having complexity $O(N)$ are reported in (Cypher et al. (1987), Nassimi and Sahni (1980)).

A simple algorithm for connected component labeling on a pyramid machine is presented in (Miller and Stout (1987)). Let us suppose that the subregions $2^i x 2^i$ have been labeled before step i. Every four adjacent regions are merged at step i to form labeled regions having $2^{i+1} x 2^{i+1}$ pixels. Region merging can be performed by examining the border pixels. Their number is of the order $O(2^i)$. Therefore, border pixels can be pushed to a smaller mesh having $O(2^i)$ PEs at higher level of the pyramid. This procedure is repeated for $i=0,...,\log_2 N-1$. Thus the total algorithm has $O(\log_2 N)$ stages. Its computational complexity is $O(N^{1/4})$ (Miller and Stout (1987).

A divide-and-conquer algorithm for labeling an N pixel image on a hypercube is presented in (Cypher et al. (1987). The image is segmented in $N^{1/2}$ square regions having $N^{1/2}$ pixels each. These regions are labeled recursively. The border inconsistencies are removed by using a graph theoretic connected component labeling algorithm. The overall algorithm has complexity $O(k\log^2 n)$. k is a relatively large constant (Cypher and Sanz (1989)).

6. Conclusions

Several parallel digital image processing architectures have been presented in this paper. It has been observed that the performance of a parallel image computer depends on the task to be performed, on the structure of the processing element and on the interconnection scheme used. According to our opinion, 32-bit processors of floating points DSPs or even specialised DIPs will be the core of future processing elements. It is advisable that such PEs have a sufficient amount of local memory, because it has been proven that it enhances PE capabilities for look-up operations, pointer based communications, histogram calculation etc. MIMD operation will be a strong feature of parallel image processing structures not only for high level vision tasks but also for cases where SIMD operation is sufficient. Mesh computers are ideal for local operations (e.g. look-up tables, convolution). They also operate fast in intermediate image processing applications (e.g. histogram, connected component analysis). Their main disadvantage is their poor performance in long-distance communications (e.g. in random access read and write). Pyramid computers perform extremely well in multiresoltuion image processing (image pyramids). They perform well in many low-and intermediate image processing tasks. However, horizontal connections seem to be useful only at the bottom level in most applications. Pyramid computers have poor performance in pointer-based communications (Cypher and Sanz (1989)). Therefore they are not the best choice for high level vision tasks. They hypercubes have very good long-distance communications. Their local communication properties vary from moderate (plain hypercube) to very good (hypercube with independent communication). Mesh computers can be easily simulated on hypercubes. Therefore it seems that it can be powerful both for low-level and for high-level vision systems. However they are inferior to the mesh and pyramid computers when performing local neighborhood operations. In general, their performance has to be studied better on practical parallel image processing systems. Their main disadvantage is the number of links required. Shuffle-exchange (Stone (1971)) and cube-connected cycles (Vuillemin (1981)) can be used instead. These networks can be used to implement hypercube algorithms effectively. However, they cannot simulate mesh computers efficiently. The are less efficient then mesh computers in local neighborhood operations (e.g. in convolutions) and they have many long-distance communications.

References

Gonzales, R.C. and Wintz, P., Digital image processing, (1987), Addison-Wesley.

Jain, A.K., Fundamentals of digital image processing, (1989), Prentice Hall.

Chiariglione, L. editor, Signal processing of HDTV, (1988), North Holland.

Burrus, C.S. and Parks T.W., DFT/FFT and convolution algorithms: theory and implementation, J.Wiley.

Elliot, D.F. and Rao, K.R., Fast transforms, algorithms and applications, (1983), Academic Press.

Pavlidis, T., Algorithms for graphics and image processing, (1982), Computer Science Press.

Lee, E.A., Programmable DSP architectures: part I, IEEE ASSP Magazine, Vol. 5, No. 4, Oct. 1988, pp. 4-19.

Plessey semiconductors, (1988), Digital signal processing IC handbook.

Wasserman, P.D., Neural Computing: theory and practice, (1989), Van Nostrand-Reinhold.

Myers, W., Lisp machines displayed at AI conference, Computer, Vol. 15, No. 11 (1982), pp. 79-82.

Golay, M.J.E., Apparatus for counting bi-nucleate lymphocytes in blood, (1965), US Patent 3, 214, 574.

Unger, H., A computer oriented toward special problems, (1958) Proc. IRE, 46, pp. 1744-1750.

Duff, M.J.B. editor, Computing structures for image processing, (1983), Academic Press.

Kittler, J., Duff, M.J.B. editors, Image processing system architectures, (1985), Research Studies Press.

Duff, M.J.B. editor, Intermediate-level image processing, (1986), Academic Press.

Uhr, L., Preston, K.Jr. and Levialdi, S., Duff M.J.B. editors, Evaluation for multicomputers for image processing, (1986), Academic Press.

Levialdi, S. editor, Multicomputer Vision, (1988), Academic Press.

Cantoni, V., di Gesu, V., Levialdi, S. editors, Image analysis and processing II, (1988), Plenum Press.

Dew, P.M., Earnshow, R.A., Heywood, T.R. editors, Parallel processing for computer vision and display, (1989), Addison-Wesley.

Sanz, J.L.C. editor, Advances in machine vision, (1989) Springer Verlag.

Special Issue on supercomputer technology, Proceedings of the IEEE, Dec. 1989.

Pitas, I. and Strintzis, M.G., An efficient and systematic way for the parallel implementation of DFT algorithms, Signal Processing III: Theories and applications, (1986), Young, I.T., editor, North Holland.

Danielsson, P-E. and Levialdi S., Computer architectures for pictorial information systems, IEEE Computer, Nov. 1981, pp. 53-67.

Duff, M.J.B., Review of the CLIP image processing system, (1978), Proc. Nat. Comp. Conf., pp. 1055-1060.

Reddaway, S.F., The DAP approach, (1979), Infotech LTD.

Batcher, K.E., Design of a massively parallel processor, IEEE Transactions on Computers, Vol. C-29, (1980), pp. 836-840.

Dudgeon, D.E. and Mersereau, R.M., Multidimensional digital signal processing, (1983), Prentice Hall.

Serra, J., Image analysis and mathematical morphology, (1982), Academic Press.

Pitas, I. and Venetsanopoulos, A.N., Non linear digital filters: principles and applications, (1990), Kluwer Academic.

Tou, J.T. and Gonzales, R.C., Pattern recognition principles, (1974), Addison-Wesley.

Sternberg, S.R., Biological image processing, Computer, Vol. 16, No. 1, (1983), pp. 22-34.

Reeves, A.P., Meshes and hypercubes for computer vision, in Multicomputer Vision, Levialdi, S. editor, (1988), Academic Press.

Reeves, A.P., Parallel Pascal: An extended Pascal for parallel computers, Journal of Parallel and Distributed Computing, 1, (1984), pp. 64-80.

Datacube, (1990), MAXbus product information.

Edwards, M.D., A review of MIMD architectures, in Image Processing Architectures, Kittler, J. and Duff, M.J.B. editors, Research Studies Press.

Kruse, B., Gudmundson, B. and Antonsson, D., in Multicomputers and image processing algorithms and programs, Preston, K. and Uhr, L. editors, (1982), Academic Press, pp. 31-45.

Krusner, T., Wu, A.Y. and Rosenfeld, A., Image Processing on ZMOB, IEEE Transactions on Computers, Vol. C-31, (1982), pp. 943-951.

Sato, M., Matsuura, H., Ogawa, H. and Iijima, T., in Multicomputers and Image Processing-algorithms and programs, Preston, K. and Uhr, L. editors, (1982), Academic Press, pp. 361-371.

Gemmar, P., in Multicomputers and image processing-algorithms and programs, Preston, K. and Uhr, L. editors, (1982), Academic Press, pp. 87-98.

Dagless, E.L., Edwards, M.D. and Proudfoot, J.T., Shared memory in CYBA-M multiprocessor, IEEE Proceedings, part E, 130, (1983), pp. 116-124.

Gottlieb, A., Grishuman, R., Kruskal, C.P., McAuliffe, K.P., Rudolph, L. and Snir, M., The NYU ultracomputer-designing an MIND shared memory parallel computer, IEEE Transactions on Computer, Vol. C-32, (1983), pp. 175-189.

Sandler, M.B., Hayat, L., Costa, L. and Naqvi, A., A comparative evaluation of DSPs, microprocessors and the transputer for image processing, Proc. IEEE Int. Conf. Acoust., Speech, Signal proc., (1989), pp. 1532-1535, Glasgow.

Nudd, G.R., Atherton, T.J., Horvarth, R.M., Clippingdale, S.C., Francis, N.D., Kerbyson, D.J., Packwood, R.A., Vandin, G.J. and Walton, D.W., WPM: a multiple SIMD architecture for image processing, Proc. 3rd IEEE Conference on image processing and its applications, (1989), Warwick.

Pitas, I. and Venetsanopoulos, A.N., A new filter structure for the implementation of certain classes of image operations, IEEE Transaction on Circuits and Systems, Vol. CAS-35, (1988), pp. 636-647.

Rumelhardt, D.E. and McClelland, editors, Parallel Distributed Processing: explorations in the microstructure of cognition, (1986), MIT Press.

Cypher, R. and Sanz, J.L., SIMD architectures and algorithms for image processing and computer vision, IEEE Transaction on Acoustics, Speech and Signal Processing, Vol. ASSP-37, No. 12, (1989), pp. 2158-2174.

Tanimoto, S.L., Ligocki, T.J. and Ling, R., A prototype pyramid machine for hierarchical cellular logic, in Parallel Hierarchical Computer Vision, Uhr, L. editor, (1987), Academic Press.

Schaefer, D.H., Wilcox, D.H. and Harris, G.C., A pyramid of MPP processing elements-experience and plans, Proc. Hawaii Int. Conf. Syst. Sci., (1985), pp. 178-184.

Merigot, A., Zavidovique, B. and Devos, F., SPHINX, a pyramidal approach to parallel image processing, Proc. IEEE Workshop Comput. Archit. Pattern Anal. Image Database Management, (1985), pp. 107-111.

Cantoni, V., Ferretti, M., Levialdi, S. and Maloberti, F., A pyramid project using integrated technology, Integrated Technology for Parallel Image Processing, Academic, (1985), pp. 121-132.

Seitz, C.L., The Cosmic Cube, Communications of ACM, Vol. 28, Jan. 1985, pp. 22-33.

Hayes, J.R., Mudge, T. and Stout, Q.F., A microprocessor based hypercube supercomputer, IEEE Micro, (1986), pp. 6-17.

Hillis, D., The Connection Machine, MIT Press, (1985).

Stout, Q.F., Algorithm-guided design considerations for meshes and pyramids, in Intermediate-level image processing, Duff, M.J.B. editor, Academic Press (1986).

Guerra, C. and Levialdi, S., Computer vision: algorithms and architectures, in Advances in Machine Vision, Springer Verlag, (1989).

Tanimoto, S.L., Algorithms for median filtering of images on a pyramid machine, in computing Structures for image processing, Academic Press, (1983).

Lee, S.Y. and Aggarwal, J.K., Parallel 2-d convolution on a mesh connected array processor, Proc. IEEE Conf. Comput. Vis. Pattern Recog., (1986), pp. 305-310.

Fang, Z. and Li, X., Parallel algorithms for image template matching on hypercube SIMD computers, Proc. IEEE Workshop Comput. Architecture Pattern Anal. Image Database Management, (1986), pp. 33-40.

Prasanna Krumar, V.K., Eshaghian, M.M., Efficient image template matching on hypercube SIMD arrays, Proc. 1987 Conf. Parallel Processing, (1987) pp. 909-912.

Pitas, I., Fast algorithms for running ordering and max/min calculation, IEEE Transactions on circuits and Systems, Vol. CAS-36, No. 6, (1989), pp. 795-804.

Reeves, A.P., On efficient global information extraction methods for parallel processors, Computer Graphics and Image Processing, Vol. 14, (1980), pp. 159-169.

Siegel, H.J., Schwederski, T., Davis, N.J. and Kuehn, J.T., PASM: a reconfigurable parallel system for image processing, Computer Architecture News, vol. 12, No. 4, (1984), pp. 7-19.

Rosenfeld, A., Parallel image processing using cellular arrays, IEEE Computer, (1983), pp. 14-20.

Cypher, R.E., Sanz, J.L.C. and Snyder, L., Practical algorithms for image component labeling on SIMD mesh connected computers, Proc. 1987 Int. Conf. Parallel Processing, (1987), pp. 772-779.

Nassimi, D. and Sahni, S., Finding connected components and connected ones on a mesh-connected parallel computer, Siam J. Comput., Vol. 9, No. 4, (1980), pp. 744-757.

Miller, R. and Stout, Q.E., Data movement techniques for the pyramid computer, SIAM J. Comp., vol. 16, No. 1, (1987), pp. 38-60.

Cypher, C.R., Sanz, J.L.C. and Snyder, L., Hypercube and shuffle-exchange algorithms for image component labeling, Proc. IEEE workshop Comput. Arch. Pattern Anal. Mach. Intell., (1987), pp. 5-10.

Stone, H.S., Parallel processing with the perfect shuffle, IEEE Transactions on Computer, Vol. C-20, (1971), pp. 153-161.

Preparata, F.P. and Vuillemin, J., The cube-connected cycles: a versatile network for parallel computation, Commun. ACM, Vol. 24, No. 5, (1981), pp. 300-309.

Kushner, T., Wu, A.Y. and Resenfeld, A., Image processing on MPP:1, Pattern Recognition, Vol. 15, No. 3, (1982), pp. 121-130.

VISION BASED ONLINE INSPECTION OF MANUFACTURED PARTS: COMPARISON OF CCD AND CAD IMAGES.

E. HIRSCH
UNIVERSITY LOUIS PASTEUR
Ecole Nationale Supérieure de Physique de Strasbourg / Laboratoire des Sciences de l'Image et de la Télédétection
7, rue de l'Université. Strasbourg. 67000. France

Abstract

This paper presents an automated system, based on a parallel computer architecture, as a solution to the 100 % control of manufactured parts in a FMS environment. The technique used is based on comparison between images acquired through a vision system and the corresponding data gained from a CAD system. Comparison takes places as well at feature level than at image level. All kind of inspections, ranging from conformity checking up to metrology, can be achieved through use of an user friendly planning system. The system described is based on work of ESPRIT project P2091 "VIMP".

1.   Introduction

Automated manufacturing of complex and expensive to produce workpieces suffers from the lack of applicable methods to detect faults immediately after critical stages of the manufacturing process. In order to prevent an expensive loss of material and labour, automated inspection must be done for each workpiece, after each critical manufacturing step. Today, only a few samples can be inspected with time-consuming methods which cannot use information on the shape provided in some cases in a CAD/CAM system.

The paper describes a low cost pre-industrial prototype to be realized in ESPRIT Project P2091, started on 1/1/1989 [1]. This prototype is aimed to be able to replace mechanical sensors with the same accuracy (of the order of 10 to 100 μm) within the overall volume of the part. The system will work on-line in a Flexible Manufacturing System (FMS), in order to increase productivity and reduce the manufacturing costs, using modern techniques of vision systems. Due to the limited resolution of the imaging sensors used today for digital image processing systems, the sensor is moved in order to scan

---

[1] P2091 Consortium:ULP/ENSPS (France), FhG-IITB (RFA), RPK/UK (RFA), Caption Sarl (France), Speroni S.P.A. (Italy)

D. Gassilloud and J. C. Grossetie (eds.), Computing with Parallel Architectures: T.Node, 173–196.
© 1991 *ECSC, EEC, EAEC, Brussels and Luxembourg. Printed in the Netherlands.*

larger workpieces in their entire extent. CAD-based knowledge is also required and used for efficient performance of such hybrid mechanical and electronical inspection tasks.

To inspect the geometrical properties, the image of the current field of view is compared with the information stored in the data-base of the associated CAD system, with or without use of structured light and Moiré Techniques. Comparison takes place after segmentation and registration of the actual image with a synthetic projection of the CAD module. Furthermore, the 3D data coming from the CAD system is used to generate a 2D representation corresponding to the angle of view of the sensor. The output of the inspection stage is used for retrofitting by the manipulator in case of a possible remanufacturing.

After description of the inspection system architecture and corresponding hardware modules, the software organisation (and connection to the FMS control computer) will be introduced. The paper is concluded by a brief description of the results already achieved. Specific application domains will also be described, even though the whole manufacturing industry is concerned by this new non-contact, CAD connected inspection system.

2. System Description and Architecture

2.1. OBJECTIVES OF THE INSPECTION SYSTEM

2.1.1 *Present Situation.* Production and assembly lines of mechanical parts will be increasingly automated. It is thus necessary to control, at each step of the manufacturing process, whether the manufacturing of parts has been realized correctly. This often implies a qualitative and/or a quantitative inspection. Manufacturing errors at the machine tool level may originate from break of the tools, fault due to the structure of the manufactured material or malfunctionning of the machine-tool. Thus the part which has just been manufactured has to be accepted, rejected, or remanufactured, depending on its state.

Today, the major part of the inspection operations are carried out by human operators either visually or through the use of a measuring apparatus, such as an optical or mechanical comparator. In the case of a very high production rate, these controls are often carried out on randomly chosen samples. The necessity to realize these controls with high accuracy led to the development of measuring equipments which allow to measure a part point by point in a programmed fashion. This measuring process requires also the removal of the part from the machine-tool in order to analyse it on a specialized measuring bench. Furthermore, the piece has to be cleaned, positioned in the referential of the measuring machine and reinstalled in the machine-tool when remanufacturing is necessary and possible. The measurement is carried out by means of mechanical contacts. This process is very slow and can considerably reduce production rates.

2.1.2 *Aim of the system.* The aim of the proposed system is to introduce a computer vision system in order to enable an exhaustive control of the production output. This leads to the development of the methods implied and the realization of a system for undertaking dimensional measurements on parts possibly left mounted on the manufacturing machine, in order to facilitate a rapid remanufacturing if needed.

Classical inspection methods compare a reference part with the set of parts to be evaluated. The method proposed for implementation in this work is based on the comparison of a conceptual reference image with actual images taken from the manufactured parts. The reference image is obtained through a CAD system, which stores in its data-base all the information necessary for the simulation of the part to be inspected. The data-base also contains the input data for the CAM system.

Figure 1 shows the principal steps of the treatment and the functional blocks of the inspection system.

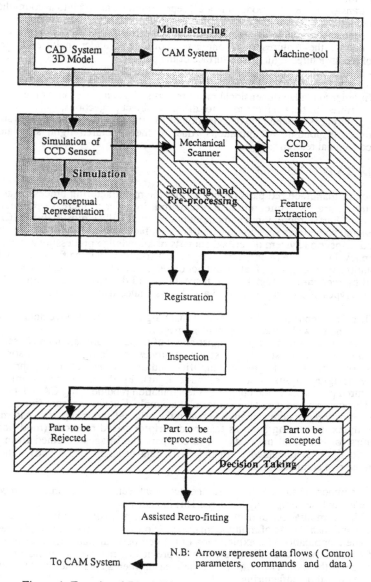

Figure 1. Functional Block Diagramm of the Inspection System.

176

In order to be able to compare the reference image with the real image, it is necessary to:
- transform the 3D model into a 2D representation, taking into account the picture-taking conditions of the camera, in order to generate a synthetic image,
- segment the real image acquired trough the camera,
- extract the features (e.g. contours ....) of the part under analysis, or the skeleton of the structured light on the surface of the part,
- compare the synthetic and transformed real images.

In order to realize dimensional measurements, the comparison involves:
- differences between contours for different object projections,
- differences between the deformation of structured light on the object's surface and the corresponding deformations, due to the structured light, simulated on the conceptual reference object.

2.2   DATA PROCESSING

Inspection of manufactured parts on-line during the manufacturing process is an essential part of the future FMS integration in production, in order to increase productivity and reduce costs. Furthermore, input and output information will be mostly visual (CAD/CAM Systems) and sometimes spoken (in case of remanufacturing assisted by an operator). The advanced inspection system described consists of knowledge processing and engineering at the top level (CAD/CAM and retrofitting after inspection), but the first layers will consist of simulation, preprocessing, feature extraction (e.g. filtering, identification, segmentation) followed by recognition (registration, inspection) and decision taking.Figure 2 indicates the various types of processing implied and the associated data structures.

The first step is to analyse the input CCD Signal so as to remove noise, enhance the images and end up with suitably segmented images.
Suitable combinations (after registration) of these pictures are then chosen as global feature to be used in the subsequent stages of processing. In the next step, some form of matching or comparison is greatly simplified and undertaken accurately through use of specially designed lightsources (structured light). Furthermore, the scanning of the manufactured part is under the control of the simulation module using CAD data.
This comparison may take the form of a simple distance measure (for example as is suitable for difference determination between the original and real parts). Alternatively, a more complex processing such as feature descriptor based methods (modified Fourier descriptors for example) may be used to compare the images obtained from the CCD sensor and those synthesized from the CAD data-base. Figure 3 shows the relation between the two comparison methods.

It is important to note that direct measurement techniques are implemented in order to be able to analyse completely the parts. This includes:
-The computation and control of the camera position with reference to the workpiece and making use of multiple images previously segmented and registered
-The computation and exploitation of the geometrical characteristics or features of the workpiece through use of multiple images previously matched with the corresponding CAD image of the part. The output of these measurements leads then to "understanding" and to sustained remanufacturing.

Furthermore, in general the images are not compared in the representation of grayscale pictures. Also, the synthetic images are gained from the analytic perspective geometric description of the outlines and surfaces of the workpiece adapted to the position of the camera.

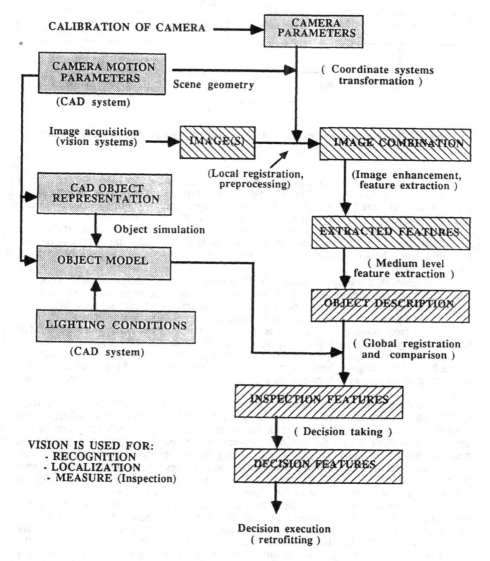

Figure 2. Processing Model of the Inspection System (off-line and on-line treatments).

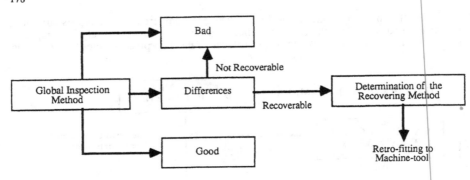

Figure 3. Relation between global and direct (difference based) Comparison Methods.

As a consequence, in the pixel plane, the synthetic image consists of a skeleton of lines which are 1 pixel broad. The pixels on the lines of the skeleton must be computed. (Also, when structured light such as Moiré is used, synthetic Moiré images are given like this).The real image will also assume this format within the vision system.

However, if a description plane is used, the synthetic image consists of datasets, describing parts of the outlines and surfaces analytically, and additional information about the relationship between these primitives and surfaces. The real image will then also be given like this.

In general, the output from the "comparison" stage is a single decision (good or bad) or a more complex response ("differences" and how to reprocess the part). A further stage of processing can then take place using, for example, a retrofitting technique to the CAD/CAM System or the associated host computer.

The most complex component is the "understanding" part which is some kind of knowledge system (possibly an expert system for remanufacturing) which uses the knowledge about the parts (and the manufacturing process) and the knowledge extracted by the lower level stages. There may be, of course, an interaction and feedback (assisted in a first step by an operator) between the inspection system and the CAM system as shown in Figure 1.

For the case of 2D graphic image generation, the system is based on a conventional CAD/CAM System associated with a fast computer (Transputer network), effort having been devoted for developing the specific hardware and software modules required by this approach. However, for the acquisition and preprocessing part, the processing has to be in real-time and solutions can only be found with highly parallel architectures realized either with specialized modules (wired processors, systolic processors) or with general purpose programmable structures (Transputer networks or array processors), as is the case for the hardware, previously developed by the project partners, used for this system.

The inspection system described here is aimed at defining and developing up to the pre-industrial stage a real-time inspection system that is designed to be compatible with CAD/CAM systems (through the use of "universal" interfaces such as defined, for example, in STEP; see, for example, /CADI-88/, /ANDE-89/). Furthermore, the compatibility within the system is ensured through the use of the same kind of computer (Transputer networks) for the feature extraction, simulation and inspection or "understanding" stages.

It is hoped that technical advantages would be obtained by supporting cooperating processing modules at the architectural and software levels through the use of common computer architectures and "universal" interfaces. (This point being suggested by the current trend of this kind of computations.) Furthermore, special attention will be paid to the man- machine interfaces (user friendly, assistance through visual and/or spoken I/O).

It is also of outmost importance to see that the inspection tasks are oriented toward metrology (measures with high accuracy have to be carried out). This calls for the assessment of following hypothesis:

- Several views of an object can be adequatly combined in order to provide a satisfactory object description.

- An object model is available (implying that all data representations have to be carefully registered, with respect to a reference frame).

3.   Software organisation

In a first aproach, one can notice that an inspection session is divided in two phases : one OFF-LINE and the other ON-LINE (see figure 4 for organization of an inspection session and figure 5 for software functionalities).

a)The aim of the OFF-LINE phase, placed before the inspection sequence, outside the FMS line, is to generate data and programs for the ON-LINE phase. This is achieved using the so-called planning and simulation systems.

The planning system creates information for :

-the simulation (input data),

-the inspection session running (program for the scanner, program for the inspection sequencer, data for the vision system, the processing of images and comparisons).

The simulation system provides "simulated data", corresponding to the real data to be acquired, stored in a STEP file.

b)During the ON-LINE phase, the inspection sequence program itself executes a program for managing the vision system, for synchronizing the FMS line and the mechanical scanner and for processing images and carrying out comparisons.

Thus, two different software ensembles can be defined for the inspection system.

-The inspection software package. It can again be splitted in two parts: The inspection sequencement software and the data processing software packages themselves.

-The planning and simulation software system, aimed to define the inspection procedures for a given part in an interactive way.

3.1   THE INSPECTION SOFTWARE PACKAGE

3.1.2 *The Data Processing Software Package.* The algorithmic organisation diagram of this package is indicated and commented in figure 6, whereas figure 7 is showing the data structures implied and the hardware used. Figure 8 indicates all the classification/comparison methods which are currently being investigated.

3.1.1 *The Inspection Sequencement Software.* The algorithmic organisation diagram of this software piece is schematically given in figure 9.This and the preceding software pieces are quite straightforward program packages, relying on well proven methods, on the contrary of the software part to be described in the next section.

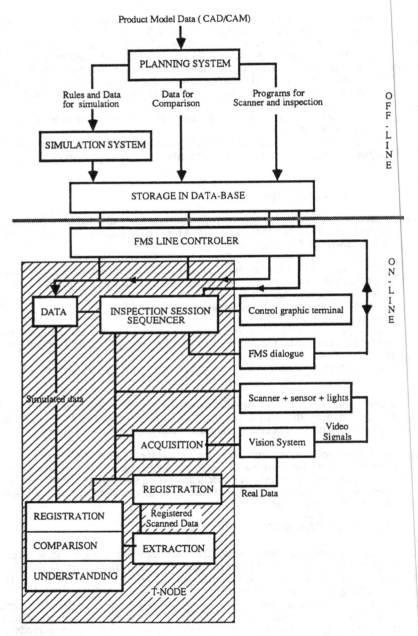

Figure 4. Organization of an Inspection Session (including off-line and on-line sessions).

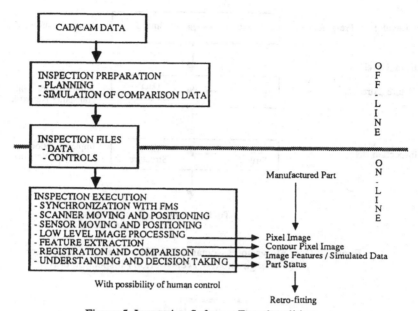

Figure 5. Inspection Software Functionalities.

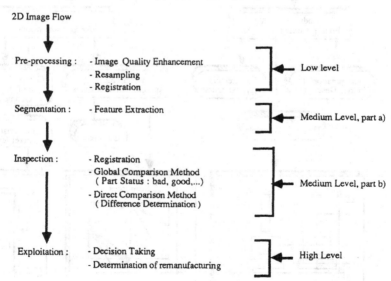

Figure 6. Software Flow of the Algorithmic Organization of the Data Processing.

182

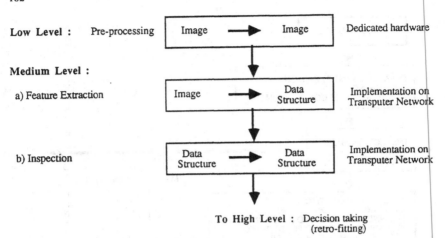

Low Level :   Pre-processing | Image → Image | Dedicated hardware

Medium Level :

a) Feature Extraction | Image → Data Structure | Implementation on Transputer Network

b) Inspection | Data Structure → Data Structure | Implementation on Transputer Network

To High Level :   Decision taking (retro-fitting)

Figure 7. Data Flows and associated Data Structures and Hardware.
(For segmentation / registration / inspection only).

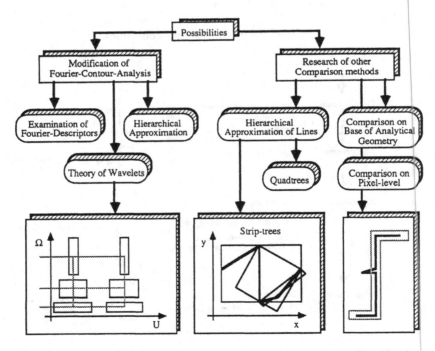

Figure 8. Methods (to be used for inspection tasks) for Comparison / Classification

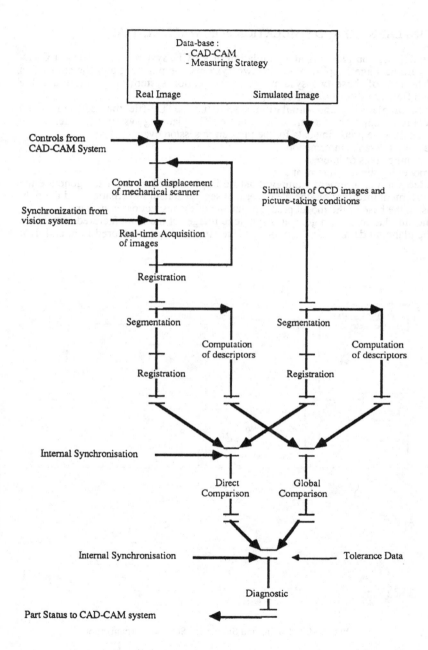

Figure 9. Software Flow of the Algorithmic Organization of the Inspection Sequencement.

3.2   THE PLANNING AND SIMULATION SOFTWARE SYSTEM

The inspection session planning and simulation of a CCD-System on the base of CAD-Data software package is splitted up into two systems, the planning and the simulation system. The role of these two systems in the inspection system architecture and the information flow are shown on Figure 10.

Base of planning and simulation system is a STEP-file that contains a 3D geometrical representation of a part to be inspected.The planning system generates on the base of these data the preparing data for the inspection session by:
- adding tolerance information
- defining areas of interest
- modelling the measurement cell

Indeed, a measurement strategy must be implemented in order to generate the camera movement information, the measurement sequencement information and the light conditions on the base of the model product data and of the inspection environment.

The simulation system generates synthetic images of the manufactured part on the base of the planning data. Main functions are the simulation of structured light and light

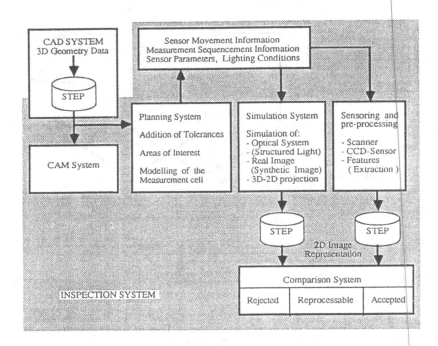

Figure 10. Planning and Simulation Software Organization.

conditions, projection of the 3D part representation into a 2D image representation (see, for example, /SUTH-74/). The result of the simulation system is a STEP-file containing, for example, a 2D polygonal representation of the image suitable for the comparison.

The planning and simulation systems contain the methods (algorithms) for generating measurement data which are stored in the data-base.

The workspace is defined once for every inspection environment by using modelling methods similar to methods used and available in CAD-systems.

Because of the high accuracy in positioning of the palettes in the measurement cell, the calibration of the workpiece in the measurement cell must be done only once. For this reason one simulation for each piece type (off-line) is sufficient.

3.2.1 *The Planning System.* In general such a software system can be divided in three parts: a communication processor, a method control system and a data-base.

The planning and simulation system will use the same data-base. This data-base must be able to store the product model of the part which should be measured. That means the 3D geometry received from the CAD-system and the technical information like tolerances and surface conditions. In addition to that, the data-base must be able to store information about the measurement cell, the camera and camera parameters, the camera movement and the synthetic images.

The planning system contains a data-base which is able to store tolerancing information. A STEP processor will convert data from the STEP file to the data-base of the planning system. In the STEP standard are defined the tolerances which are exchangeable using the STEP format. After having stored each part of the inspection model data (measurement machine, measurement equipment, inspection task(s), inspection sequencement, geometry, tolerances, surface conditions,...) in the data-base, an inspection session is defined.

Figure 11 indicates the architecture of the planning system (and of the simulation system). Planning is concerned with:
- the modelling of the measurement system,
- the inspection planning (choice of the area of interest on the part and how to inspect it),
- the addition of tolerances to standard CAD models.

The planning system generates off-line its data, stored in the inspection data-base and then, in a second time, uses this data on-line in order to carry out an inspection session.

3.2.2 *The Simulation System.* The simulation of a CCD-image requires three different models to represent all necessary data:
- A geometric model (that describes the complete geometry of the object) and a model of the measurement cell, that are to be simulated. The geometric model is the starting point for constructing the required models which, in turn, are needed for synthesizing an image comparable to the one obtained from the CCD camera.
- A parametrical camera model, that is able to describe the optical system with regard to aperture, focal length, lens, depth of field and distortion.
- A physical model for light-effects, that can describe the patterns projected onto the surface of the object.

For the representation of these data on the screen or in a STEP-file, two projections are necessary regarding the position of camera and workpiece:
- A projection that transforms the object-data corresponding to the camera position.
- A projection that transforms 3 dimensional object data into 2 dimensional data.

186

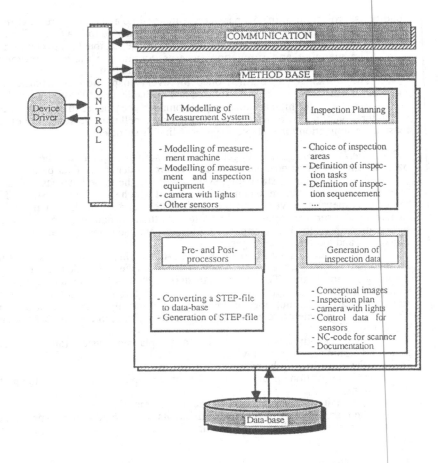

Figure 11. Planning and Simulation System Software Organisation.

The research for existing projection algorithms from 3D to 2D data led to a classification of three different projection types:
- Object oriented hidden surface algorithms.
- Image space based hidden surface algorithms.
- Ray tracing algorithms.

Taking into account these different characteristics, the object oriented hidden surface algorithms seem to be suitable algorithm types because the simulation of structured light is practicable with a tolerable amount of data. Implementation and investigation of existing object oriented hidden surface algorithms are currently performed.

The connection to the planning system (and the sequencement of the operation of the two software pieces) is exemplified on figure 12.

It is noteworthy to mention that the exchange of data between the different software packages has been standardized through use of STEP files.

3.2.3 *Integration of the Inspection in a FMS.* Figure 13 gives the schematic representation of the inspection set-up in a manufacturing cell.

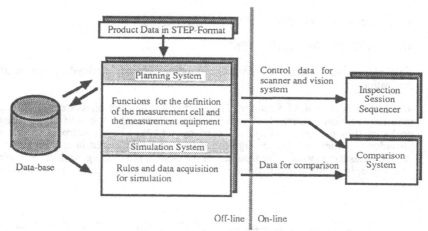

Figure 12. Planning and Simulation System Operation Sequencement.

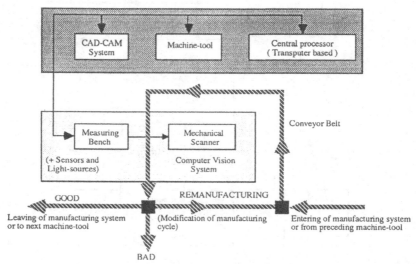

Figure 13. Inspection System Set-up in FMS Environment.

Figure 14 shows, then, what is the integration in FMS (the general manufacturing organisation makes explicit reference to the analysis outputed by the COSIMA Esprit project). The manufacturing controler uses a standard MMS library in order, first, to manage the different actors, second to favour standardization. This part of the work is carried out in collaboration with a FMS manufacturer providing all the facilities needed for the integration of the inspection system in FMS.

4. Achieved results

4.1 HARDWARE COMPONENTS

This section summarizes the hardware modules already defined and currently under realization.

4.1.1 *The Mechanical Scanner.* This part of the inspection system is built around a modified version of a standard conventional mechanical inspection robot. Roughly, the probe of this system has been replaced by a 512x512 CCD-camera. The robot also provides facilities to carry the lighting system to be described later.Due to the use of a proven measuring system, the accuracy of the camera positioning, with respect to the piece to analyse, is within a few microns. This system is currently used to define the scanning

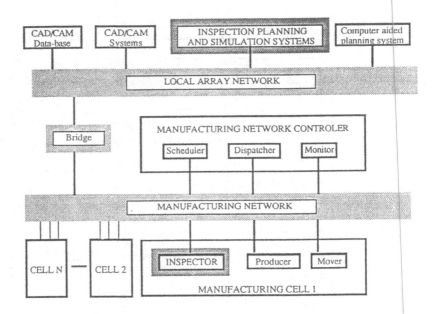

Figure 14. Integration of Inspection System (off-line and on-line parts) in FMS.

pathes of a piece, in order to be able to analyse the part in its full extent (measurement strategy and definition of the area of interest for specific pieces).

4.1.2 *The Vision Systems*. Two systems, already developed and tested, are used:
- The first one is a modular vision system, built around dedicated hardware modules, having in charge each a specific processing task. This system, described in detail in /PAUL-88/, is able to work at video realtime and its output is fed to the comparison stage (see section 3). This system is aimed for industrialisation, once the processing chains are defined and tested.
- The second is a fully programmable image processing system of general purpose. Its role is to facilitate the development of the processing chains and to validate them. It can be seen as a development tool, used interactively by the user, in order to design its inspection tasks. Usually, complex vision tasks can be sub-divided into three types of processing, reflecting the nature of the treatments and of the data structures. This is due to the fact that the processing of images imply very different processing tasks with respect to the target applications. In order to optimize the overall system performance, one has then to match to each processing level the best suited hardware. The resulting system can, as a consequence, be seen as a heterogeneous pipe-lined processing structure. Figure 15 defines the three usual processing levels. On figure 16 is illustrated how these levels can then be applied, in order to reduce the image data, for the solution of a given application.

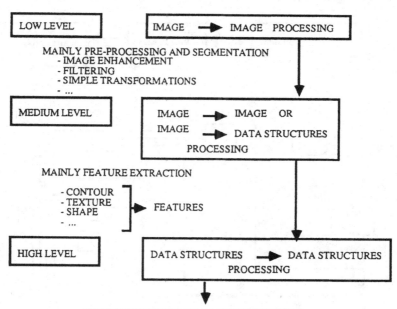

Figure 15. Processing Levels for Vision based Applications (see also figures 6 and 7) .

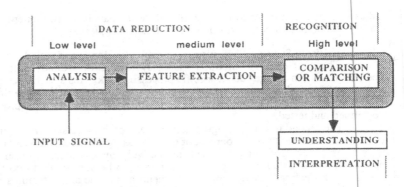

Figure 16. Data Reduction Steps (from raw data up to symbolic data).

The two vision systems, used for implementation of the inspection system, have an architecture corresponding to the described data processing. This can be seen in figure 17, which gives a block diagramm of the vision system developed partially during ESPRIT Project P26 (Advanced algorithms and architectures for speech and image processing).

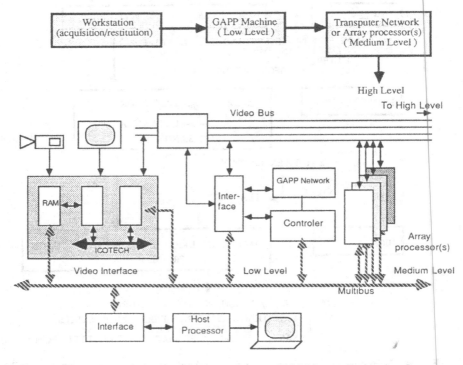

Figure 17. Heterogeneous Pipe-lined Architecture of P26 Image Processing System.

Without going into detail (the system is fully described in /PIER-88/, /PERU-88/), figures 18 and 19 show the structure of the low and medium processing parts of the vision system.

The P26 Transputer-based processing module is however to specifically oriented toward image (or signal) processing, and, for that reason, a similar approach is quite difficult to use for the realization of the inspection system described in this paper. In our case, it is more advisable to use a Transputer-based system of general purpose. A system based on this second approach will allow much more flexibility with respect to the very various kinds of processing involved in our system.

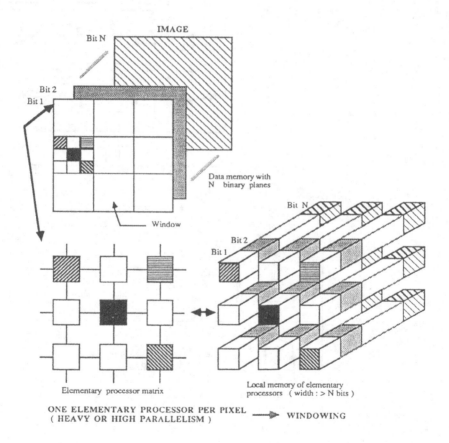

Figure 18. Principle of the GAPP-based Low-level Module of P26 Vision System.

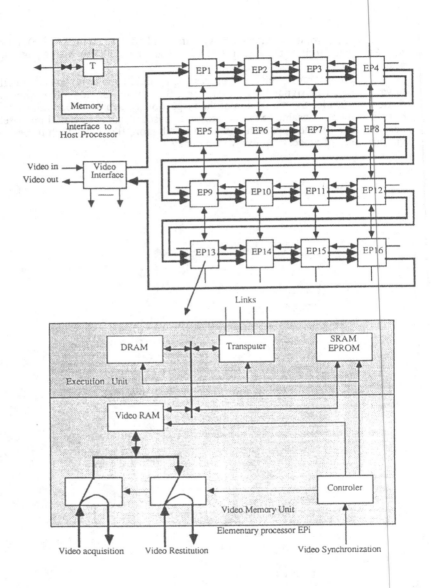

Figure 19. Transputer-based Medium-level Processing Module of P26 Vision System.

4.1.3 *The Sensoric System.* Lighting conditions play a crucial role for the quality of the acquired data. Strong use is thus made of special lightsources and illumination techniques.

Among standard methods such as structured light and shadowing techniques, special methods are used:
- Use of diffuse light using a ring of light emitting diodes.
- Use of a laser fan.
- Use of Moiré techniques. For this latter technique, a Moiré pattern is acquired, whereas the corresponding synthetic pattern is generated using CAD data. The two images are then compared and the shape differences of the piece with its model can thus be estimated (see, for instance, /TEAN-88/, /GASV-89/, /MORS-89/).

4.1.4 *The Central Computer System.* The design of the system architecture, the study of input and output techniques in order to achieve good performances (real time) and to avoid bottlenecks for the whole system have been carried out.

The choice has been made to use a transputer based system (TNODE) which assumes:
- The synchronisation of scanner movements.
- The acquisition of real images from the vision system.
- The medium and high level processing of real images.
- A part of the simulation process (low level).
- The comparison of real and simulated parameters.

Figure 20 gives the functional architecture of the parallel Transputer-based processing system TNODE and figure 21 shows how the central computer system is integrated in the inspection system (Remenber that figure 4 describes the functional architecture of the whole system).

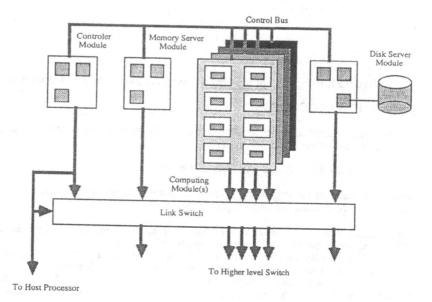

Figure 20. Functional Architecture of the TNODE parallel processing System.

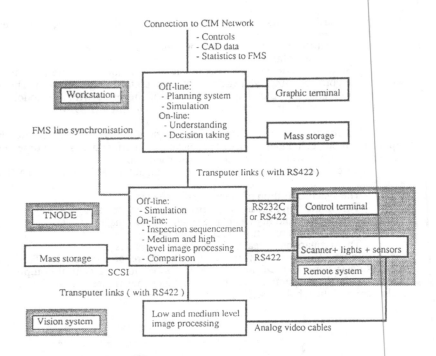

Figure 21. Integration of the Central Computer System in the Inspection System.

4.2   SOFTWARE COMPONENTS

The software described under heading 3 is currently being implemented on the different hardware pieces of the inspection system.

4.3   INSPECTION TASKS (Application Domains)

In order to validate the inspection system, the inspection tasks have first been classified and secondly representative target applications have been defined.

4.3.1 *Classification of Inpection Tasks.* Four application tasks have been defined, covering all the inspection tasks one has usually to face in industry :
    - Conformity checking: the part is analysed globaly in order to verify the conformity of the piece. No accuracy problems arise in this verification.
    - Range inspection: A specific part of the piece is analysed and measurements are carried out with an accuracy of 0.1 mm. The attention is only focused on specific features of the piece.

- "Scanning inspection": The part is analysed in its full extent with an accuracy of the order of 10 microns. This inspection task makes full use of the inspection system.
- High resolution inspection: with a precision of the order of one micron, specific features of a piece are measured.

All these inspection tasks are oriented toward metrology. In order to test and validate these tasks, a model part has been defined. The closed loop shown schematically on the figure below illustrates how these model parts will be used in order to improve the inspection system specifications.

4.3.2 *Free Form Inspection.* An alternative task is to verify the shape of free form pieces such as for example turbine blades. In contrast to the tasks defined in the previous section, the position of surface points, which are not situated at particular regions of the object like edges or corners, must be measured. In this case, the Moiré technique is extensively used. After extraction of the Moiré pattern skeleton, comparison with the corresponding conceptual pattern allows to estimate the shape of the piece. The tangential plane to a given point on the surface of the piece can be determined with an accuracy of 0.02 degrees. Carrying this out for a given set of points allows then to define the shape and the deviations with respect to a master piece. This calls for a careful calibration of the system. This part of the work is carried out in collaboration with a turbine blade manufacturer.

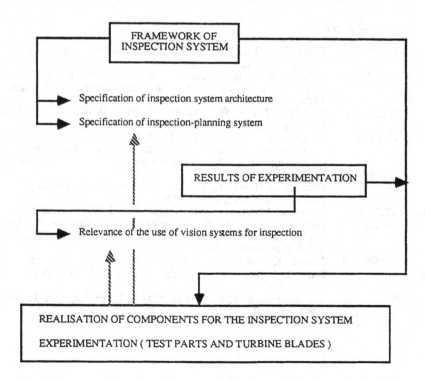

FRAMEWORK OF
INSPECTION SYSTEM

Specification of inspection system architecture

Specification of inspection-planning system

RESULTS OF EXPERIMENTATION

Relevance of the use of vision systems for inspection

REALISATION OF COMPONENTS FOR THE INSPECTION SYSTEM

EXPERIMENTATION (TEST PARTS AND TURBINE BLADES)

5. Conclusion

In this paper, a non contact inspection system, based on real time computer vision, has been extensively described. Inspection is carried out through comparison of conceptual images and actual object pictures. The system is oriented toward metrology, measurements having to be carried out with an accuracy of 10 to 100 microns. This necessitates a careful calibration of the inspection system as well as the definition of references. The method is based on the fact that several images of an object, after combination, lead to a satisfactory object representation. The inspection is on-line and controls 100 % of the parts. This is aimed to decrease inspection time and increase production rate.

The hardware and software components have been described and some specific application domains have been defined. The project, however, does not aim to developp a restricted system, as the whole manufacturing industry is concerned by this non contact, CAD connected and FMS integrated inspection system.

Acknowledgements

The author wishes to address his thanks to the people working on this project (ESPRIT P2091) and for the kindful permission to use some of the illustrations presented in this paper.

References

/SUTH-74/   Sutherland T.E. , Sproul R.F., Schumacker R.A., ACM Computing Surveys, Vol 6, N. 1, 1974.

/CADI-88/   Schlechtendahl E.G. (Ed.), " Specification of CAD*I neutral file for CAD geometry, version 3.3 ", Research report, Vol. 1, Springer Verlag, 1988.

/PAUL-88/   Paul D. , Hättich W. , Nill W., Tatari S., Winkler G., IEEE Transactions PAMI, Vol. 10, N. 3, 1988, pp 399-407.

/PERU-88/   Perucca G. , Giorcelli S., De Couasnon T., Hirsch E., Mangold H., " Advanced algorithms and architectures for speech and image processing ", in " Putting Technology to use ", CEC/DGXIII Ed., North-Holland, 1988, pp 543-561.

/PIER-88/   Pierre F. , Herve Y., Eugene F., Draman C., Wendling S., Proc. of 2th PIXIM Conference, Paris, 1988.

/TEAN-88/   Technical Annex of ESPRIT Project P2091 "VIMP", 1988.

/ANDE-89/   Anderl R., Schmitt M., " State of the art of interfaces for the exchange of product model data in industrial applications ", CEN/CENELEC/AMT/WG STEP 8, december 1989.

/GASV-89/   Gasvik K.J, Hovde T., Vadseh T., Proc. 5th Cim-Europe Conference, Halatsis C. and Torres J. Eds., IFS Publications, springer Verlag, 1989, pp 301-308.

/MORS-89/   Morshedizadeh M.R, Wykes C.M. , J. Phys. E. Sci. Instrum., Vol. 22, 1989, pp 88-92.

A PROBLEM-INDEPENDENT PARALLEL IMPLEMENTATION OF SIMULATED ANNEALING: MODELS AND EXPERIMENTS

P. ROUSSEL-RAGOT and G. DREYFUS,
Senior Member, IEEE

ABSTRACT. We suggest a problem-independent parallel implementation of the simulated annealing algorithm which is guarantied to exhibit the same convergence behaviour as the serial algorithm. We introduce two models of parallelization, depending on the value of the temperature, and we derive statistical models which can predict the speed-up for any problem, as a function of the acceptance rate and of the number of processors. The performances are evaluated on a simple placement problem with a Transputer-based network, and the models are compared with experiments.

1. Introduction

The simulated annealing algorithm (Kirkpatrick et al. (1983)) is a flexible and powerful optimization method which has proven successful in the search of optimal or near-optimal solutions for complex engineering applications, such as the placement of components in integrated circuits. This non deterministic approach is particularly well adapted to problems for which conventional methods get trapped in local minima, for it allows transitions of the system that increase the cost function to be minimized. The probability that such a transition will be accepted is controlled by parameter, called the temperature. Finely tuned cooling schedules (Lam and Delosme (1988), Otten and van Ginneken (1988)) may ensure fast convergence to near-optimal solutions, but, as the complexity of the problem grows, the best schedule may still require a very large computational time.

In this paper, we propose a problem-independent, parallel simulated annealing algorithm which guarantees the same quality of convergence as the sequential algorithm, and a statistical model of its behaviour is derived. This study provides a straightforward way to implement in parallel any sequential schedule and to evaluate the expected acceleration factor as a function of the number of processors used in parallel.

2. Summary of Previous Approaches to Parallel Simulated Annealing

In an optimization problem, one tries to find the best state, or configuration, of a system, according to a given cost function, often referred to as the "energy". The simulated

D. Gassilloud and J. C. Grossetie (eds.), Computing with Parallel Architectures: T.Node, 197–214.

annealing algorithm is a variant of an iterative improvement method: starting with an initial state, the algorithm generates a sequence of attempted perturbations, usually termed "elementary moves".

The moves improving the cost function to be minimized are accepted (as they are in classical methods), and the moves increasing the energy are accepted with a probability which depends on the value of a control parameter, the temperature. The value of the temperature is decreased stepwise: the length of each temperature step is controlled by rules which will be described below. The implementation of simulated annealing on a multiprocessor is not straightforward, because of the sequential nature of the method. Simulated annealing is commonly described as a sequence of homogeneous Markov chains: each computation step of a chain starts only when the previous step is completed. This is the condition for the whole process to lead to a unique feasible configuration. In order to reduce the computation time required, two kinds of parallelism can be used:

i) A parallelism in the evaluation of each move: the computation of a given step of the Markov chain depends only on the configuration of the system before the step and is performed without further interaction with the other steps; therefore, each move evaluation can be parallelized inasmuch as the computations of the variation of the cost function and of the acceptance criterion can be made parallel. This kind of parallelism, which is completely problem-dependent, will not be discussed here.

ii) A global parallelism on the Markov chain level, which can obviously be combined with the first kind of parallelism, if necessary.

Several attempts to parallelize the simulated annealing algorithm were reported in the literature. The differences lie in the way in which the problem implemented in parallel, and the main issue are:

i)   the convergence conditions of the parallel algorithm,

ii) the dependence of the parallelism on the problem to be solved.

The placement problem - which is used as a test example in the present paper - is of central importance in Computer Aided Design. The approach to the parallel implementation of this problem suggested by (Casotto et al. (1987)) consists in partitioning the set of cells to be placed into a number of subset equal to the number of processors available; each subset is assigned to a given processor. The processors run asynchronously as long as the moves occur in a given set of cells; exchanges of cells from different sets are allowed, but imply that one of the two processors involved stops. The moves within a set of cells are translations, rotations or exchanges of the cells. This method is well adapted to problems with short-range interactions. The asynchrony of the processors implies that each processor never knows exactly what the current configuration is, which introduces some chaos in the determination of the energy. This method was implemented on a Sequent Balance 8000 with up to 8 processors running in parallel. (Casotto and Sangiovanni-Vincentelli (1987)) also experimented massive parallelization of the simulated annealing algorithm on the Connection Machine.

Clusters of cells are also used by (Mallela and Grover (1988)) in order to reduce the number of cells to be placed in each sub-problem. The placement of the cells in each cluster involves a reduced search space, thus a reduced computation time, each cluster being evaluated in parallel if desired.

Another approach of the cell placement problem is suggested by (Darema et al. (1987)); in this case, each processor evaluates one perturbation of the Markov chain, under the condition that two processors are not allowed to move the same cells simultaneously; therefore, there is no conflict between processors and the final configuration is always a valid one. Whenever a perturbation is accepted, the configuration of the cells is updated, regardless of the moves which are being computed. At low temperature, when the acceptance ratio is low, this does not introduce a large bias as compared to the sequential method. At higher temperature, the behaviour of the parallel method deviates significantly from that of the sequential method. The measurements in this study were performed in a parallel emulation environment, allowing simulation of a shared memory multiprocessor system with up to 64 processors.

A comparable approach was suggested by (Brouwer and Banerjee (1988)) for channel routing: sets of adjacent tracks are assigned to parallel processors and nets are moved between tracks which are assigned to a given processor; information about the moves are then broadcast to other processors to update their data structures.

A different approach was used by (Kravitz and Rutenbar (1986), Rutenbar and Kravitz (1986)); they introduce the notion of serializable subset of moves. a set of moves is serializable if the moves do not interact with each other. If the moves of such a subset are evaluated in parallel, the result is the same as it is in sequential. But the determination of these subsets is more and more difficult and time consuming as the number of processors increases. The suggested solution to this problem is the following: they consider the "simplest serializable subset", where only of the accepted moves is accepted, while all the rejected moves are counted. Then, the parallel algorithm is quite different from the sequential one at high temperature since the acceptance ratio is not the same. This issue will be discussed in detail in the next section. The experiments were performed on a DEC VAX 11/784, consisting of four VAX 11/780 processors connected to a shared 8 Mbyte memory.

Yet another approach was suggested by (Aarts et al. (1986)) who used, at high temperature, different processors to work on different short Markov chains. When the temperature is changed, one of the final configurations is used as the initial configuration of the next temperature step. As the temperature decreases, less and less Markov subchains are evaluated in parallel, while more and more processors are used for the generation of each subchain. At low temperature, all processors evaluate a single Markov chain. The behaviour of this method at high temperature is very different from the behaviour of the sequential algorithm since the configurations transmitted from one Markov chain to another are obtained after a shorter number of steps than in the sequential chain. Aarts used a parallel machine consisting of fifteen Motorola 68000 microprocessors with local memory and a shared 8 Mbyte memory.

3. Principle and Models

The present section describes the principle of the parallel implementation of simulated annealing that we suggest. We first explain and justify the principle of the parallelization. We subsequently propose a statistical model of this stochastic parallel computation.

3.1. GENERAL CONSIDERATIONS

We first define the acceptance rate $\chi(T)$ as the ratio of the number of accepted moves to the number of attempted moves, averaged over a given temperature One of the salient features of simulated annealing is the decrease of $\chi(T)$ as the temperature is reduced. This is due to two facts: first, the system approaches a minimum and it is unlikely that a move decreases the energy; moreover, the value of $\exp(-\Delta E/T)$, where ΔE is the variation of the cost function and T is the temperature, becomes very small, so that the probability of accepting a move which increases the energy vanishes. Most parallel simulated annealing methods take advantage of this fact: in the low temperature regime, when the acceptance rate χ is small, one can use a number K of processor such that $K < 1/\chi$. Thus, at most one move will be accepted while K moves are evaluated, so that the computation time in the parallel mode can be expected to be smaller than the computation time in the sequential mode by a factor of the order of K.

However, the computation time is not the only performance criterion. One wants, of course, to obtain a valid solution, and hopefully the optimal one (or one of the optimal ones). Therefore, the convergence of the algorithm is of central importance. Several theoretical studies of the sequential algorithm have been published (Aarts and van Laarhoven (1985)), (Geman and Geman (1984)), but the theory is much less developed for parallel simulated annealing. However, some parallelization schemes may hamper greatly the convergence of the algorithm, and even make it impossible in some cases. For instance, in the context of massively parallel implementations of simulated annealing for image processing, it was proved by A. Trouvé (private communication), that the algorithm may converge towards states of high energy of the system. Therefore, it seems desirable to design a parallel scheme which complies with the convergence conditions of the sequential algorithm, so that one can capitalize on the accumulated knowledge related to sequential simulated algorithm.

In the following, we suggest a parallel simulated annealing scheme which
i)   is problem-independent;
ii) has the same convergence properties as the sequential algorithm.

3.2. PRINCIPLE

As stated above, we use K processors in parallel, each of them evaluating one move. Each processor has its own memory. We want to design a parallel scheme which is equivalent to the sequential one, as far as convergence is concerned.

The usual, sequential, Metropolis algorithm at fixed temperature T consists in generating a Markov chain of states, the energies of which would have a Boltzmann distribution if the chain were infinitely long; since the chain is of finite length L, the resulting distribution will actually be "close to" the Boltzmann distribution. We want to find a parallel scheme which generates a Markov chain, the states of which have the same probability distribution as the sequential chain, all other parameters being equal. This guarantees that the convergence behaviour of the parallel algorithm will be similar to the behaviour of the sequential one. We shall see in the next section that the acceptance rate $\chi(T)$ is of central importance. its value leads us to consider two different regimes:
- a low temperature regime: if $\chi(T) < 1/K$, less than one move out of K will be accepted;

thus, the scheme proceeds as follows: the processors attempt moves on their own, asynchronously, in parallel, until one of the K processors accepts a move; when an accepted move is found, the processors are synchronised, their memories are updated with the new configuration and the next evaluation step takes place.

- a high temperature regime: ($\chi(T) > 1/K$): in this regime, each processor is allowed to evaluate one move only and waits until all the other processors complete their evaluation. Then, one of the accepted moves is chosen at random, the processor memories are updated with the new configuration and the next evaluation step takes place. The reason why we choose one of the accepted move at random, instead of choosing the first accepted move, is the following: since the computation time of a single move can vary substantially, choosing the first move would greatly favour the short computations (for instance, moves of weakly connected blocks, or downhill moves which do not require the computation of the exponential).

In addition to the above mentioned K "slave" processors the scheme required one "master" processor which monitors the annealing schedule, chooses the accepted move in the high temperature regime, updated the memory of each processor and keeps track of statistics.

3.3. MODELS

In all the following, we use the standard annealing schedule, whereby the temperature is decreased stepwise according to $T_{n+1} = \alpha T_n$, where T_n is the nth temperature and α may range from 0.9 to 0.99. We denote by

- L_a, the maximum number of accepted moves at a given temperature,
- L_t, the maximum number of attempts at a given temperature,
- τ_0, the average computation time necessary to evaluate one move in the sequential mode.

The meaning of τ_0 is clear if only one type of elementary move is used; otherwise, it would represent the average value of the computation time of the various types of moves occurring during annealing. In both case, it can be estimated as the duration of a temperature step divided by the number of attempted moves. If the perturbations vary with the temperature (for example, if exchanges of blocks occur mainly at high temperatures and translations mainly at low temperatures), the value of τ_0 will vary with temperature.

The temperature is decreased either when the number of accepted moves at the current temperature reaches L_a, or when the number of attempted moves at the current temperature reaches L_t, whichever limit is reached first.

Note that τ_0, the average computation time to evaluate one move in the sequential mode, is not exactly the same as that in parallel, because the master processor can take care of the necessary statistic while the slave processors evaluate the moves. Therefore, τ_0 is an upper limit of the average computation time for one move in the parallel implementation.

3.3.1. Model of the high temperature mode.
In the high temperature mode, each processor evaluates one move, and all processors are synchronized at the end of each evaluation; we denote by τ_r the average overhead due to communications with the K slaves and their

synchronization: therefore, the average time necessary for the K processors to perform one evaluation is $\tau_o + \tau_r$.   Note that τ_r takes into account the fact that the moves may be of different durations, so that the time to complete a parallel evaluation is equal to the duration of the longest attempted move.

Since the length of the Markov chain depends on the number of accepted moves and/or on the number of attempted moves, we first have to evaluate these quantities. Assume that, after one parallel evaluation of K moves, r moves out of K are rejected; K-r moves are found acceptable, but only one of them will actually be accepted in the Markov chain, the other ones being discarded. The ratio of the number of accepted moves to the number of attempted moves, in the serial mode, would be (K-r)/K; however, in the parallel mode, only one move is accepted. How do we construct a chain which has the same acceptance ratio as the sequential one? The procedure is as follows: we number the processors in an arbitrary, but definite order, from 1 to K. We denote by n, the number of the first processor in the list which accepts a move and we construct the Markov chain with the n first moves in the list. A Markov chain of n-1 rejected moves, followed by one accepted move, would have been found with the same probability in the sequential mode. It can be shown that the average value of n is equal to $n^* = (K+1)/(K-r+1)$ (see appendix).

If all K processors reject their attempted moves, the number of the first processor cannot be found using this approach, but since there is no accepted move, the number of attempted moves to be taken into account is clearly K.

To summarize, when K evaluations are performed in parallel:
- if at least one move has been accepted, one of the accepted moves is chosen randomly and we consider that $n^* = (K+1)/(K-r+1)$ moves have been attempted,
- if no move has been accepted, we consider that K moves have been attempted.

This provides a good estimate of the effective number of attempted moves since, on the average, the ratio of the number of accepted moves to the effective number of attempted moves in the parallel mode is equal to the sequential acceptance rate. This can be shown as follows.

The average number n^*_a of accepted moves for one parallel evaluation is equal to the ratio of the number of parallel evaluations for which at least one move is accepted (since, in this case, one move is taken into account) to the total number of parallel evaluations. The probability that i moves out of K are accepted is equal to

$$\binom{K}{i} (1-\chi)^{K-1} \chi^i;$$

the probability that all K moves are rejected is $(1-\chi)^K$. Thus,

$$n^*_a = \sum_{i=1}^{K} \binom{K}{i} \chi^i (1-\chi)^{K-1} = 1-(1-\chi)^K.$$

When i moves out of K are accepted, the number of attempted moves is taken equal to $K+1/(i+1)$, so that the effective number of attempted moves n^*_t in the parallel mode is equal to

$$n_t^* = (1-\chi)^K K + \sum_{i=1}^{K} \binom{K}{i} \chi^i(1-\chi)^{K-i} \frac{K+1}{i+1}$$

Therefore, the acceptance rate in the parallel mode is equal to

$$\frac{\sum_{i=1}^{K} \binom{K}{i} {}^i(1-\chi)^{K-i}}{(1-\chi)^K K + \sum_{i=1}^{K} \binom{K}{i}\chi^i(1-\chi)^{K-1}\frac{K+1}{i+1}}$$

This ratio can be shown after some algebra to be equal to . Thus, we obtain the same convergence behaviour in the parallel mode and in the sequential mode since the parallel algorithm has the same transition probability matrix as the sequential one.

We now evaluate the total effective number of attempted moves N^*_t, and the total number of accepted moves, actually taken into account, N^*_a, once N parallel evaluations of K moves have been performed.

The average effective number of attempts is given by

$$N_t^* = N \left[(1-\chi)^K K + K \sum_{i=1}^{K} \binom{K}{i}\chi^i(1-\chi)^{K-1} \frac{K+1}{i+1} \right]$$

or equivalently

$$N_t^* = N \frac{1-(1-\chi)^K}{\chi}$$

The limit of L_t attempted moves is reached after a number N_t of parallel evaluations of K moves which is given by

$$N_t = L_t \frac{\chi}{1-(1-\chi)^K}$$

The number N^*_a of accepted moves actually taken into accounts is equal to the number of parallel evaluations of K moves leading to at least one acceptable move, hence

$$N_a^* = N[1-(1-\chi)^K]$$

Therefore, the limit of L_a accepted moves is reached after a number N_a of parallel evaluations of K moves which is given by

$$N_a = \frac{L_a}{1-(1-\chi)^K}$$

Therefore, in the high temperature mode, the number of parallel evaluations at a given temperature is

$N_p = \min(N_t, N_a)$.

The corresponding computation time is

$t_p = N_p (\tau_0 + \tau_r)$.

In the serial mode, the computation time is

$t_s = \tau_0 L_a / \chi$ if the L_a limit is reached first

$t_s = \tau_0 L_t$ if the L_t limit is reached first

Therefore, whichever limit L_a or L_t is reached first,

$$\frac{t_p}{t_s} = \frac{\chi}{1-(1-\chi)^K} \left(1 + \frac{\tau_r}{\tau_0}\right) \tag{1}$$

Note that $\lim (t_p/t_s) = 1 + \tau_r/\tau_0$ when $\chi \to 1$ and $\lim (t_p/t_s) = 1/K.(1 + \tau_r/\tau_0)$ when $\chi \to 0$.

At high temperature, the efficiency is low because the parallel mode skips rejected moves and only few moves are rejected at high temperatures when the acceptance rate is high; at low temperature, the computation time is roughly divided by the number of processors, as expected, if the overhead time τ_r is small compared to τ_0.

The average value of τ_0 is known from the serial implementation of the simulated annealing algorithm. The determination of τ_r is not straightforward and depends on the problem. If τ_0 is constant, τ_r may be approximated conservatively by K times the communication time: if the K parallel computations end at the same time, K successive communications will be required for the master to know all the results and restart the slaves.

3.3.2. Model of the low temperature mode. In the low temperature mode, each processor evaluates moves independently until one processor out of K accepts a move. At the end of each individual evaluation, the processors send asynchronously to the master the result of their attempt; if no move was accepted by any processor since the previous communication, another move is attempted. If one move was accepted, the memories of the slave processors are updated and the processors are synchronized. In this mode, all the rejected moves are counted as steps towards equilibrium.

In order to model the behaviour of this low temperature mode, it is necessary to evaluate the number of moves required for one move to be accepted. This can be done in two ways: (Aarts et al. (1986)) evaluate the number of parallel calculations required. Their estimation leads to a number of parallel calculations equal, on the average, to $1/1-(1-\chi)^K$. Since it is easier to estimate the time characteristics of individual moves from the sequential results, we find it preferable to evaluate the number of such moves. One configuration is accepted on the average when $1/\chi$ moves are evaluated. The process has then performed $1/\chi$ steps towards equilibrium in the serial mode. Since we want to obtain a feasible configuration of the system, if another move is accepted by one of the K-1 other processors, we do not take it into account: the perturbations are chosen at random and, if, for example, one block is exchanged in two different moves, the resulting configuration is not a valid one since this block would be placed in two different locations. When the processors are synchronized, $1/\chi + K-1$ moves have been evaluated and, on the average

$(1/\chi + K\text{-}1)$. have been accepted. Since we discard all the accepted moves, but one, we count only

$$(1/\chi + K\text{-}1) - (1/\chi + K\text{-}1)\cdot\chi + 1 = 1/\chi + (K\text{-}1)(1\text{-}\chi)$$

steps in the Markov chain.

If τ_m is the time required to obtain one accepted move in parallel, we can model the behaviour of the low temperature mode as follows:

i - when L_a in reached first,

$t_p = L_a \cdot \tau_m$ and $t_s = L_a/\chi \cdot \tau_o$, thus

$$\frac{t_p}{t_s} = \frac{\tau_m}{\tau_o} \cdot \chi \tag{2}$$

ii- when L_t is reached first,

$$t_p = \frac{L_t}{1/\chi + (K\text{-}1)(1\text{-}\chi)} \tau_m \tag{3}$$

and

$t_s = L_t \tau_o$, thus

$$\frac{t_p}{t_s} = \frac{1}{1/\chi + (K\text{-}1)(1\text{-}\chi)} \frac{\tau_m}{\tau_o}$$

Note that for $K = 1$, one has $\tau_m = \tau_o/\chi$, so that $t_p = t_s$, as expected.

Here again, the average value of τ_o is known, but the determination of τ_m is not an easy task and depends on the problem, If τ_o is constant and if $1/\chi$ is much larger than K, the value of τ_m can be approximated by $(\tau_o + \tau_c)/K\chi$, τ_c being the time required by one slave to communicate its result to the master.

4. Results

4.1. A SIMPLE PLACEMENT PROBLEM

We tested our parallel methods and models on a simple placement problem. It consists of a two dimensional array of b^2 chips arranged on a square grid. In the ground state configuration of the system, each chip is connected to its nearest neighbours by two-terminal connections. the elementary move is the exchange of two chips, chosen at random; the cost function is equal to the total length of the wires. The parameters of the standard sequential annealing schedule are the following:
- the initial configuration is chosen at random,
- the initial temperature is chose so that the acceptance rate is larger than 0.9.
- the temperature is modified when $5.b^2.(b^2\text{-}1)$ moves have been evaluated or when

$b^2.(b^2-1)/2$ moves have been accepted,
- the cooling parameter α is equal to 0.9,
- the simulated annealing process is stopped when the temperature reaches the value 0.2 or when no move is accepted at a given temperature.

This annealing schedule was not intended to be optimal: we only wanted to evaluate the performances of the parallel algorithm as compared to those of the serial algorithm, subject to the same conditions.

4.2. THE TRANSPUTERS

We implemented the parallel algorithm on a network of Transputers. A Transputer is a 32-bit processor with its own memory. Communications occur only through four high-speed serial links, so that each Transputer can communicate with four neighbour Transputers. One link is used for communications between two Transputers only, so that parallel architectures are implemented simply by connecting the serial links between the pairs of communicating Transputers. T800 Transputers have an on-chip floating-point processor, which T414 Transputers have not. Instructions for communications are available in the software (OCCAM) and no data can be lost since these communications are synchronized. We use one Transputer as the master processor and we perform the computations on Transputers linked to the master. The architecture can be improved so that no Transputer has to be used only for communications, but this does not restrict the validity of our model.

Experiments were performed with 25, 49 and 81 chips on 3 and 6 Transputers. We shall present the most relevant results here, obtained on 81 chips in two cases: the communication time τ_r is small as compared to the computation time τ_0 ($\tau_0 \simeq 4.2$ msec and $\tau_r \simeq 0.5$ msec), and the communication and computation times are of the same order of magnitude ($\tau_0 \simeq 0.6$ msec and $\tau_r \simeq 0.3$ msec).

4.3. NUMERICAL RESULTS

Both temperature modes were investigated independently on a complete annealing, although they are not intended to be actually used on the whole temperature range.

We compared the behaviour of the high and low temperature modes to the behaviour of the sequential mode, on 100 different initial configurations. Figure 1a is a plot of the average final energy of each temperature step as a function of temperature; it can be seen that the high temperature mode behaves similarly to the sequential mode, whereas the low temperature mode decreases the energy quickly for high temperature values. This is due to the fact that, in the low temperature mode, the first accepted move is taken into account for updating the system. Since we used T414 Transputers without floating-point computations, the computation of the exponential is very long as compared to the execution of a simple instruction; thus, the first accepted move often happens to be a move which decreases the energy. In addition, the low-temperature mode is not expected to have the same acceptance rate as the sequential algorithm at high temperature: since all rejected moves are counted as steps of the Markov chain, and since the total number of moves at a given temperature is the same as in the sequential mode, the number of accepted moves is lower than in the sequential computation; therefore, the

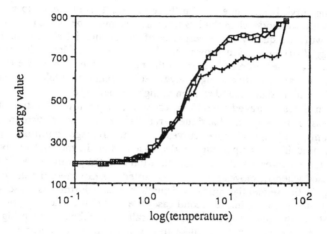

Figure 1a. Final value of the energy for a temperature step for the sequential mode (squares) and the high temperature (dots) and low temperature (crosses) modes.

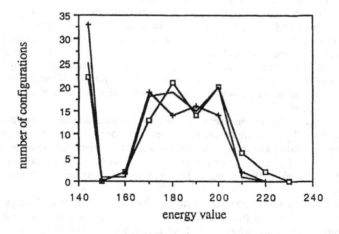

Figure 1b. Energy distribution of the initial configurations (right-hand peak), and energy distributions of the configurations after annealing (left-hand peaks).

probability of escaping from a local minimum is lower than it should be at the considered temperature, thus the average energy is lower. This introduces a bias which does not affect the final result in this problem, but might do in others; therefore, it is definitely not desirable, in general, to use the low-temperature mode at high temperature. At low temperature, the annealing curve is the same for the three modes. This allows us to switch from high to low temperature mode when the low temperature mode becomes more efficient, still complying with the quality of convergence of the sequential algorithm. The final and initial energy distributions are shown on Figure 1b: no significant difference between the three modes can be observed because of the nature of the problem we investigated; a difference should appear when using finely tuned annealing schedules, since the low temperature mode exhibits significant deviation at high temperature.

The computation times, averaged over 10 experiments, for each temperature step of the annealing process for the sequential and the parallel algorithms, are shown on Figure 2. On all diagrams, the upper three curves are the average duration of a temperaturestep measured if the temperature is decreased when L_t moves have been attempted; the lower three curves are the average duration of a temperature step if the temperature is decreased when L_a moves have been accepted. As expected, the duration of a temperature step in the sequential mode is virtually constant in the first case and increases sharply at low temperature in the second case. We find that the acceleration is poor at high temperature: the time required for the parallel algorithms is even higher than the time required for the sequential algorithm when the communication and synchronization time is close to the computation time (Figure 2b and 2c). This results from the high value of the acceptance rate: few moves are rejected, so that the parallel mode is not efficient. In contrast, at low temperature, the duration is almost divided by the number of processors. It can be seen on Figure 2c that the average duration of a temperature step, when the limit L_t is used, is small at high temperature for the low temperature mode; this is due to the fact that, in this mode, as mentioned before, the energy decreases quickly at high temperature; thus, the acceptance rate decreases too, and the number of rejected moves is high. Moreover, in this mode, all the rejected moves are counted as steps of the Markov chain. When the L_a limit is used, the overall annealing time is divided by 2 with 3 processors when the communication time is large, and by 2.5 when it is small. This value depends strongly on the annealing schedule: if more time is spent at low temperature, as is frequently the case in real optimization problems, the overall speed-up factor is higher.

Since we use a linear scale for temperature, whereas the decrease of the temperature is geometric, the overall gain in annealing time does not appear clearly; thus we present, on Figure 3, the cumulated annealing time for the sequential algorithm and for the parallel algorithm, using the L_a limit in the case where z_r is close to z_0. The total time is divided by 2 with this parallel method when 3 Transputers are used and by 3 when 6 Transputers are used.

Figure 4 exhibits a very good agreement between the measurements performed in the parallel temperature mode and the estimated values of t_p/t_s when the L_a limit is reached first (relations 1 and 2), and when the L_t limit is reached first (relations 1 and 3). The acceleration is higher when the L_t limit is used in the low temperature mode, but, since each temperature step is much longer than in the case of the L_a limit, it is definitively worthwhile using the L_a limit when it is reached first. To compute the estimates from the model, we evaluated $z_0 + z_r$ as the average duration of a temperature step divided by the number of parallel evaluations, and z_m as the average duration of a temperature step divided by the number of accepted moves. The average value of $\chi(T)$ was estimated from the sequential results.

Figures 2. Average duration of a temperature step versus temperature; results obtained in the sequential mode (squares), high temperature mode (dots) and low-temperature mode (crosses); upper three curves: temperature decreased when Lt moves have been attempted; lower three curves: temperature decreased when La moves have been accepted.

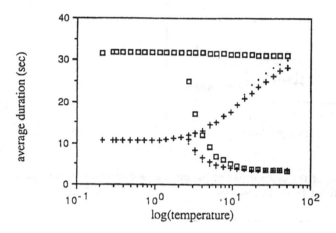

Figure 2a. Overhead time much smaller than computation time; measurements performed with three T414 Transputers.

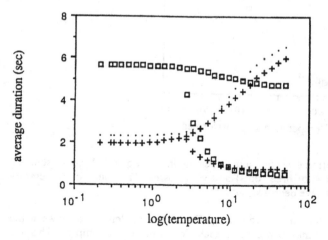

Figure 2b. Overhead time of the same order of magnitude as computation time; measurements performed with three T414 Transputers.

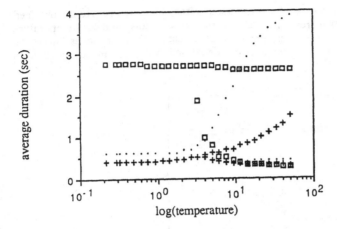

Figure 2c. Overhead time of the same order of magnitude as computation time; measurements performed with six T800 Transputers.

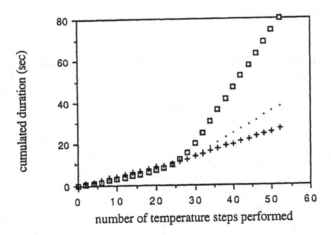

Figure 3. Cumulated duration of a complete annealing in the sequential mode (squares) and in the parallel mode with three (dots) and six (crosses) Transputers; temperature decreased when La moves have been accepted.

In the low temperature mode, communications were implemented between the working processors and the master processor each time a move is attempted. This was required for measuring the number of moves actually attempted in order to evaluate the model. For real implementation of this parallel algorithm, only synchronization on the accepted moves is required, so that the accelerations obtained in our example are the

Figures 4. Ratio of the duration of a temperature step in the parallel mode to the duration of a temperature step in the sequential mode; measurements performed with three Transputers; overhead of the same order of magnitude as computation time; squares: measurements results; +: results computed from the model when the La limit is used; black squares: measurements results; x: results computed from the model when the Lt limit is used.

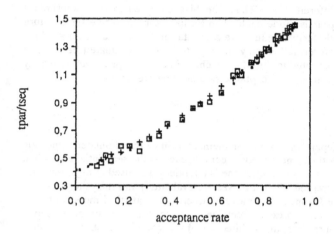

Figure 4a. High-temperature mode.

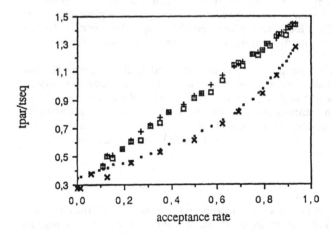

Figure 4b. Low-temperature mode.

worst case. A further modification of the parallel mode can be used: the low temperature mode is not used at high temperature because the first accepted move is the shortest to compute, which may introduce a bias, as observed in our experiments. If the processors are not synchronized when a move is accepted, that is, if the processors communicate the result of the move they have evaluated and start a new move as soon as their configuration is actualized, then, the computations become asynchronous, and the first accepted move may not be the one which is the shortest to compute, since the processors start their individual evaluations at different time. Thus, the bias observed in our experiments should vanish. This asynchronous mode could then be used for the whole temperature range and this method should further reduce the computation time, because no synchronization time is required. Nevertheless, only the rejected moves evaluated before one move is accepted should be counted in the Markov chain in order to preserve the quality of convergence of annealing, since the acceptance rate must be preserved.

5. Conclusion

We propose a problem independent parallel implementation of the simulated annealing algorithm, which guarantees the same quality of convergence as the sequential algorithm. The parallel algorithm consists of two modes: one is intended to be used at high temperature (at least one move is accepted when K moves are evaluated) and the other one is to be used at low temperature (at most one move is accepted). Statistical models of both modes are derived and compared to experiments on a simple placement problem, implemented on a network of Transputers; the architecture of the system consists of a "master" processor linked to K "slaves" processors. These models are expressed as functions of the acceptance rate, which enables an estimation of the acceleration for any optimization problem. They take into account the fact that, depending on the implementation of the sequential algorithm, the length of the Markov chain for each temperature step may be taken either equal to a given number of accepted moves or equal to a given number of attempted moves. The condition for switching from the high temperature mode to the low temperature mode will depend on the number of processors used, and on the length of the Markov chains.

As mentioned above, it is possible to increase the speed-up if the synchronization between the slaves is used only when a move is accepted. Thus, the speed-up evaluated from the models is the worst case and can be improved for real implementations.

Acknowledgments: The authors are very grateful to A. Trouvé and O. Catoni for their critical comments on the derivation of the effective number of moves. They wish to thank the Groupe de Soutien aux Utilisateurs of the CIRCE Computer Center.

6. Appendix

We denote by K the number of processors numbered from 1 to K, and by i, the number of accepted moves among the K moves attempted in parallel. We show in the following that the average value of the number of the first processor in the list which accepts a move is equal to $n^* = (K+1)/(K-r+1)$ (Catoni and Trouvé).

We denote by σ the number of the first processor in the list which accepts a move. The probability that τ is equal or higher than n is

$$P(\tau \geq n) = \frac{\binom{K-n+1}{j}}{\binom{K}{i}} = \frac{(K-n+1)(K-n)...(K-n-i+2)}{K(K-1)...(K-i+1)}$$

Thus,

$$P(\sigma=n) = P(\tau \geq n) - P(\tau \geq (n+1)) = \frac{\binom{K-n+1}{j} - \binom{K-n}{j}}{\binom{K}{i}}$$

which can be written as follows

$$P(\tau = n) = \frac{i(K-n)(K-n-1)...(K-n-i+2)}{K(K-1)...(K-i+1)}$$

The expectation value of σ, n^*, is equal to

$$n^* = \sum_{n=1}^{K-i+1} n.P(\sigma=n) = \sum_{n=1}^{K-i+1} P(\sigma \geq n)$$

Thus,

$$n^* = \sum_{n=1}^{K-i+1} \frac{(K-n+1)(K-n)...(K-n-i+2)}{K(K-1)...(K-i+1)} = \frac{1}{K(K-1)...(K-i+1)} \sum_{m=i}^{K} m(m-1)...(m-i+1)$$

The summation

$$\sum_{m=i}^{K} m(m-1)...(m-i+1)$$

is equal to the ith derivative for $x=1$ of

$$\sum_{n=0}^{K} x^n = \frac{1-x^{K+1}}{1-x} = \sum_{j=0}^{K} \binom{K+1}{j+1} (x-1)^j$$

Thus, the expectation value is

$$n^* \frac{i! \binom{K+1}{i+1}}{K(K-1)...(K-i+1)} = \frac{K+1}{i+1}$$

If we denote by r, the number of rejected moves, we have $i = K-r$, and

$$n^* = \frac{K+1}{K-r+1}$$

7. References

Kirkpatrick, S., Gelatt, C. and Vecchi, M., Optimization by Simulated Annealing, Science, Vol. 220, (1983), pp. 671-680.

Lam, J. and Delosme, J-M., Performance of a new annealing schedule, Proceedings of the 25th IEEE Design Automation Conference, (1988), pp. 306-311.

Otten, R. and van Ginneken, L., Stop criteria in simulated annealing, Proceedings of the IEEE International Conference on Computer Design, (1988), pp. 549-552.

Casotto, A., Romeo, F. and Sangiovanni-Vincentelli, A., A parallel simulated annealing algorithm for the placement of macro-cells, IEEE Transactions on CAD, Vol. CAD-6, No. 5, (1987), pp. 838-847.

Casotto, A. and Sangiovanni-Vincentelli, A., Placement of standard cells using simulated annealing on the connection machine, Proceedings of the IEEE International Conference on Computer Design, (1987), pp. 350-353.

Mallela, S. and Grover, L., Clustering based simulated annealing for standard cell placement, Proceedings of the 25th IEEE Design Automation Conference, (1988), pp. 312-317.

Darema, F., Kirkpatrick, S. and Norton, V.A., Parallel algorithms for chip placement by simulated annealing, IBM J. Res. Develop., Vol. 31, No. 3, (1987), pp. 391-402.

Brouwer, R. and Banerjee, P., A parallel simulated annealing algorithm for channel routing on a hypercube multiprocessor, Proceedings of the IEEE International Conference on Computer Design, (1988), 4-7.

Kravitz, S. and Rutenbar, R., Multiprocessor-based placement by simulated annealing, Proceedings of the 23th IEEE Design Automation Conference, (1986).

Rutenbar, R. and Kravitz, S., Layout by annealing in a parallel environment, Proceedings of the IEEE International Conference on Computer Design, (1986), pp. 434-437.

Jayaraman, R. and Rutenbar, R., floorplanning by annealing on a hypercube multiprocessor, Proceedings of the IEEE International Conference on Computer Aided Design, (1987), pp. 346-349.

Aarts, E. and de Bont, F., Habers, E. and van Laarhoven, P., Parallel implementations of the statistical cooling algorithm, Integration, the VLSI journal, Vol. 4, (1986), pp. 209-238.

Aarts, E. and van Laarhoven, P., Statistical cooling: a general approach to combinatorial optimization problems, Philips Journal of Research, Vol. 40, No. 4, (1985), pp. 193-226.

Geman, S. and Geman, D., Stochastic relaxation, Gibbs distributions, and the Bayesian restoration of images, IEEE Proceedings on Pattern analysis and machine intelligence, (1984), pp. 722-741.

Catoni, O. and Trouvé, A., A propos du recuit simulé synchrone, unpublished.

PARALLEL IMPLEMENTATION ON TRANSPUTERS OF KOHONEN'S ALGORITHM.

J.M. AUGER
INSTITUT NATIONAL DES TELECOMMUNICATIONS
9 rue Charles Fourier
91011 EVRY
FRANCE

1. Introduction

The study of neural algorithms generally necessitates a more or less intensive period of simulation. This is necessary in order to provide a better idea of the behaviour of the model and it allows to adjust the values of the coefficients that describe the algorithm. After this testing and learning step, one is able to use the model on real size applications and sometimes even to design dedicated VLSI chips (THEE, MEAD).

However this simulation time is often excessive even if one is using a very fast monoprocessor computer and this can lead to giving up the model simply because of prohibitive computation time. Kohonen's self-organization algorithm (KOHO1, LIPP) which has been already extensively used for several types of applications (KELL, KOHO2, ANGE, LALO, RITT) is one of the best known time-consuming neural algorithm.

To tackle this problem, different approaches have been followed. A first one, introduced by Oja (OJA) consists in simplifying the subproblem of finding the best matching unit. A second one proposed by Rodriguez et al (RODR) is a modification done to the initial algorithm, which they demonstrate does not alter the properties of the model. At the beginning of the learning step, the neural network is composed of very few cells. Then, dynamical creation of cells takes place. Consequently the total number of operations is decreased and so is the computaton time. A third one, we shall discuss longer, consists in distributing the algorithm. We shall see that the use of a loosely coupled architecture like a network of transputers allows to significantly reduce the computation time. The same approach has been used with success on the Backpropagation Algorithm (PETR, BOUR, ERNO). We will also consider the extension of the Kohonen algorithm to the solution of the Traveling Salesman Problem . This has been shown (ANGE) to be a very interesting and demonstrative example. This new implementation introduces some non trivial problems.

2. Self-Organising Maps

2.1. generalities on neural networks

Neural networks are massively parallel interconnected networks of simple and adaptive elements or neurons. A synaptic coefficient is attached to every connections between two neurons. Typically each neuron, performs a task similar to the one described by fig.1. It receives informations from its neighbors and computes its activity level according to the formula.below.

D. Gassilloud and J. C. Grossetie (eds.), Computing with Parallel Architectures: T.Node, 215–226.
© 1991 *ECSC, EEC, EAEC, Brussels and Luxembourg. Printed in the Netherlands.*

216

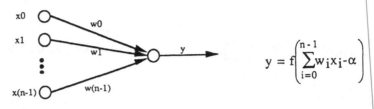

$$y = f\left(\sum_{i=0}^{n-1} w_i x_i - \alpha\right)$$

figure 1.

More complex nodes may include temporal integration or other type of temporal dependencies and more complex operations than summation.

Neural net models are specified by the net topology, neuron characteristics, and training or learning rules. These rules specify an initial set of synaptic coefficients and indicate how they should be adapted during use to improve performances. Both design procedures and learning rules are the topic of much current research.

2.2 Description of the Self-Organizing Maps Model

The self-organizing maps algorithm has been introduced by T. Kohonen (KOHO1) and further used in several types of applications (cf. 2.4). This model basically extracts the topological structures of the data presented to it. The responses from the network will be ordered spatially forming the "feature map". The basic principle is a unsupervised learning scheme. It learns from examples in an unsupervised way. In other words, there is no need for a teacher to tune the network; it is not supposed to learn associations between pairs of input patterns and expected output patterns. The cells compete in their activities. The winner and its neighbors developp into specific detectors of input signal pattern. The presence or absence of response in a special location is important not its value. Localized response is a central characteristic of the model.

The model proposed by Kohonen is a non-linear adaptive dynamical system with lots of lateral feedback connections whose evolution is described by a system of differential equations. It should be noted that the feedback is strongly distance-dependent and plays a prominent part in the formation of the feature maps.

On the following discussion we shall concentrate on its computational form obtained after simplifications that preserve the main characteristics of the model. Neurons are arranged in a two-dimensional grid. Each neuron j is connected to every input cells and its weights vector is denoted by w_j (fig.2).

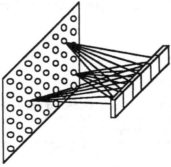

figure 2.

The topology of the interactions in the network defines which neurons are neighbors. It's the use of these neighborhoods that introduces the topological constraints in the final representations. they are responsible for spatially ordering the responses of the network. In a simplifyed way, they play the part of the lateral feedback connections in the original model. Fig.3 illustrates a 2-dimensionnal hexagonal grid on which we can define six or more immediate neighbors to each neurons.

2.3.   Algorithm

Notations:

m   : number of input neurons
n   : number of neurons on the map
W   : synaptic matrix (n X m)
w_{ji} : $W(j, i)$
w_j : vector corresponding to the jth line of W

> *Random initialization of the adaptive synaptic coefficients;*
> *Initialization of the size of the neighborhood;*
> **While** *not end* **do**
> > *choose an example x(t);*
> > **For** *j from 1 to n* **do**
> > > *(Compute the distance d_j between x(t) and neuron j)*
> > > $$d_j{}^2 = \sum_{i=0}^{m-1} \left(x_i(t) - w_{ji}(t) \right)^2$$
> > *done;*
> > *Compute the neuron j* whose distance to x(t) is minimal;*
> > **For** *j from 1 to n* **do**
> > > *If neuron j is located in the neighborhood Nj*(t) of neuron j* then*
> > > > $w_j(t + 1) = w_j(t) + \alpha(t)(x(t) - w_j(t))$
> > > *else*
> > > > $w_j(t + 1) = w_j(t)$
> > > *endif*
> > *done;*
> > *t=t+1;*
> > *end=$\alpha(t)<\alpha_{min}$*
> *done.*

During the learning process, the parameter α as well as the size of the neighborhood decrease. In a first period, α should start whith a value which is close to unity, thereafter decreasing gradually. The ordering of the w_j takes place during the initial step, while the remaining step is only needed for the fine adjustment of the map. As for the neighborhood, if it were too small at the beginning, the map would not be ordered

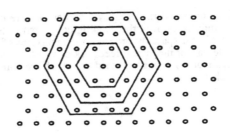

figure 3.

globally. According to Kohonen, he initial size of the neighborhood could even be more than half of the diameter of the network and shrinks linearly with time. This algorithm is computionaly time consuming.

2.4. Practical Applications

The self-organizing algorithm has been used in a variety of applications. Let's mention some of them.

Image Processing:
- Application of the Topological Maps Algorithm to the Recognition of Bi-dimensional Electrophoresis Images (KELL).
- Vector Quantization of Images Based Upon the Kohonen Self-Organizing Feature Maps", (NASR).

Speech Processing:
- "The "Neural" Phonetic Typewriter", (KOHO2)

Optimization:
- "Self-Organizing Feature Maps and the Travelling Salesman Problem", (ANGE).
- "Self-Organizing Feature Maps for the Multiple Travelling Salesman Problem" (GOLD).

Robotics:
- "Neuroplanners: Mechanisms for Subcognitive Control", (LALO).
- "Topology-conserving Maps for Motor Control", (RITT)

A.I.:
- "Applying Neural Computing to Expert Systemd Design" , (TIRR)

3. Parallel Implementation on Transputers

3.1 Transputer main characteristics

First let's do a brief recap about the parallel machine we shall use in our experiments. The transputer contains a complete CPU, local memory, a hardware task-scheduler and four serial communications links on a single chip. This allows it to be used to implement the Communicating Sequential Process model of parallel computing. CSP considers a parallel program to be equivalent to a number of sequential programs running concurrently while exchanging messages over synchronous messages channels. The vertices of the graph representing the communications are the processes and the edges the channels. The problem is to choose a topology for the network of Transputers and then to map the graph of communications on it.

3.2.   The distributed algorithm

We are aiming at distributing the algorithm mentioned above. For all that we decompose the domain, i.e. we distribute the n neurons among different processes. Thus, the synaptic matrix is divided into blocs W^k of equal size n^k. Each bloc, made of a subset of the synaptic coefficients vectors, corresponds to a specific process. W^k is a local variable for process k. This decomposition is very simple because every neurons play the same part; i.e. every neuron perform the same computation. As the domain is regular, no problem of load-balancing occurs. The algorithm becomes:

Notations:
p   : number of processes
W^k : sub-matrix (n^k X m) of W
//   : // means "every processes compute in parallel"

//*Random initialization of the adaptive synaptic coefficients;*
//*Initialization of the size of the neighborhood;*
While   *not end* **do**
    Choose an example x(t);
    Presentation of x(t) to all the processes;
    //*For j from 1 to n^k do*
        (Compute the distance d_j between x(t) and neuron j)

$$d_j{}^2 = \sum_{i=0}^{m-1} \left(x_i(t) - w^k{}_{ji}(t) \right)^2$$

done;
//*Compute the neuron j^{*k} whose distance to x(t) is minimal;*
Compute neuron $j^* = min(j^{*k})$ and communicate its identity to all the processes;
//*For j from 1 to n^k do*
    *If neuron j is located in the neighborhood $N_j^*(t)$ of neuron j^* **then***
        $w_j(t + 1) = w_j(t) + \alpha(t)(x(t) - w_j(t))$
    else
        $w_j(t + 1) = w_j(t)$
    endif
done;
t=t+1;
    end=$\alpha(t) < \alpha_{min}$
done.

Every process run the same algorithm very similar to the sequential one except the two steps involving communcations. Communications take place during the presentation of the example $x(t)$ to the k processes and during the search for the best matching unit.

3.3. Topology for the network of Transputers

In the previous paragraph we saw the principle of the distributed algorithm without refering to a particular configuration for the network of transputers. Our choice is driven by performance optimization purpose. the configuration takes into account the graph of communications and the limitation of the transputer architecture (four serial links).

The efficiency of a distributed algorithm is linked to the fact that the graph of communications is or is not included in the topology of processors. As we shall not use extra multiplexing code because such software is slow and tedious to write, two processes will be able to communicate only if they are allocated to neighboring transputers. The topology of processors should also take advantage of the link connectivity possible in a network of transputers.

The n-dimensional hypercube has become a popular topology for parallel supercomputers, because it can minimize the lengths of the path between processors.

With the current transputer architecture only a four-dimensional hypercube (sixteen transputers) can be built. We choose this topology for the performances are closely linked to the maximal distance between the processors.

Moreover Inmos plans to have ready for 1991 a new processor (POUN). Multiplexing hardware wil be added so that the physical links can be shared transparently. Inmos is also designing a matching routing chip so that transputers can be connected by a full-blown packet-switching network. The current limitations should be overcome (16,384-node hypercube claimed).

Other topologies like the ring, the torus, etc... allow to build biger networks of processors because the number of links per node doesn't grow when the size of the network increase (SIEM)

3.4. Communication steps

The algorithms are written so that only one process is allocated to a transputer (no time-slicing) and channels correspond to physical links. The graph of communications is included in a n-dimensional hypercube.

3.4.1. Propagating an example

The network of transputers communicates with the host computer through an additional transputer named root. It is mainly in charge of initiating the network and managing the host ressources access.

In a n-dimensional hypercube, if the distance between two nodes is L ($L \leq n$), L distinct paths exit between the two nodes. Fig.4 illustates the paths followed by an example from the root node to every nodes in the network.

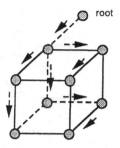

figure 4.

In the case of transputers, the time needed to transmit a m-dimensional real vector over a communication link can be approximated by a linear function of the size of the message.

$$t = t_s + m.t_c$$

where t_s is the time needed to start a communication and t_c the time needed to exchange a real value. The time required fro the propagation of the example from the root processor to every nodes of the network can therefore be estimated by:

$$T_{prop} \approx (t_s + m.t_c)\log_2(p)$$

where $p = 2^d$ is the number of processors.

3.4.2 Finding the best matching unit

The problem is to determine the minimum of a set of real values; each value belongs to a node of a n-dimensional hypercube. The following algorithm is divided into n steps.

> *For i from 0 to d-1 do*
> > *Concurrently*
> > > *-send to (d-i) processes among its d neighbors, the value of variable Min*
> > > *-receive from (d-i) processes among its d neighbors, the value of their variable Min and store them in the vector received_value;*
> >
> > *(update the content of Min)*
> > *For j from 1 to d-i do*
> > > *if received_value[j]< Min then*
> > > > *Min := received_value[j]*
> > >
> > > *endif*
> >
> > *done*
>
> *done*

For a process, the (d-i) neighbors are any of its d neighbors provided that if process i send a data to process j, process j must be waiting for data to come from process i.
After the n steps, the local variable Min in each process is the minimum of the initial set of real values. fig.5 illustrates the three steps of the algorithm on a 3-dimensional hypercube. We use the Occam symbols ? and ! to describe the communications.

222

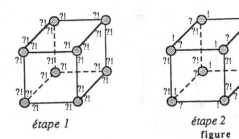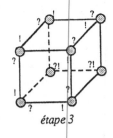

étape 1   étape 2   étape 3

figure 5.

Several creteria exist to evaluate a distributed algorithm. We consider the following:
Degree of distribution.
This notion is linked to the symmetry of the tasks perfomed by the different processes.
From that point of view, the previous algorithm offers a "textual symmetry" (RAYN). It
means that every processes run identical programs, but reference is made to the name of
the process, and each process has a specific name. Here, the name of the process
determines the neighbors to which it sends messages and from which it waits for
messages.
Computation time.
Communications are performed concurrently over transputer links. The computation time
can be approximated by:

$$T_{comp} \approx o(\log_2(p))$$

Number of messages.
It can be approximated by:

$$N = p. \sum_{i=1}^{d} i$$

$$N \approx o(\frac{1}{2}p.\log_2{}^2 p)$$

4.   Parallel Resolution of the Traveling Salesman Problem

4.1.   Description

Angeniol et al intended to show the potential of the self-organizing maps for optimization
problems and proposed a slightly modifyed algorithm to solve the Travelling Salesman
Problem (ANGE).
The TSP can be easily stated as a search for the shortest path passing once and only once
through every city in a given set. The problem has been shown to be NP-complete. An
approximate tour in their approach is given by a set of cells joined together in a one-
dimensional ring, evolving in a continuous manner toward the ultimate solution path. An
iteration step consists in the presentation of one city. The cell closest to the city moves
toward it and it induces its neighbors to do so as well, but with a decreasing intensity
along the ring. At the beginning of the process, the ring is made of a single cell. Then the
number of cells evolves according to cells creation and cells deletion processes. A cell is
duplicated if it was choosen more than once during a survey of all the cities. On the

contrary, a cell is deleted if it has not been choosen after three consecutive surveys. For more precise details, refer to (ANGE).

The main modification that has to be considered while distributing this algorithm is that the size of the network is no more fixed. Therefore, to reach good performances, the load has to be dynamically balanced between the processors.

4.2. Dynamic load-balancing

An important characteristic of this algorithm is its homogeneity. In other words each of its elements, cells, correspond the same computation (FOX). Such an algorithm can be load-balanced by allocating an equal number of elements by processor.

4.3. Parallel implementation

The ith row of matrix W corresponds to the cell with number i on the ring. In addition, let's consider a ring included in the n-dimensional hypercube. Processors are numbered from 1 to p along this ring as illustated by fig.6.

W is divided into p blocs W^k. The blocs of the synaptic matrix are assigned to the different processes in a way preserving the ring topology; i.e. two adjacent neurons on the ring belong either to the same process or to two different processes, directly connected in the hypercube. The main variables local to processor k are:

- W^k

- $v(k), v(k+1)$

where $v(k)$ is the number of the first row of W allocated to processor k. Consequently $W^k(i) = W(v(k)+i)$. The condition for load-balance is:

$$v(1)=0$$
$$v(k)=E[v \cdot v(k-1)] \qquad 1 < k \leq p$$
$$v(p+1)=p$$

- Δ^k

Where Δ^k is the relative variation of the number of cells on processor k.

Creation and deletion processes run concurrently on the p processors. For processor k, the duplication of the ith row of W is:

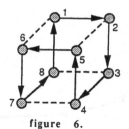

figure   6.

224

$$For\ j\ from\ v(k+1)-v(k)\ to\ i+1\ step\ -1\ do$$
$$|\ \ w^k_{j+1}=w^k_j$$
$$done;$$
$$w^k_{i+1}=w^k_i;$$
$$\Delta^k=\Delta^k+1$$

For processor k, the deletion of the ith row of W is:

$$For\ j\ from\ i\ to\ v(k+1)-v(k)-1\ do$$
$$|\ \ w^k_j=w^k_{j+1}$$
$$done;$$
$$\Delta^k=\Delta^k-1$$

For all k, $v(k)$ is updated by the transmission of Δ^k along the ring. The load is balanced after a complete survey of the cities. The process is initiated by processor number p which knows the number n of cells and sends it to processor number 1. The latter computes the value of $v(1)$, sends it with n to processor 2 and begins a communication step if the computed $v(1)$ doesn't match the actual value. And so on between processor 2 and its successors. If the load is already balanced, a real value is just transmitted along the ring. As more communications take place, lower performances have to be expected by comparison with the distributed algorithm discribed in chapter 3.

5.   Results

The results reported in this chapter were obtained using programs written in OCCAM language running on INMOS boards B012 with T800 processors. The examples were two-dimensional vectors. Analytical results show that the speed-up is a growing function of the examples dimensionality. So higher performances have to be expected for input signals of larger dimensionality.
Fig.7 describes the computation time evolution related to the number of processors.
The size of the network (1000 neurons) and the number of examples (688000) are fixed.

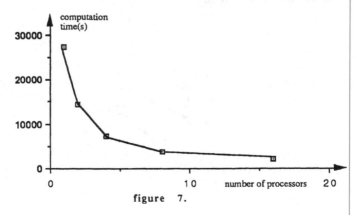

figure   7.

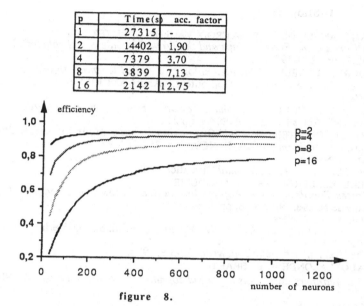

p	Time(s)	acc. factor
1	27315	-
2	14402	1,90
4	7379	3,70
8	3839	7,13
16	2142	12,75

figure 8.

Fig.8 describes the efficiency evolution related to the number of neurons.
Concerning the algorithm that solves the TSP, fig.9 describes the efficiency evolution related to the number of neurons. In the tab below, performances are compared to the previous one for 100 neurons and 34200 examples.

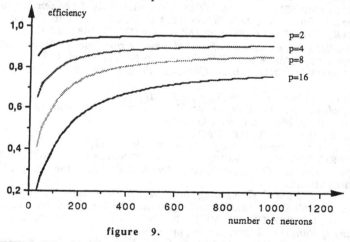

figure 9.

efficiency (%)	p=2	p=4	p=8	p=16
Kohonen	91,1	83,0	66,9	42,9
PVC	90,6	77,0	60,7	39,2

226

6. Bibliography

(ANGE) ANGENIOL B., DE LA CROIX VAUBOIS G., LE TEXIER J.Y.
"Self-organizing Feature Maps and the Travelling Salesman Problem", Neural Networks, Vol. 1, pp. 289-293, 1988.

(BOUR) BOURRELY J. *"Parallelization of a neural learning algorithm on a hypercube"*, Hypercube and distributed Computers,F.André and J.P.Verjus Editors North holland, 1989.

(ERNO) ERNOULT C. *"Performance of Backpropagation on a parallel transputer-based machine"*, Actes NEURO-NIMES 88, pp 311-324.

(GOLD) GOLDSTEIN M., *"Self-Organizing Feature Maps for the Multiple Travelling Salesman Problem"*, Procs. INNC90, pp. 258-261.

(INMO) INMOS,
"OCCAM 2, Reference Manual", Prentice-Hall.

(KELL) KELLER M., FOGELMAN-SOULIE
"Cartes Topologiques & Application en Reconnaissance d'Images d'Electrophorèse", Actes de NEURO-NIMES 88, pp 403-414.

(KOHO1) KOHONEN T.
"Self-organization and Associative Memory", Berlin: Spring-Verlag, 1984.

(KOHO2) KOHONEN T.
"The "Neural" Phonetic Typewriter", IEEE, 1988.

(LALO) LALONDE W. R., GRAF D.H.
"Neuroplanners: Mechanisms for Subcognitive Control", Actes NEURO-NIMES 88, pp 34-48.

(LECU) LE CUN
"Modèles connexionnistes de l'apprentissage", thèse de doctorat, Juin 1987.

(LIPP) LIPPMANN R. P.
"An Introduction to Computing with Neural Nets", IEEE ASSP Magazine, April 1987.

(MEAD) MEAD C. and MAHOWALD M. *" A silicon model of early visual processing"* Neural Networks, vol.1,pp.91-97, 1988.

(OJA) LAMPINEN J. and OJA E.*"Fast Computation of Kohonen Self-Organization"*, to appear in Proc. NATO ARW Workshop, Les Arcs, France, Feb.27-Mar.3,1989

(PETR) PETROWSKI A., PERSONNAZ L., DREYFUS G., GIRAULT C.
"Parallel Implementations of neural network simulations", Hypercube and distributed Computers, F.André and J.P.Verjus Editors North holland, 1989

(POUN) POUNTAIN D., *"Virtual Channels: the new generation of transputers"*, BYTE April 90.

(RITT) RITTER H., MARTINETZ T., SCHULTEN K.
"Topology-conserving Maps for Motor Control", Department of Physics, Technical University of Munich, D-8046 Garching.

(RUME) RUMELHART D.E., ZIPSER D.
"Competitive Learning", Cognitive science, 9:75-112, 1985.

(THEE) THEETEN J.B., MAUDUIT N., DURANTON M., SIRRAT J.A.*"The LNEURO-CHIP: a digital VLSI with On-chip Learning Mechanism"*, Procs. INNC90, pp. 593-596.

(TIRR) TIRRI H.
"Applying Neural Computing to expert system design", actes de la 3ème conf. internationale sur les fondations d'organisation de données et des algorithmes, Juin 1989.

(RODR) RODRIGUEZ S., ALMEIDA B. *"Improving the Learning Speed in Topological Maps of Patterns"*, Procs. INNC90, pp. 813-816.

(SIEM) H.P. SIEMON, A. ULTSCH *"Kohonen Networks on Transputers: Implementation and animation"* Procs. INNC90, pp 643-646.

LEARNING ON VLSI: A GENERAL-PURPOSE DIGITAL NEUROCHIP

M. DURANTON and J.A. SIRAT
Laboratoires d'Electronique Philips
3 avenue Descartes, B.P. 15
94451 Limeil-Brevannes Cédex, France

ABSTRACT. We present a general-purpose digital neurochip for the resolution and the learning stages of neural algorithms. It updates neuron states and synaptic coefficients in parallel on input neurons. Using a standard technology (1.6 m CMOS), a chip may implement 32 input and 32 output neurons with 16-bit synaptic coefficients. Typical on-chip operation time is 2 s for updating one neuron state or 32 coefficients and with 8-bit input neurons. Moreover, many circuits can be assembled to simulate structured or large-size nets, as well as higher-order nets. By choosing adapted parameters, most of the learning rules considered so far for neural networks can be programmed. In particular, the error backpropagation algorithm is implemented by a simple arrangement of chips with optimal use of the chip parallelism and minimal interchip communications. Specification of the required precision for synaptic weights is given by theoretical arguments and numerical simulations: 16 bits per synapse should be sufficient for almost all the considered cases.
Keywords: architecture, cascadability, digital, learning, neural networks, parallelisms, VLSI.

1. Introduction

Existing computers are stretched to their limits when performing complex activities such as image or speech recognition, whereas solutions to these problems are obvious for human beings. Artificial neural networks are inspired by the massively parallel and interconnected structure of the brain. The simplest mathematical model considers neurons as threshold units which achieve the weighted sum of their inputs and emit a signal if the threshold is exceeded. The learning behaviour is implemented by adjustment of the strengths (weights) of the connections between neurons, called synapses, in order to create the behaviours of classification, associative memory and generalization which are expected from artificial neutral networks.

Neural network simulations are very time-consuming tasks for ordinary sequential computers and the need for fast evaluation of large networks becomes more and more acute.

The learning procedures are also very computer intensive: there is a definitive need for hardware able to perform most common learning rules. In order to improve the

D. Gassilloud and J. C. Grossetie (eds.), Computing with Parallel Architectures: T.Node, 227–241.

performances of the simulations, parallel dedicated circuits have already been developed, mostly with an analogue and fully parallel approach (Graf et al. (1988), Alspector et al. (1987)), but generally without learning schemes or for specific learning rules (Widrow-Hoff algorithm (Personnaz et al. (1989)), Boltzmann machine (Alspector et al. (1987), Farhat (1987))).

In spite of the great computational power that specific analogue or optical devices (Wagner and Psaltis (1987) can offer, they involve technological problems that prevent their ability from being an efficient answer to today's neural problems. Furthermore, the interface between these non-standard devices and the environment also decreases their performances, because postprocessing is usually carried out through a conventional computer. These considerations led us to propose a fully digital CMOS VLSI which allows various kinds of neural networks and learning algorithms to be implemented. It is designed to be highly efficient in matrix operations as well as in implementing most learning rules. To validate theoretical assumptions and to analyse a large range of solutions and learning algorithms, a fully digital device offers the undeniable benefit of a known precision, well-defined states and full control of the parameters.

Special attention was paid to making the device as cascadable as possible, so that networks of virtually any structure and any size can be built with several chips. The degree of parallelism is also increased by simultaneous use of several circuits.

The implementation of a fully parallel digital circuit implies size and connectivity problems. To overcome them, we have chosen to parallelize only the loop on input neurons: the effects of "input" neurons on one "output" neuron are computed in parallel, in the resolution phase as well as in the learning phase. This choice of parallelism allows the updating of the neuron states or the synaptic coefficients converging to one output neuron with any succession of output neurons; a complete evaluation of neurons is not necessary in order to update only one of them. (This particularity is useful for implementing certain kinds of learning algorithms such as minimal overlap (Krauth and Mezard (1987)) or the self-organizing feature map of Kohonen (Kohonen (1984))). Implemented on conventional computers with software, a fully connected neural network requires a computation time growing as the square of the number of neurons. For one circuit, the computing time grow only linearly, giving a significant improvement over software simulations. This improvement persists during he learning phase; the whole set of synaptic coefficients related to a given "output" neuron is parallelly updated.

In Section 2.1 we describe the overall architecture of the chip and how it performs the evaluation of new states of neurons. In Section 2.2 we give a description of the circuits involved during the learning phase and the arithmetic operations that are performed. In Section 3.1 we explain how to implement local learning algorithms on the chip. We chose to use the Kohonen learning rule because it highlights many problems that may appear when implementing local rules. The implementation of non-local learning rules is a more difficult task because it involves information distributed in the whole network. However, with our circuit some of these can also be implemented; this will be described in Section 3.2 for the error backpropagation method. In Section 4, we briefly present our simulations for the numerical precision required for synapses. Section 5 deals with the association of several chips in order to simulate large networks.

2. A Digital Circuit for Neural Networks

2.1. IMPLEMENTATION OF THE RESOLUTION STAGE

A first version of the circuit which did not include on-chip learning has already been presented (Duranton et al. (1989)). We describe it briefly in this section. The core of the chip is the synaptic matrix (Figure 1). It contains N^2 "synapses" (for N input and N output neurons) that are coded in 2's complement over 8 or 16 bits (below, we give simulations and calculations showing that learning algorithms with floating point numbers can be emulated with 16-bit integers in most cases). This matrix is a RAM, which means that the synaptic coefficients are modifiable as required by learning rules. The state of neurons (signed or not) is coded over 1 to 8 bits. The state of output neuron i, V_i, is updated according to:

$$V_i(t + 1) = f\left(\sum_{j=1}^{N} W_{ij} \times V_j(t) \right) ,$$

where f is a one-variable function, e.g. a sigmoid. The circuit computes the argument of f, $\sum_{j=1}^{N} W_{ij} \times V_j(t)$, which is the main part of the calculations. The multiplications of synaptic values by one bit of the state of each neuron (V_j) and the additions of these products

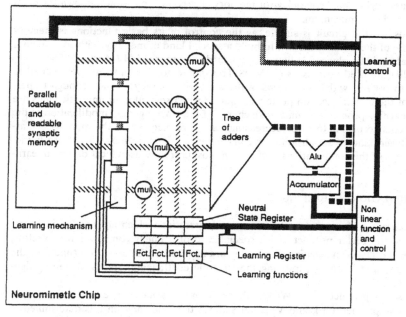

Figure 1. Circuit architecture (for the sake of clarity, only a four-neuron circuit is shown).

are fully parallel. The multiplication step $W_{ij} \times V_j$ is serialized over the different bits of V_j, N 8-bit by 8-bit parallel multipliers being replaced by N 8-bit AND gates, to save the silicon area that parallel multipliers would require. The partial products are accumulated in a shift register.

The need for maximum flexibility of the circuit leads to the application of the function f off chip (for example with look-up tables), as long as the new neuron' states go off chip serially. The new state of the ith neuron may then be written back into the neural state register of the same or another integrated circuit. Some other facilities could also be offered by the chip:

- A dual neural state register may be used to allow for different updating schedules, for example in Hopfield nets. In this case, output is fed back to the input synchronously or asynchronously (Cheung et al. (1987)). In synchronous mode, the computed state of neurons waits in a register until all neurons are updated; then the whole register is written into the register used for the calculations. In asynchronous mode, the newly computed neuron is written directly into the register used for the next calculation.
- An arithmetic unit could be used to accumulate internal partial products, but also to allow for accumulation of external partial products. Thus arrangements of neurochips may implement structured, larger-sized, higher-precision, or higher-order networks.
- A column of latches would enable free access to the synaptic memory while the rest of the circuit performs an updating. In fact, this columns of latches is a part of the learning processors.

The last feature is more useful with 8-bit neurons: the on-chip computation loop being executed eight times, the delay for memory access - without slowing down the computation rate - is at a maximum.

The use of the circuit is simple, as the control of its basic functions is memory mapped. One of the initial ideas was to build a special kind of memory, with some neural abilities, that could be plugged in lieu of a standard computer RAM (Morton (1988)).

Parallel oriented processors (INMOS Transputer, for instance) are well suited to the design fo systems with associations of these circuits, as they are fast enough to perform part of the communication protocol required when several neuromimetic chips are used. The learning processors, which take charge of the learning task (modification of the W_{ij} coefficients according to error-decreasing rules) are placed with the memory cell array. The chosen kind of serialisation and the inner architecture make it easy to implement the steps of the computations required in most currently used local or global learning schemes.

2.2. IMPLEMENTATION OF LEARNING

The VLSI circuit performs two generic vectorial operations which are needed in neural computation: the scalar product and a special case of a linear combination of vectors, which we call a "Hebbian learning step". They are involved in the execution (updating the neuron states) and learning (updating the synaptic coefficients) stages of neural algorithms.

The scalar product $\sum_{j=1}^{N} W_{ij} V_j$, where W_{ij} is the synaptic coefficient from input neuron j to output neuron i, and V_j is the state of the input neuron j, is determined in parallel on input neurons. Final updating of the state V_i of the output neuron i - application of a sigmoid or a threshold function - is realized off chip.

The Hebbian learning step modifies all the synaptic coefficients W_{ij} converging to a given output neuron i in a single time step according to $W_{ij}(t+1) = (W_{ij}(t) + _iV_j$, where $_i$ is an integer (scalar) "increment" that depends only on the output neuron i. V_j is the state of the input neuron j which may be replaced by some other quantity related to input neuron j in special cases.

It is worth noting that, after running a Hebbian learning step, the norm of the ith row of the synaptic matrix, i.e. $\sum^N_{j=1} (W_{ij})^2$, is updated with no read operation on the synaptic coefficients:

$$\sum_{j=1}^{N} [W_{ij}(t+1)]^2 = \sum_{j=1}^{N} [W_{ij}(t) + _iV_j]^2$$

becomes:

$$\sum_{j=1}^{N} [W_{ij}(t+1)]^2 = \sum_{j=1}^{N} [W_{ij}(t)]^2 + 2\Delta_i \sum_{j=1}^{N} W_{ij}(t) V_j + {}^2_i \sum_{j=1}^{N} (V_j)^2.$$

The first term is the previously determined norm at step t. The second term is a calar product that is computed as described previously. As the last term does not depend on the W_{ij}, it is calculated off chip. In the case of a limited range of W_{ij}, the formula holds as long as the W_{ij} coefficients remain within their bounds.

2.3. HARDWARE IMPLEMENTATION OF THE BASIC OPERATIONS

The principle is the simultaneous modification of the coefficients W_{ij} related to one output neuron i. This is carried out by N learning processors acting in a single-instruction multiple-data (SIMD) architecture. Each of the N processors determines the modification of its synaptic coefficient according to a piece of data related to neuron i (this information is shared among the N learning processors) and data which are related to neuron j (this information is not shared with the other learning processors). The modification of the synaptic coefficient could be an increment, a decrement or no change.

To latch the synaptic weights, the resolution part of the calculation uses the learning processors. The first steps of learning and retrieval processes are the same: for the modification of the weights of the output neuron i, the N modules are loaded in parallel with their coefficients. Then they compute the weight change according to the data stored in the related neural state register and a learning register used to store the value related to the neuron j, and the N weights are written back in parallel into the memory.

The learning processors perform the following operations on the synaptic coefficients: $W_{ij} = W_{ij} + DW_{ij}$ with $DW_{ij} = g(V_i, V_j) \times \delta_i$. The term δ_i is associated with the output neuron i while the function g depends on values related to neuron i and neuron j. In fact, the g function can have one of three output values: +1, -1 or 0. Thus the modification of W_{ij} could be $W_{ij} = W_{ij} \pm \delta_i$, or $W_{ij} = W_{ij}$. With this mechanism, it is possible to implement true multiplications for modifying the weights in several steps.

To calculate the relevant synaptic coefficient increment, the learning processors are composed of two units:
- One general unit, shared by all processors, selects the type of operation to be processed according to the data stored in the learning register. This unit also generates the common increment δ_i.
- N local units (for input neurons) produce the control signals for the adder-subtractors. The local units receive their information from the general unit and from the portion of the neural state register storing the state of the input neuron related to the particular synapse to be modified.

The various learning rules are implemented only by modifying the truth table of the general unit, and by performing several elementary learning phases. We now give a non-exhaustive review of the learning algorithms we can implement with this chip.

3. Programming Learning Rules

3.1. LOCAL LEARNING RULES

In many learning rules, modification of W_{ij} involves only the input neuron state V_j and the output neuron state V_i (V_j and V_i might be replaced by other quantities related to neurons j and i respectively, e.g. desired states). We call them local as the procedure needs no information from neurons that are not connected by the considered W_{ij}. This class of learning rules includes the following:
- Prescriptive rules of different forms: auto- and heteroassociative Hebb rules (Hopfield (1982), Meir and Domany (1988)), Hebb rule generalized to higher-order nets (Sirat et al. (1990)), Hebb rule with linear and constant terms (Peretto (1988)).
- Iterative rules for hetero- or autoassociative memories: perceptron rule (Minski and Papert (1969)), Widrow-Hoff delta rule (Widrow and Winter (1988)), gardening the basins of attraction (Poppel and Krey (1987)), minimum overlap rule (Krauth and Mezard (1987)).
- Non-supervised learning rules to extract feature maps (Kohonen (1984)), perceptive fields (Linsker (1988)), principal (Sanger (1988)) or independent components (Jutten).
- Stochastic rules such as that used for the Boltzmann machine (Farhat (1987)).

All the above-mentioned algorithms can be programmed with a specific choice of the variables Δ_i and V_j. More details will be given in a further publication. For the sake of brevity, we only consider one example here, namely the self-organizing feature map of Kohonen as described in (Lippmann (1987)). This programming case is non-trivial as it requires some transformations of the learning parameters to take into account the particular form of the learning rule.

3.1.1. *Example of Programming: Kohonen's Self-Organizing Map.*
Let us take a Kohonen network with N input units and M output nodes. The state of input unit j is denoted by V_j. The vector corresponding to node i is given by its N components $(W_{ij})_{j=1,N}$. As the modification of the W_{ij} is a linear combination of W_{ij} and V_j, we are led to use the variable change $W_{ij} = \gamma_i \Gamma_{ij}$ where the W_{ij} remain the actual synaptic coefficients and the Γ_{ij} are stored in the synaptic memory of the chip. The γ_i are scaling factors associated with out-

put nodes i. With an appropriate adaptation of the Υ_i, we reduce the coefficient modification into a Hebbian learning step:

$$W_{ij}(t+1) = W_{ij}(t) + \eta(t)[V_j - W_{ij}(t)]$$

become:

$$\gamma_i(t+1)\Gamma_{ij}(t+1) = \gamma_i(t)\Gamma_{ij}(t) + \eta(t)[V_j - \gamma_i(t)\Gamma_{ij}(t)].$$

When we take $\gamma_i(t+1) = \gamma_i(t)[1-\ (t)]$, and carry out simple algebra, the modification formula with the new variable reduces to:

$$\Gamma_{ij}(t+1) = \Gamma_{ij}(t) + \frac{\eta(t)}{\gamma_i(t)[1-\eta(t)]}\,V_j.$$

Then, the learning procedure is written as follows:

(1) Set the initial values $\gamma_i(t=0)$ to 1. Initialize weights: write into the memory of the chip the chosen random values of $[\Gamma_{ij}(t=0)]_{j=1,N} = [W_{ij}(t=0)]_{j=1,N}$ and compute the initial square moduli $[m_i(t=0)]^2 = \sum_{j=1}^{N}[\Gamma_{ij}(t=0)]^2$ for every output node i (off chip).

(2) Present the new input V_j to the chip and compute its square modulus $m_V^2 = \sum_{j=1}^{N} V_j^2$ (off chip).

(3) Compute distances to all output nodes i:
  • compute the scalar product $s_i = \sum_{j=1}^{N} \Gamma_{ij}(t)V_j$ (on chip);
  • deduce the squared distance between node i and input vectors (off chip):

$$d_i^2 = \sum_{j=1}^{N}[W_{ij}(t) - V_j]^2,$$

$$d_i^2 = \sum_{j=1}^{N}[W_{ij}(t)]^2 - 2\sum_{j=1}^{N} W_{ij}(t)V_j + \sum_{j=1}^{N} V_j^2,$$

$$d_i^2 = [\gamma_i(t)m_i(t)]^2 - 2\gamma_i(t)s_i + m_V^2,$$

where

$$[m_i(t)]^2 = \sum_{j=1}^{N}[\Gamma_{ij}(t)]^2.$$

(4) Select the output node i_0 with minimum distance d_{i_0}.

(5) Update stored weights Γ_{ij}, scaling coefficients γ_i, and row norms m_i of the stored matrix Γ at nodes i in the neighbourhood of i_0:

$$\Gamma_{ij}(t+1) = \Gamma_{ij}(t) + \frac{\eta(t)}{\gamma_i(t)[1 - \eta(t)]} \, V_j,$$

$$\gamma_i(t+1) = \gamma_i(t)[1 - \eta(t)],$$

$$[m_i(t+1)]^2 = [m_i(t)]^2 + 2s_i \frac{\eta(t)}{\gamma_i(t)[1 - \eta(t)]} + \left\{ m_V \frac{\eta(t)}{\gamma_i(t)[1 - \eta(t)]} \right\}^2.$$

(6) Go to step 2.

3.2. ERROR BACKPROPAGATION

This very popular rule has given a great impulse to neural network research and applications (Rumelhart et al. (1986), Proc. NIPS Conf. (1988)). In contrast to the previously enumerated rules, it is non-local, so efficient hardware implementation is not straightforward. We propose here a simple arrangement of a few chips that uses them with maximum computing speed and minimum interchip communication. It is based on algorithmic decomposition into local stages, namely scalar products and Hebbian learning steps. Hence the chip described before needs no modification.

We girst give a formal description of the algorithm. Let us take a multilayer perceptron with $K+1$ layers of neurons, and N_k neurons at layer k. The state of neuron i in layer k (k=0 to K) is denoted by V^k_i. The synaptic coefficient connecting input neuron j (layer k-1) to output neuron i (layer k) is W^k_{ij}. f is the sigmoid response function of the neurons.

Backpropagation learning is performed by successive steps:
1) Initialize the W^k_{ij}.
2) Present a new input V^0_i.
3) Compute the neurons' states in the following layers $(V^k_i)_{k=1,K}$ iteratively:

$$V^k_i = f\left(\sum_{j=1}^{N_{k-1}} W^k_{ij} V^{k-1}_j \right);$$

4) compute the error at output neurons i, i.e.

$$\delta^K_i = 2f'\left(\sum_{j'=1}^{N_{K-1}} W^K_{ij'} V^{K-1}_{j'} \right)[(V^K_i)^{\text{desired}} - V^K_i],$$

where f' is the derivative of the function f;
5) backpropagate errors from layer K to layer 1:

$$\delta^{k-1}_j = 2f'\left(\sum_{j'=1}^{N_{K-1}} W^k_{ij'} V^{k-1}_{j'} \right) \sum_{i=1}^{N_k} \delta^k_i W^k_{ij};$$

6) update the synaptic coefficients:

$$W_{ij}^k(t+1) = W_{ij}^k(t) + \eta \delta_i^k V_j^{k-1} \qquad (k = 1 \text{ to } K),$$

where η is the learning rate;
7) go to step 2.

Parallel computation is required for steps 3), 5) and 6). Steps 3) and 5) involve a scalar product with the rows of the synaptic matrix (input: states V_{j}^{k-1} of the neurons) and of the transposed synaptic matrix (input: errors δ_i^k at the output neurons) respectively. Step 6) can be viewed as a Hebbian learning step either with the synaptic matrix (input: states V_{j}^{k-1} of the neurons) or with the transposed synaptic matrix (input: errors δ_i^k at the output neurons). Now, architecture and programming of the backpropagation system comes naturally: one subsystem stores the direct synaptic matrix, W_{ij}^k, for k=1 to K (DS). The second stores the transposed matrix W_{ji}^k for k=K to 2 (TS). Input values are the V_{j}^{k-1} and the errors δ_i^k (for DS and TS respectively). Increments are $\Delta i = \eta \delta_i$, and $\Delta j = \eta V_{j}^{k-1}$ respectively. Figure 2 shows an example of the arrangement of chips for this algorithm.

We now give some remarks.

The coherent initialization (step 1)) and modification (step 6)) of the synaptic coefficients guarantees that the matrix stored in TS is always the transposed matrix of DS.

An apparently similar system architecture has been proposed recently (Paulos and Hollis (1988)). It performs steps 3) and 5) on two separate subsystem. However, step 6) needs external computation on a conventional-sequential-processor. Therefore communication flow between subsystem and processor is a bottle-neck (read-write of the W_{ij} at

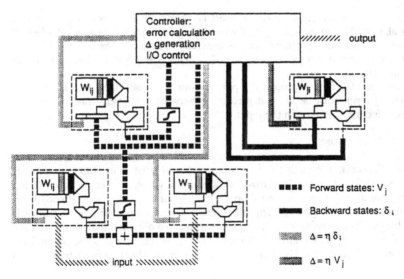

Figure 2. Multilayer perceptron with error backpropagation learning rule.

236

each learning step). Our system overcomes this drawback. Moreover, we use a general-purpose neurochip.

We only considered here the simplest version of the backpropagation algorithm. Variants which need the moduli of the synaptic rows - as defined in the preceding example - can easily be programmed (e.g. the partial conjugate gradient (Kramer and Sangiovanelli-Vincentelli (1988)) or the rationalized backpropagation (Makram-Ebeid et al. (1989))). Moreover, we could implement a more sophisticated variant - which contains a momentum term (Rumelhart et al. (1986)) - with minor modifications of the chip.

4. Neural Learning with Integer Synapses

4.1. PRESENTATION/FORMULATION OF THE PROBLEM

Most of the simulations and theoretical predictions for neural algorithms assume that synaptic coefficients are of the real type. In the case of a dedicated hardware implementation - as we use - architecture complexity is greatly reduced when limited-range integer-type coefficients are used. What is the precision required on the synaptic coefficients for the different algorithms? We give here a first estimate based on numerical arguments and on computer simulations.

4.2. THEORETICAL CONSIDERATIONS

A first estimate of the required precision can be given by theoretical considerations in simple cases:
1) Hopfield nets: when the Hebbian rule is used, random walk analysis (see for example (Sirat et al. (1990))) shows that a typical value of W_{ij} during learning is $\pm \sqrt{P}$, where P is the number of learned patterns. As P is generally of order N, the number of input neurons, the precision has to be about $\log_2 P/2$. This is in good agreement with numerical simulations.
2) Single- and multilayer perceptrons: if input neurons are "real", the relative precision on the (first) layer must be at least greater. Otherwise the quantification noise reduces the effective precision on the input.

4.3. COMPUTER SIMULATIONS

4.3.1. *Hopfield Networks.* We focus here on iterative learning rules in Hopfield content-addressable memories. For the Widrow-Hoff algorithm which converges towards the pseudoinverse solution (Diederich and Opper (1987)), some results have already been published (Personnaz et al. (1989)). The numerical simulations give the required precision: about $\log_2 N$ bits per synapse for N input neurons. We obtained a similar result for the minimum overlap rule (Krauth and Mezard (1987)) which provides the optimal capacity for supervised learning in Hopfield or single-layer networks (binary patterns).

4.3.2. *Multilayered Networks.* We have studied two cases which correspond to "real application" conditions:

1) Classification: a three-layer perceptron (56 inputs, 20 hidden, 5 hidden, 1 output) was trained with the backpropagation algorithm to classify objects. Inputs correspond to different extracted and processed features. Inputs are real values with a typical relative variation range of 10. Learning times vary a little when accuracy on synaptic coefficients is decreased from real type to 16 bits. However, this time diverges below 16 bits. It is important to notice that in this case the momentum term does not help in learning.

2) Real data compression (autobackpropagation in a two-layer, linear network): this algorithm had been proposed to compress information coded on several "real" symbols such as blocks of pixels (Cottrell et al., Bourlard and Kamp (1988)). The architecture of the net is N real input neurons, n real hidden neurons, N real output neurons ($n < N$). Figure 3 shows the performance - signal-to-noise ratio - achieved with the original algorithm vs. the number of bits per synaptic coefficient during learning (Cottrell et al.) (i.e. autobackpropagation with linear neurons ($f(x)=x$) and no momentum term). Quantization effects appear below 16 bits per synapse. We also have verified that quantization on the different variables used during learning does not alter the results (V_j, 8 bits; δ_i, less than 6 bits; Δ, less than 8 bits).

These first studies show that 16-bit coefficients should be sufficient to achieve learning in most of the cases. As no special quantization procedure has been used, we expect that algorithms dedicated to learning with integers will need far less precision on the synapses. Moreover, not implementing the momentum term should not be critical for most of the applications, as already observed (Makram-Ebeid (1989), Diederich and Opper (1987)).

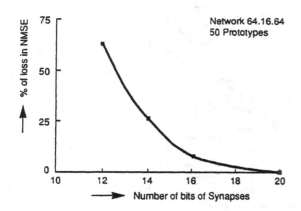

Figure 3. Loss of performance of the network used for image compression as a function of the number of bits per synapse during the learning stage (NMSE, normalized mean square error).

238

5. Examples of System Architecture

The circuit can fit into various systems for many neural network architectures.

The first possible use of one chip is a Hopfield net (fully connected) with N input and output neurons (32 with the current technology), as described in Figure 1.

The performance of a single circuit is estimated to be about 4.000.000 binary neuron updatings per second. Synaptic coefficients are then updated at a rate of 4.000.000xN (= 128.000.000 for 32 input neurons per chip) modifications per second. If input neurons are coded on 8 bits, there are 700.000 updatings per second.

Several chips can also be used simultaneously to extend the limits of the Hopfield net. For instance, the number of neurons can be doubled (2xN) by using four chips, and so on (Figure 4).

Figure 2 displays a special arrangement of circuits for the error backpropagation algorithm. Two subsystems perform forward propagation of neural states (three chips on the left) and backpropagation of errors (one chip on the right). This also illustrates the cascadability abilities of the circuit: the new state of a neuron can be stored from the nonlinear function output into the neural state register of another layer. The possibilities offered for connections between two layers, i.e. $N_1 \rightarrow N_2$ (network with N_1 input cells, and N_2 output neurons), may be any size from $N \rightarrow N$ to $Nx8 \rightarrow N/8$.

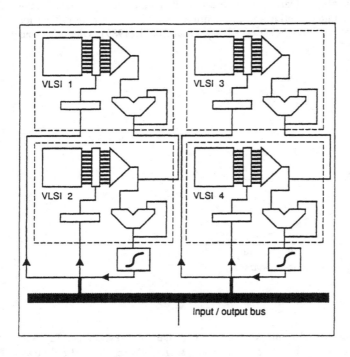

Figure 4. A 2xN fully connected network made with four circuits of N neutrons.

For the Nxp → N/p case, the calculation of the state of one neuron is performed in p steps, and the results of each step are added without shifting. Under those circumstances, the synaptic matrix is considered as a succession of sets of p columns of weights, each set representing the connections of input neurons to one output neuron. In this case, the state of the input neurons can be encoded in 1 bit for $p = 8$, 2 bits for $p = 4$,... and 8 bits for $p = 1$.

For instance, a 256 $\underset{8}{\rightarrow}$ 32 $\underset{1}{\rightarrow}$ 32 multilayer perceptron is built with 256 binary input neurons, and 32 8-bit hidden and output neurons (the numbers above the arrows represent the numbers of circuits involved in connecting the two layers). The example of Figure 2 shows an architecture that can map a 64 $\underset{2}{\rightarrow}$ 32 $\underset{1}{\rightarrow}$ 32 network of 8-bit neurons, as well as a 512 $\underset{2}{\rightarrow}$ 4 $\underset{1}{\rightarrow}$ 32 network with 512 binary input neurons and all the other neurons coded in 8 bits.

6. Conclusion

We have described a general-purpose neurochip for the resolution and learning stages of neural computing. Parallelism on input neurons is achieved for output neuron state evaluation and for synaptic weight updating. The latter follows a Hebb-like local formula. The digital realization guarantees exact integer calculations. According to our simulations and theoretical considerations, 16-bit precision on the weights should yield the same accuracy as with real-type variables.

Arrangement of several chips and adapted programming allows most of the formal neural nets (Hopfield, Kohonen, multilayer perceptrons) to be emulated. Our architecture may implement most of the learning schemes, including the minimum overlap rule, Kohonen's self-organizing map and error backpropagation. The chip is fully cascadable, allowing any size and architecture of neural nets.

A typical on-chip running time for updating one output neuron state (resolution stage), or all synaptic weights related to one neuron (learning stage), is less than 250 ns for neurons in a Hopfield network. Larger networks can be built with several circuits, and with Transputer microprocessors these chips could realize fine-grain parallel machines that achieve computing times shorter by several orders of magnitude compared with conventional computers.

Future work will include improvement of the chip to embed other variants of learning schemes, many-chips system architecture and programming, and an exhaustive study of the algorithms to be implemented on this kind of neuromachine.

7. Acknowledgements

We would particularly like to thank J. Gobert and P. Martin (LEP) for fruitful discussions about the architecture of the circuit, N. Mauduit (LEP) for first design of the circuit, J.L. Zorer and J.R. Viala (LEP) for simulations of learning with integers, and S. Makram (LEP) for discussions on his work before publications.

240

8. References

Graf, H.P., Jackel, L.D. and Hubbard, W.E. (1988), Computer, 21, 41.

Alspector, J., Allen, R.B., Hu, V. and Satyanarayana, S. (1987), Stochastic learning networks and their electronic implementation, Proc. NIPS Conf. Denver, CO, November 8-12, 1987, IEEE, New York.

Personnaz, L., Johannet, A., Dreyfus, G. and Weinfeld, M. (1989), Towards a neural network chip: a performance assessment and a simple example, Proc. "nEuro": Neural Networks from Models to Applications, IDSET, Paris.

Farhat, N.H. (1987), Appl. Opt., 26, 5093.

Wagner, K. and Psaltis, D. (1987), Appl. Opt., 26, 5061.

Krauth, W. and Mezard, M. (1987), J. Phys. A, 20, L745.

Kohonen, T. (1984), Self-Organization and Associative Memory, Springer, Berlin.

Duranton, M., Gobert, J. and Mauduit, N. (1989), Digital VLSI module for neural networks, Proc. "nEuro": Neural Networks from Models to Applications, IDSET, Paris.

Cheung, K.F., Atlas, L.E. and Marks II, R.J. (1987), Appl. Opt., 26, 4808.

Morton, S.G. (1988), Electron. Syst. Des. Mag., 18.

Hopfield, J.J. (1982), Proc. Natl. Acad. Sci. USA, 79, 2554.

Meir, E. and Domany, E. (1988), Phys. Rev. A, 37, 2660.

Sirat, J.A., Jorand, D. and Philips, J. Res. (1990), 44, 501 and references cited therein.

Peretto, P. (1988), J. Phys. (Paris), 49, 711.

Minski, M. and Papert, S. (1969), Perceptions: An Introduction to Computational Geometry, MIT Press, Cambridge, MA.

Widrow, B. and Winter, R. (1988), Computer, 21 (3), 25.

Poppel, G. and Krey, U. (1987), Europhys. Lett., 4 (9), 979.

Linsker, R. (1988), Computer, 21, 105.

Sanger, T. (1988), An optimality principle for unsupervised learning, Proc. NIPS Conf., Denver, CO, November 28 - December 1, 1988, IEEE, New York.

Jutten, C., Calcul neuromimétique et traitement du signal-analyse en composantes indépendantes, Thesis, Université Scientifique et Médicale de Grenoble, Institut National Polytechnique de Grenoble.

Lippmann, R. (1987), IEEE ASSP Mag., 3, 4.

Rumelhart, D.E., Hinton, G.E. and Williams, R.J. (1986), Learning the internal representations by error-backpropagation, in Parallel Distributed Processing, Vol. 1, MIT Press, Cambridge, MA.

Proc. NIPS Conf. (1988), Denver, CO, November 28 - December 1, 1988.

Paulos, J.J. and Hollis, P.W. (1988), Neural Networks, 1 (suppl. 1), 399.

Kramer, A. and Sangiovanelli-Vincentelli, A. (1988), Efficient parallel learning algorithms for neural networks, Proc. NIPS Conf., Denver, CO, November 28 - December 1, 1988, IEEE, New York.

Makram-Ebeid, S., Sirat, J.A. and Viala, J.R. (1989), A rationalized error backpropagation algorithm, Proc. INNS, Washington, DC, June 18-22, 1989, IEEE TAB Neural Network Committee.

Diederich, S. and Opper, M. (1987), Phys. Rev. Lett., 58, 949.

Cottrell, G.W., Munro, P.W. and Zipser, D., Image compression by error backpropagation: a demonstration of extensional programming, in Advances in Cognitive Science, Vol. 2, Norwood, NJ.
Bourlard, H. and Kamp, Y. (1988), Biol. Cybern., 59, 291.

9. Authors

Duranton, M., Ing. degree (Electronic Engineering), ENSERG, Grenoble, France, 1984; Drs. degree (Information Processing), INPG, Grenoble, France, 1985; Ing. degree (Computer Science), ENSIMAG. Grenoble, France, 1986; LEP, 1986. His research interests are in neural networks, massively parallel computers and processors.
Sirat, J.A., Ing. degree, Ecole Polytechnique, Palaiseau, France, 1983; Ph.D (Nouvelle Thèse), Université Scientifique et Médicale de Grenoble, France, 1986; LEP, 1986. His main topics of research were successively low-temperature solid-state physics (thesis) and neural networks.